A Fish Like Grampa's

THOMAS MCCABE

A Fish Like Grampa's

Published by Zaveair Press
tkbtsg@gmail.com

Printed in the United States of America

FIRST EDITION

Library of Congress Catalog-in-Publication data
Library of Congress Control Number: 2017901777
McCabe, Thomas Keith
A Fish Like Grampa's / Thomas McCabe
p. cm.
ISBN – 978-0-9842624-1-0
ISBN 0-9842624-1-5
United States--Memoir—1959-2003

To Grampa, for the way he made those wet, windswept days the best ones of all while encouraging us to persevere despite high skies and calm sunshine

And to Dad for being there, especially when he was needed most

…Grampa's calm, baritone voice was explaining something about the fish. His stories were told in a way that always defied my best efforts to repeat them with any hope of extracting the same awe from others he never failed to produce in my adolescent mind. It was a musky, held by a much younger version of Grampa in the antique photograph. He had it on a gaff hook, hoisted with some effort for the photographer as it hung by Grampa's side.

I usually absorbed every word of Grampa's stories; tales that had been distilled over time until every nuance, each minute inflection in his voice was there for a reason. That day however, it was all I could do to acknowledge that he was speaking to me at all. All I seemed capable of doing was to stare at the photo, engrossed by the sheer size of the brute.

It had been caught over thirty years earlier in the fall of 1925 off Indian Point in Pelican Lake, Wisconsin. The waves were approaching three feet on that rainy, windswept day. It was all Grampa and his friend Lynn Moyer could do to maneuver the wooden rowboat north of the reef then cast as quickly as possible before the howling north wind pushed them into the point itself. There were very few motors then, just oars. With the boat bucking amidst the waves Grampa let fly a wooden, white and red Pikie Minnow with amber eyes. Two, maybe three cranks later the huge, needle toothed predator slammed into Grampa's lure with such force it was all he could do

1

to keep the taut line from snapping. His reel didn't have a drag system, so it was up to Grampa's thumb.

Lynn Moyer strained at the oars, barely forcing the boat through the unrelenting wind. After making it a hundred feet north that felt like a thousand, Lynn reached for the gaff just as Grampa brought the musky to the side of the boat. Working quickly, Lynn made three, then four futile attempts to get the large hook through the mouth and past the gill plate. On his fifth attempt the fish was out of the water. Lynn Moyer may not have been an expert gaffer, but the same couldn't be said about his proficiency with firearms. One shot fired from his long barreled .22 pistol, with the boat heaving about in the waves, struck the writhing brute squarely between the eyes.

Catch and release was unheard of in 1925, but Grampa's musky wasn't destined for the wall. By evening it had been gutted and placed in a wooden crate crammed with enough ice to keep it fresh for the long train ride back to Naperville, Illinois. Grampa had six sons under the age of fourteen waiting for him, and after working half the day in her kitchen Gramma served a musky feast with all the trimmings that was talked about for years.

The only thing left was the head. My father and all of my uncles remembered that needle toothed memento being around for decades. My brothers, cousins and I got to see it as well, whenever we were lucky enough to get Grampa to show it to us, unaware he had been, as always, planning to all along. It was nailed to a timeworn wooden beam in Grampa's basement, hovering above his workbench, but after Grampa's passing no one knew what became of it.

**

The head was gone, but Grampa's photo wasn't. It has inspired four generations of our family, and not just because of the musky. The man holding it had made indelible impressions as well. Everyone in our family who knew and loved him knows what I mean. His expansive arrowhead collection represented decades of traversing freshly plowed, blue/black soil after a steady rain along the banks of the DuPage River in and around McDowells Forest Preserve, or near the vicinity of Messingers Spring. He regaled his grandchildren with tales of the Native Americans who had fired the arrows - the tiny arrowheads towards birds and small prey, the larger ones towards bigger game. One was so huge it had to have been the tip of a spear; one that, in the young minds of his grandchildren, must have been used in mortal combat.

Because of Gramma's unwavering faith he was obliged to attend Sunday services from time to time, but Grampa's true place of worship was the pristine forests, rivers, streams and lakes of the rural Midwest and northern Wisconsin. He had steadfastly maintained nothing was closer to God than unspoiled nature, and since humans were incapable of reproducing such natural wonders with any degree of equal splendor, it stood to reason folks would be well advised to leave it as they found it.

He was a blue-collar workingman by trade, but to me and my siblings as well as my numerous cousins and other relatives, he was the artist of mesmerizing oil paintings, a Mark Twainian philosopher, an earth-toned writer and exceptional storyteller. His passing in the fall of 1959 was devastating, and although we had been lucky to have known him at all, I guess I'll always wish we could be together in a boat again, tossing out a few more casts, probing the depths. I want to ask him about the things still moving around down there, confounding things that began stirring long after his departure; I want to know if my priorities are as valid as they feel, if his infallible ear hears anything out of tune. I guess I still need his approval, to know I stayed on the path he encouraged me to follow.

Chapter 1

My cousins and I had spent numerous hours along the banks of the West Branch of the DuPage River in Naperville, Illinois, fishing for bluegills, sunfish and hopefully an elusive bass that was hunting for our small prey as well. We usually just wrapped some line around our hand with a small hook and a smaller still section of worm, hoping to lure the darting little fish from their hiding places along the old, limestone walls that ran along the banks by the venerable, wooden walking bridge west of downtown in the mid to late 1950's.

There was an old dam just west of the bridge, and above it was where Grampa said the fishing was best. As much as I enjoyed being there with him listening to his stories as he patiently watched our clumsy efforts at hooking the little bait stealers, nothing compared to the first and only time I was lucky enough to be with him in northern Wisconsin.

***

In 1910 my grandparents had spent their honeymoon at the Resthaven Resort that years later was called Don's Northern Resort (except as far as I knew everybody called it Northern Don's) along the western shore of Musky Bay in Pelican Lake. Although Grampa had been to Pelican since then, our family trip in August 1959 was the first time my grandparents had been there together since their honeymoon.

Our 1953 light green Plymouth station wagon was loaded to the hilt the sunny summer morning we left; my grandparents, two older brothers, my kid sister plus my parents and our mutt Scamp were all jammed together along with the luggage, fishing and camping gear. I don't recall it being crowded, however, because I wasn't able to stop thinking about our destination - Pelican Lake - *the* Pelican Lake.

There would be no fishing line wrapped around my eleven-year-old hand on this trip. I had a brand new South Bend pole, an open faced baitcasting reel just like Grampa's only newer, super strong black Nylon line and an assortment of lures I had personally picked out because they looked just like a small fish, the exact type of lure I would strike if I were a musky, I reasoned. There was no way a huge brute similar to Grampa's wouldn't hit, I just knew it. The question was when - maybe not on my first cast off the dock, but after the initial splash of that fateful cast, all kinds of muskies would no doubt gather around, and after my second or third attempt the fight would be on.

***

As Dad drove north (crawled, as far as I was concerned) Grampa attempted, on several occasions, to inject a modicum of reality into the upcoming hunt. For the first time in my life, however, I was forced to dismiss his advice and wise council. After all, hadn't it been thirty-four years since he had landed his musky? Just think of all the muskies that had been born since then, I reasoned. Why, there has to be hundreds, maybe *thousands* of monster muskies lurking about in the fertile waters of *the* Pelican Lake! I believed that sacred body of water was so pristine you could dip a tin cup from the side of the boat if you were thirsty, but only at great personal risk. The flash from the metal alone could cost you a finger or two. No, I had to insist to myself, Grampa was wrong this time; he just had to be.

***

Rain had been predicted, but not the near tornado conditions we encountered by the time we dropped my grandparents off at Northern Don's. The rain was coming in sheets, driven by a howling wind that showed no signs of letting up. Gramma wanted us to stay at the resort, but Dad, hoping for a break in the late afternoon weather, drove us around the lake to the small hamlet of Pelican Lake and parked next to the train depot across from the Old Hotel on Route 45. Our Plymouth station wagon rocked as the gale force winds and rain battered against its side, and Mom was visibly upset. My brothers and I were fascinated by it all. Our kid sister Suzie was almost four, and Mom had her arms around her so she was okay. Besides, there was no need to worry. Dad was there. Nothing bad could happen that couldn't be set right if Dad was there.

Later that evening after the storm let up we made our way to a campground. The gravel road, County Q, was washboard bumpy. Dad, along with my brothers and I had to get out several times to drag large branches and other debris out of our way. We made it though, but it wasn't until morning before the aftermath of the storm was truly appreciated. Huge pines and other trees had been snapped in half or uprooted. Debris was everywhere as we made our way to Northern Don's. Gramma and Grampa were relieved that we were okay. They'd had their own scare when a huge Norway pine crashed just outside the second story window of their upstairs room, a tree that had no doubt been there decades before during their honeymoon.

As much as I enjoyed wandering through the nearby woods and climbing on some of the broken trees, it was the lake I wanted to explore. It seemed as if Dad was taking forever to bail out the rowboat he had rented, and longer still to get the 8 hp Johnson to cooperate. There was so much debris floating by the dock I decided to hold my casts until we were on the lake.

Grampa said the high, cloudless skies, especially after the weather we had just experienced, would likely keep the fish away and it was too bad we hadn't been on the water a few hours before the storm arrived. "You should've been here yesterday" or "you should've been here last week" were phrases destined to be repeated for decades to countless musky hunters, but when you're eleven, remarks such as those carry no weight at all. We were on Pelican Lake, approaching Indian Point with fishing gear in hand, and I was as ready as I could be to hook into a descendant of Grampa's huge trophy.

***

Dad cut the motor along the northwest corner of Indian Point, about a hundred yards into the mouth of Treacherous Bay.

Grampa looked at the point, then over his shoulder at Meckanac Point located on the other side of the bay. He had been staring at that point when Dad drove past it with a disconcerted look upon his face as he glanced back and forth between the two points. In 1925 the locals had told him his musky had been landed off Indian Point, after he and Lynn Moyer had described their location. That morning however, Grampa wasn't so sure. It had been thirty-four years since his last time on Pelican, one of the largest inland lakes in Wisconsin, and he remarked that it might have been Meckanac Point after all.

Personally, I didn't understand why that should make a difference. We were on *Pelican Lake*, so all we had to do was throw out our lures! Water was water, muskies lived in water, so where we threw our lures didn't matter as long as they landed somewhere in the lake. To prove my point, I let fly a soaring cast that went much farther than my older brothers could throw, and it landed right in front of a fifty-pound musky and the fight of my life was on, but not really, as much as I needed all that to be true. In reality, all I had accomplished was a backlash of monumental proportions. Cherry bombs in a fishing line factory couldn't have created a bigger mess.

My impatient attempts to correct the situation only made things worse and my two older brothers, Don and Larry, made sure everyone in the boat was acutely aware of that fact. Grampa took my gear and with a gentle urgency went to work. To my wonderment, he had set things right in no time at all.

"Cast smooth, not hard," he instructed. "Keep your thumb lightly on the spool as you cast, lightly now, as if you were stroking the head of a canary..." My hand-picked lure flew effortlessly through the air and landed a good forty feet away.

"Bring it in faster Tommy boy, you can't reel faster than a musky can swim, no one can, not in water this warm." Grampa kept a sharp eye on my lure as he spoke, or so I thought. Actually, he was training his eyes on the area two or three feet behind my lure and to either side, and did the same for my two brothers as well. Then panic struck. I looked around and noticed we had forgotten the net. I mentioned our dilemma to Dad, but he just smiled.

"Don't worry, Mot. You hook 'em, we'll get 'em in." Dad sometimes called me Mot because that's how I used to spell my name when I was four. He only said it when he was amused, and over the years I had grown accustomed to it, appreciating how special it made me feel even if it reminded me of a jar of applesauce.

I trusted Dad, but I still wanted the net. Then Grampa reached behind himself and produced a timeworn gaff hook, the same one that Lynn Moyer had used to land Grampa's musky in 1925.

"You get one to the boat, Tommy boy," Grampa said with a smile on his face, "and this will do the rest. Now cast away." Grampa put down the gaff, reached in his pocket for a wooden farmer's match and lit his old, Kaywoodie pipe filled with Kentucky Club Mixture. The clear air was so still the flame barely flickered. Grampa gave out a contemptuous snort as he searched the sky in vain; not a cloud or even a light breeze to blow some inclement weather our way could be found. We had been there over ten minutes, yet the boat remained in the same spot as if we had dropped anchors from the stern and bow. Undeterred, my brothers and I kept casting away, pausing occasionally to untangle the inevitable backlashes.

***

By lunchtime we had fished Indian Point, a spot called Town Bar, all around Crescent Island and most of Mud Bay. Nothing. Not even what Grampa called a "follow". Eventually, bitter disappointment finds us all, but when you're eleven and it comes without any warning you had felt obliged to acknowledge, it can be particularly devastating. Grampa would have none of that however, not in his boat.

"Musky fishing is special because they have always been cantankerous, cagey brutes that can be darn near impossible to catch," he said. "Even the local Indians and pioneers of long ago told tales of boat loads of northern and perch, but only an occasional musky, comparatively speaking. You boys have done good today, and now you know why most fishermen would rather chase the same fish muskies do," Grampa said as he effortlessly lit his pipe in the still air, sending a curl of smoke slowly skyward. "When it happens though, when you finally hook into one, you'll be a cut above the bobber and worm crowd. They'll never know the thrill of thrills, because they gave up. You won't want to rub it in or brag. You won't feel the need, because you are musky fishermen. Simply show them your fish, that's all you'll have to do. Just don't give up. Don't *ever* give up."

***

We headed into Outlet Bay where Grampa said we could hopefully practice on a few northern, but as he had predicted the high skies and cool, still air had driven our prey away from their feeding spots. Grampa said the fish were confused that day, probably sick, as if the cold front had given them upset stomachs. Somehow, that made sense to me; I didn't know why.

Still, I had found comfort in Grampa's words. For weeks on end I had thought of little else other than landing a fish like Grampa's, but as we made our way back to Northern Don's, skunked and defeated, I knew the search was far from over. I knew, or at least suspected, there was no shame in coming back empty handed, not if you were hunting muskies.

The fight had just begun, and if I had any doubts about my participation in the coming years, they were erased later that day in front of the country grocery store near the Old Hotel. I was in the parking lot kicking gravel about, looking for perfect sized stones for my slingshot when Grampa called me over.

He was standing in front of an old, metal cooler about six feet long. The top was up, and there was a rectangular piece of glass in its place. Grampa pointed to the glass, and I peered in. Lying upon a bed of ice was a silver and rainbow hued musky, and it was a monster. I was awestruck; even death hadn't diminished the essence of its ferociousness.

One thing, however, left me perplexed; if the weather that day couldn't have been worse for catching muskies, how was the person who caught the musky able to do it? I asked Grampa that very question as we stood there staring through the glass. When he didn't answer right away I finally pried my eyes away from the behemoth and looked at him; he was already looking at me, and when he had my full attention he placed his hands on my shoulders. His baritone voice was as calm as it was sincere.

"The only certainty about musky fishing is uncertainty. And the best way to minimize that uncertainty is something you already know, because you and your brothers learned it today. Don't give up. Don't you *ever* give up."

"I won't, Grampa."

"Promise?"

"Promise."

"Then your battle is half won, Tommy boy."

His eyes followed mine back to the musky. No matter how many times I looked at it or how long I stared, the emotions that had been generated when I had first looked inside the cooler didn't lesson in their intensity. It was a magnificent sight.

Millionaires could keep their millions, kings could keep their thrones, because from that moment on I knew what I wanted, and nothing, not even Time, was going to stop me from attaining my goal. *A fish like Grampa's.*

The Quest had been joined.

Chapter 2

"**G**rampa died."

I was sitting upon my favorite chair that afternoon in the living room watching television when Mom said those words to me. She went back to the kitchen then, hoping in vain to busy herself in a way that might diminish her own grief. Things had been looking grim ever since Grampa had suffered a stroke a few days earlier while visiting my Uncle Ben and Aunt Ricky in Amherst, Massachusetts. Even so, Mom's words couldn't have cut deeper if they had been delivered on a freshly honed butcher knife. Tears stung my eyes as I stared straight ahead, oblivious to whatever program I had been watching.

Some of the adults had been maintaining Grampa's stroke was perhaps just a warning. They also repeated other things people say in order to at least partially rationalize away their grief and fear at such times, and I had believed with everything inside me those things were true, that they *had* to be true. It had only been a few months since our trip to Pelican Lake, and just as I had been naive enough to believe I'd be landing muskies on about every third or fourth cast, I had taken the adults' words to heart as well, refusing to believe Grampa had actually been near death. By age eleven, I hadn't been able to prepare myself for the realities of musky fishing anymore than the inevitable flow of time that had caught up with Grampa. Except for two dogs, no one I loved had ever died; let alone a human family member; let alone *Grampa*.

***

In retrospect, the unparalleled thrills of life's major accomplishments when first achieved have their antitheses, and Grampa's evening visitation and funeral a day later brought that home full force. A few hours after the funeral when our large, extended family had gathered at Gramma's and Grampa's 19th century Italianate in Naperville, I found myself wandering about, paying attention to things I had always appreciated, but generally took for granted; not anymore. A lifetime's worth of Grampa's books, various collections, paintings; even his old pipes brought back elusive, disjointed fragments of his essence, as if part of him was still with us. Then reality would intrude and grief would set in again. When I came across Grampa's photo though, and looked again at the large musky and the amazing man holding it, the focus remained clear, and Grampa stayed with me as well. He had, in a sense, come back, and he has never gone away. He never will.

Chapter 3

In June of 1960 sixth grade was finally over and my family was just a few weeks away from another fishing adventure in northern Wisconsin. We were going to stay in a cabin, a real cabin on Lake Tomahawk, not all that far from Pelican Lake. My brothers and I had managed to acquire more fishing gear and lures during the previous year thanks to birthdays, Christmas, and money earned from more than a few shoveled walks whenever a snowstorm was thoughtful enough to bury our neighborhood. Heavy spring and early summer rains were also a financial blessing, causing our neighbors' lawns to grow.

In 1960 however, I wasn't taking any chances. All bases would be covered and every angle would be scrutinized to such a degree that even the smartest muskies in Lake Tomahawk would be in trouble. I had even spent a few nights in our backyard with a flashlight, catching nightcrawlers. Muskies liked nightcrawlers, they must like them I reasoned; what kind fish doesn't like nightcrawlers? Despite what Grampa had said about the bobber and worm crowd, what if we arrived at Lake Tomahawk and found out from the locals that nightcrawlers were all the muskies were hitting on, and the local bait shops were fresh out due to the demand? Nope, that wasn't going to happen to us.

I captured about four dozen, just in case. Besides, they were fun to catch and I liked putting them in fresh dirt mixed with old coffee grounds. The coffee would make them wiggle more; that's what Dad told me anyway. As usual, I hadn't noticed or chose to ignore the barely perceptible smile on his face. We were going to be there two whole weeks, which meant regardless of how duplicitous the weather decided to behave we'd be able to wait it out for that perfect, or perhaps several perfect days on the water.

The only drawback was Dad had been offered the opportunity to paint the outside of the cabin instead of paying cash for our stay. It wasn't a big place, and Dad painted houses most of the summer anyway to supplement his teacher's salary, so he'd be able to finish the whole job in two or three days. Dad told my brothers and me it was our job to find the hot spots on the lake while he finished the cabin. The three of us thought that was an excellent plan. Even so, my brothers and I would miss having him in the boat. As it turned out, that proved to be especially true for brother Larry, and for the same reason, only different, for me.

***

My brothers were in their mid-teens and the three of us could swim, so Mom and Dad didn't have too much of a problem with us out on the lake. We fished all the first day and even ate lunch on the water. The only fish we caught were panfish, having switched to nightcrawlers and bobbers after being skunked all morning casting lures. We felt varying degrees of ambivalence from having deviated from what Grampa had told us, but any action was better than the boredom of being skunked all morning. We rationalized our tactics by reassuring each other that muskies not only liked nightcrawlers but loved them; no doubt about it.

Finally, Larry couldn't take it anymore; he couldn't rationalize away his guilt. He had always been the spiritual brother even if none of us knew it at the time, and was convinced Grampa's disapproval transcended everything, including the grave. He switched back to a lure, and started casting.

None of us knew where, exactly, we should've been fishing, having no knowledge of structure or anything else locals and experienced anglers took for granted. Well, almost nothing. We did know that fish could be found near lily pads, so we stayed in the bays and other areas that had visible signs of cover. We had never even heard of submerged rock reefs or underwater structure of any kind, let alone why they might produce what we were after - the elusive, trophy musky.

We pulled into another bay north of where we were staying and began to cast away. By then Don, my oldest brother, had also returned to casting a lure; a Pikie Minnow just like Grampa's. I was ready to switch myself, and had even begun to reel in my bobber and nightcrawler when it happened. I didn't see the strike, but I sure heard Larry's hollering. Out of nowhere a huge fish (by our standards) had slammed into his lure and the fight was on! Don had just cast, and since I was almost reeled in and closest to Larry, it fell upon me to grab the net. Larry did a good job of maneuvering the fish towards the boat, and when we got our first look at it our eyes grew twice their size. Larry had done it;

he had hooked a musky! At least we thought it was a musky, having never seen a northern pike before in our lives.

"Give Don the net! Give *Don* the net!" Larry demanded, after noticing our eldest brother had brought in his lure and was poised to help.

"Don't worry!" I yelled, shaking with anticipation, "I'll get 'em, just bring 'em closer, Larry!"

Although all three of us were pretty good at sports, Don was clearly the agile, most coordinated one of us all, and his reflexes were legend. I knew Larry would have preferred Don was in charge of the net, but time had run out and I was reluctant to hand it over anyway. I was twelve, almost a teenager, and wanted desperately to prove myself to my older brothers.

Larry fought the writhing fish right up to the side of the boat and I lunged after the beast as hard and fast as I could, jamming the net into the water like a net-man possessed. All I accomplished was to hit the alleged musky on its snout with the outer rim of the net, knocking the lure out of its mouth. As quickly as it had appeared, Larry's trophy was gone.

"GOSH DARN IT!!" Larry bellowed, loud enough for half the residents on the lake to hear, or so it seemed; only that's not what he yelled. If Mom and Dad had heard what Larry *really* bellowed and recognized his voice, which was a distinct possibility, Larry was a goner. His only hope was for us to stay on the lake as long as possible. *My* only hope was Don would keep Larry from strangling me.

As rare as such occurrences were, whenever Larry became truly unhinged it was a very good idea to get away from him. That was hard to do in a small fishing boat, but Don came to my rescue by switching seats with me. He figured I deserved to be strangled and thrown overboard as much as Larry did, but since he was the oldest and would have to explain my disappearance, I was spared. That's how it felt anyway.

What occurred next cemented the concept of what would, in our later years, be described as karma, although it was Larry who eventually chose that path in earnest. Later on, I saw it as poetic justice. I'm not sure how Don took it, at least at the time. Judging by his stoic behavior as he just kept casting away prior to the incident that was about to occur, I could only surmise that I was one lucky little brother for not having lost *his* musky, even if it was just a northern.

***

Racked with remorse, I went back to nightcrawlers and maintained as low a profile as possible. Then it happened. My bobber didn't just dance a little, like when a good-sized panfish was toying around, it disappeared in nothing flat. I immediately set the hook as hard as I could, even though my pole was already bent nearly in half as the powerful tugging was making both my arms shake. I had done it! I had hooked into what felt as if it must have been the biggest musky Lake Tomahawk, a prime musky lake, had produced in decades!

I tried to reel it in, but the line kept peeling off my reel as if it were an old-fashioned tape recording spool nearing the end of its rewind. Larry's fish was temporarily forgotten as both my brothers frantically reeled in their lures as fast as possible, as if we all had single-mindedly resolved not to let this one get away. I didn't understand the concept of the drag system on my reel, none of us did, or that it was even there, so I used my thumb just like Grampa would have done.

The fight was mind-boggling; I had never experienced anything like it before in my life. After what seemed an eternity, the huge fish, my first *musky* no doubt, had begun to tire so I reeled it in as fast as I could. As if preordained, Don was on the ready with the net, eyeing the action with a concentration only he could conjure up with such intensity. The huge fish was at the boat, still too deep for any of us to get a good look at my prize of prizes. Suddenly the water erupted in an explosion of fury and Don, true to his reputation, ripped the net through the water and netted the monster! Netted the monster carp, with its round, stupid looking lips and all. Rather than looking into the fiery eyes of a ferocious Northwoods predator, we were gazing into the eyes of a creature that looked as if it were as stupid as I felt. Actually, I was feeling pretty sorry for myself.

"A *carp?*" I whined. "A stinking carp, all the way up *here?*" Carp were more than abundant in the Fox River that ran through our hometown of Aurora, Illinois, but none of us had ever imagined we would find one in the sky-blue waters of a northern Wisconsin musky lake.

Despite his best efforts, Don could barely contain himself. Justifiably, Larry didn't even try. I guess Don unhooked my "trophy" and let it go; I was too dumbstruck to really notice. I recall wanting to gut the impostor, and years later Don admitted that prompted his actions. I regretted not killing that eater of game fish eggs, and a few lively debates ensued because of my stance, but I didn't care. Still, I had to give that bottom feeding mud sucker credit - it had put up a very good fight.

***

As it turned out, Larry had been lucky. No one had heard his blasphemous outburst, at least not Mom and Dad. They did hear about my ineptitude with the net, however, and more than once. Dad said it was all part of fishing and the best thing to do was to go out and hook into another one.

I maintained that I should again be allowed the opportunity to man the net, something about if you fall off a horse it's imperative to get back on immediately, but my brothers decided that wasn't an option unless I wanted to net one of my own catches. My kid sister Suzie said I could man the net for her, but since she never wanted to fish and was not quite five my prospects of regaining my self esteem were left largely up to me.

Be that way, I said to myself. The following morning, I grabbed my bow and arrows and decided to go big game hunting instead. As soon as I departed, Don and Larry wasted no time getting down to the dock and scrambling into the boat. I went into the woods, bow and arrow at the ready, but big game must have been scarce that time of year. Lucky for them, I concluded, because the new arrows I had purchased with my snow shoveling and lawn money were top of the line, razor blade heads and all.

I could only afford three of them, so it was imperative that I hit whatever target was presented. Still, game was indeed sparse. No moose or bear, or anything except a chipmunk that looked as if it would have made a better pet than target. Figuring I needed target practice anyway, I decided to fire into a large pine about twenty feet in front of me. I missed three times in a row. To my disappointment, the new razor-headed arrows were never seen again either, at least by me. It was time for the heavy artillery, I concluded.

I made my way through the wilderness, a whole twenty yards of it or so, back to the cabin to retrieve Old Daisy, my high-powered hunting rifle; except she wasn't high-powered since she was only a B.B. gun, and only looked like a high-powered rifle – sort of. Since the moose and bear weren't cooperating, I decided to try my luck with a little "anything that moved" hunting. That's when it hit me, the brainstorm of the decade, maybe even the entire twentieth century!

Muskies were known to sometimes feed near shore, and my stroke of genius would place Old Daisy and me there at the ready! Actually, she wasn't really old, having been a present that prior Christmas, but the "old" part gave her a sense of dignity. I never understood why such a lethal weapon was named after a flower, but since that was beyond my control I left it for others to contemplate. Maybe the inventor's name was Daisy, and he went into gun making to atone for the cruel fate of having to take his name to school every day. Whatever the explanation, the Lake Tomahawk muskies were about to meet their match, even if I had to walk the shoreline around the entire lake.

***

Suzie was alone on the dock as I approached. Don and Larry were about a hundred feet away in their boat casting. I began to search the water from shore by the side of the dock, keeping a sharp eye out for my elusive prey. I spotted a school of minnows and a cautious crawfish, but that was about it. I missed the crawfish, who didn't seem overly concerned I was shooting at it.

That's when I heard the splash, a big one. Looking up, I noticed my kid sister had disappeared from the dock where she had been balancing herself as she walked along the dock's outer edge. I dropped Old Daisy and flew into the water; belly flopped really, and began swimming as fast as I could. Suzie had fallen in near the end and on the other side of the dock, so when I arrived at the vicinity of the splash I cut underneath the dock itself, through a maze of spider webs that were home to these huge dock spiders. I had to assume they were more than capable of gnawing half my face off, and besides, my phobia of spiders was well known. I needed to submerge anyway in order to find my sister and that was definitely the perfect time to do so.

I could hear my brothers hollering as I went under and opened my eyes. Five feet or so in front of me I saw her, at least two feet under and sinking slowly. She wasn't kicking or anything, just sinking, in what I would later find out was called the fetal position. Whatever it was, I had to move fast. I got there in no time, grabbed Suzie and brought her to the surface. It was too deep for me to stand, but I managed to get her to grab onto the side of the dock then I climbed onto it myself.

She was scared, coughing and crying, but she was okay. My brothers shouted, asking if she was all right, and when I told them I thought so, they concluded the situation was well in hand and kept on casting. After all, musky fishing was musky fishing, and besides, Dad and Mom were already sprinting towards the dock.

I was labeled a hero, but when I found Old Daisy where I had hastily dropped her in six inches of lake water I discovered adulation and fame came with a price. She never fired again. We didn't see another musky on that trip either, assuming we had seen one at all, and with Old Daisy out of commission my brain storm of the century was dead in the water as well.

The muskies were still out there though, swimming around, stalking their prey. They were still out there, big and mean, and no way were we going to give up. The Quest was still alive, more than ever, and the following year Dad was to join the hunt as well. Join the hunt, and make family history in the process.

Chapter 4

Carrol Lake wasn't very large, but the following year it sure looked like prime musky water to me. Then again, every single body of water in Wisconsin bigger than a pond, and many of those as well, looked like prime musky water as far as I was concerned. Everyone in my family was accomplished campers, having had plenty of practice in the mountains of Colorado years before while Dad, thanks to the G.I. Bill, was attending summer school at Colorado State to get his Masters. Suzie hadn't been born prior to our four summers in Greeley, but she caught on to camping fast. She had little choice since she would have been forced to endure several more boring stories about our mountain camping adventures and especially our advice that was as condescending as it was inevitable.

The human members of our family weren't the only ones whose excitement escalated as we approached our Northwoods destination. Standing in the rear section of our station wagon with the back window down, our mutt Scamp was literally shaking with anticipation as one intriguing scent after another found its way to his hypersensitive nose.

To this day, Mom still suspects he was pushed but that's not what happened. I don't know what scent enthralled him so, but when it hit, that tough little mutt wasn't going to be denied. In a flash, Scamp leapt through the open back window and landed unceremoniously upon hard-packed gravel of the old county road Dad was driving down at about thirty miles an hour. My brothers and I watched in amazement as that short haired, muscular mutt bounced several times before coming to a halt. We thought for sure he had finally managed to kill himself, but we should have known better. After all, it was Scamp, the toughest, meanest mutt in our neighborhood and points beyond.

His reputation was the stuff of legends back home; he liked to chase cars and slam into whizzing hubcaps only to shake his head and trot away, usually growling, and sometimes bleeding. 1961 Chevy Biscaynes were his favorite target because the driver's side mirror made a whistling noise as they passed by, which for whatever reason was unacceptable to Scamp. Many were the male dogs, regardless of size, that rued the day they ventured anywhere near Scamp's turf. He lorded over his harem with a vengeance, and although "tough love" was a phrase yet to be invented its meaning wasn't lost on the female dogs within at least a four-block radius of our home.

True to his reputation, the county road's hard packed gravel that morning proved no match for Scamp's shot-put of a head. By the time Dad managed to wheel around, Scamp was already trotting back to the car, a little scraped up but still displaying his usual contempt towards the world in general. After hopping back into the rear of the station wagon (with the back window rolled up) Scamp predictably began to lick himself shamelessly as if nothing out of the ordinary had occurred, and just as predictably paid little attention to his wounds while doing so.

***

We pitched our tent and set up tarps over the picnic table at a prime campsite on the south shore of Carrol Lake. The weather was perfect. There was a slight, pine-scented breeze, apparently unable to budge a foggy mist that enshrouded the lake; perfect musky weather, we surmised.

I had been formulating a plan of attack ever since our departure from Lake Tomahawk the prior year, and as Dad, Don, Larry and I headed out on the lake I began to prepare the key to my strategy. I had found what I believed to be the perfect lure while browsing the isles at Crosby's Sporting Goods back home in Aurora. It was a silver and black Heddon Pumpkinseed, with just enough red about its gills and mouth to make it irresistible to any self-respecting musky; I'd have bet anything. Moreover, I had read about the importance of leaders in a Boy's Life article and had one of those on my line as well. My very own "High Noon" had arrived and I was locked and loaded.

Three hours later my miracle lure was back in my galvanized tackle box as I sullenly watched my bobber bounce about in the undulating waves. My brothers were casting away, changing lures on about every fourth or fifth cast. Dad, however, had employed a different tactic, that as teenagers my brothers and I didn't fully appreciate but didn't completely dismiss. Dad was summoning the musky gods by not only throwing Grampa's old Pikie Minnow (the same one that had hooked Grampa's musky) but going so far as to actually be using Grampa's old, hickory fishing pole and one of Grampa's old reels.

The concept of a wooden pole seemed archaic to me, but I had to admit it looked pretty cool even if it was older than Dad by at least twenty years. Its most impressive feature was the fact that it was a two-piece rod joined at the middle. The handle was rather long as well, as opposed to the ones we had on our South Bend poles that weren't much longer than the breadth of our palms. Even so, after five hours on the water the only fish caught were some small panfish on my bobber and worms, at least until we were just about ready to head back to camp.

Boredom and frustration were instantly transformed into adrenaline charged excitement as my bobber instantly shot out of sight. I yanked hard on my rod, driving home the needle-sharp Eagle hook and the fight was on! Unlike the carp from the previous year, whatever was on the other end of my line was shaking so furiously my hands were actually vibrating. The carp had fought hard, but those had been heavy tugs which had seemed to move my arms with each pull.

I not only didn't understand the drag system on my reel - I still didn't even know of its existence. It must have been inadvertently tightened down because although the fish was putting up a furious fight, at least I was able to keep reeling it in. I finally had it to the boat, visibly relieved it wasn't another carp. It sure wasn't a musky either, unless Carrol Lake muskies had blue, irregular stripes on their gill plates. I had caught enough bluegills in my life to recognize the species, but I had never seen one that big; none of us had. It was almost the size of a flattened junior league football, and weighed close to two pounds.

I had been cleaning bluegills a fourth that size and smaller for years. They didn't amount to much more than appetizers, but they tasted good once Mom worked her magic with boiling Crisco and cornmeal. I was looking forward to cleaning one that would produce an actual meal that evening, but Dad, as it turned out, would play a much bigger role in deciding that evening's menu.

***

Scamp was standing on the dock when we made it in, impatiently wagging his stub of a tail. He was mostly a white, shorthaired mutt of average size. His day in the woods, however, rolling in who knew what, had turned most of him brown. He didn't smell very good either, reeked actually, so none of us were too offended when he took off after greeting us to chase some chipmunks that for some reason were chattering at him.

The rest of us went about our business, enjoying the camping experience in a variety of ways. I had a bluegill to clean, a *big* bluegill, and decided to get at it right away. Don and Larry built a fire while Mom and Suzie began to get things ready for supper. Dad disappeared behind some trees down by the shore, taking Grampa's hickory rod with him. In many ways, it was like any other day we had spent camping in the Northwoods, but thanks to Dad that was about to change.

Dad would listen patiently when my brothers and I would go on about how we were going to locate and catch a musky, and how cool it would be and everything. He listened patiently then acknowledged what we said with a smile whose probable meaning was so imperceptible we were left to merely suspect he *may* have thought we had a lot to learn. He wasn't thrilled by the hunt or overly enthralled with fishing, at least as it applied to him actually catching something. He liked to catch fish, I don't mean that, but spending time on the water with his children was what put Dad in the boat.

If he knew about the specifics of musky fishing, weather, drag systems, structure, lures, leaders and lines, he generally kept it to himself, but it was just as likely whatever knowledge he possessed about fishing was limited to what he had learned along the banks of the DuPage River in Naperville with his five brothers.

Dad would rather do things than talk about them, for the most part. Born in a farmhouse on 75th Street in Naperville in 1913, he grew up in a quintessential Americana hometown. His generation, a lot of them anyway, felt an obligation towards themselves and others to scorn bravado. They saw the "Look at me!" attitude some felt compelled to display as a sign of at least weakness, and to be avoided at all costs.

Dad and all five of his brothers saw combat in World War II, but rarely talked about it, and never amongst themselves in the company of their children. After all of the "Six Micks" as they were called growing up (assuming the speaker was smiling when he said it) returned home safely from that brutal conflict, Life Magazine wanted to do a story and put them on the cover. "The real heroes are still over there, and they're never coming home" was the only response Life Magazine received from my father and his brothers when they declined the request.

Dad had been a very good athlete and a star halfback in high school and a starting quarterback in college. He got into coaching and eventually became the athletic director of West Aurora Junior High, later known as Franklin Junior High. He wasn't the type of coach who screamed and went ballistic, but when he did raise his stentorian, baritone voice everyone, and I mean *every*one, fell silent and paid attention. Dad reminded me of the movie star Gary Cooper in both appearance and demeanor. As a child growing up, I wondered which of them would win if they had a fight, then surmised they would have liked each other too much for that scenario to ever unfold. Lucky for Gary Cooper - I believed that as well.

As family-oriented as Dad happened to be and as much as he enjoyed our company while fishing, on that late afternoon he had made his way to the shoreline in front of our campsite by himself. I had just about finished cleaning my large bluegill when I heard staccato splashing coming from the other side of the thick tree and brush cover near shore. At first I thought Dad was giving an uncooperative Scamp an overdue bath, then I remembered Dad had taken Grampa's pole with him. Grampa's pole...Grampa's pole....*Grampa's pole!* The realization of what must have been going on struck like an inspiration and within seconds I was sprinting through the maze of trees towards shore with my brothers in hot pursuit.

We burst through the trees and came to an abrupt halt upon seeing Dad trying to control a large fish that was thrashing wildly, not twenty feet from shore. The fish put up such a struggle that Grampa's old wooden pole, long overdue for retirement, finally succumbed by snapping in two before our non-blinking eyes. That's when things really grew intense. The large fish took off for the deep with Grampa's old Pikie Minnow still stuck in its mouth. Dad immediately rushed into the lake up to his knees and grabbed the line right out of the water with his left hand, while still holding onto the broken butt end of the pole with his right. The broken top half bounced and thrashed about in the water like a large, homemade bobber fashioned from a stick. Dad quickly made his way back to shore and tossed the butt end of the pole a few feet behind him, then began to pull in his still flailing prey, one hand over the other.

When Scamp arrived upon the scene, the fish was still fighting and splashing not ten feet from shore as Dad kept trying to land it by hand. My brothers and I were convinced it was a musky, but regardless, Scamp wanted in on the action. Barking the whole time as he ran back and forth along the shore, that crazy mutt finally backtracked into the trees then turned and charged, leaping right into the lake directly towards the writhing fish.

"Scamp! Scamp! Get the heck out of there!" My brothers and I screamed, but it wasn't until Dad bellowed "SCAMP!!" before our courageous mutt paid any attention. Like I told you, when Dad raised his baritone football coach's voice, everyone, and I mean *every*one, fell silent and paid attention. Scamp paid attention all right, but he was anything but silent. Back on shore he was barking so furiously a small crowd of campers had formed, half expecting, in all probability, to find a body.

Before long Dad had managed to get the fish within netting range, but by the time Don had sprinted to the boat and back with the net Dad had already reached down and grabbed the writhing fish by hand. It was a musky all right, around thirty inches or so. That doesn't sound big to most folks, but to my brothers and me it was huge - not near as big as Grampa's, but judging from what we had been catching, huge.

When Dad quickly brought it to our campsite a vacationing state trooper took one look at it and said it was probably a northern, after he found out Dad's intention if it was a musky;

he was going to get it to the water before it was too late and let it go. It had measured out at twenty-nine inches, and since a musky had to be thirty inches to be legal, Dad wasn't going to keep it. Dad played hard, but by the rules.

"Nope," the state trooper said, "that's a northern all right. I'd clean and cook it right away if I were you, but watch out for the Y bones." Then he left.

Dad wasn't about to argue with one of Wisconsin's Finest, not as far as fish identification was concerned. It was 1961, and back then hardly anyone had even heard of catch and release if at all, even if it had been a musky. Most folks adhered to "catch and eat" regardless of game fish species.

I was given the enviable task of cleaning that fish, and there weren't any Y bones. Not a one. It looked like a northern though, if a northern has pointed, reddish fins and muted, vertical stripes along its body...

Years later I had some very impressive shore lunches prepared by guides whose culinary expertise in filleting and cooking extremely fresh northern was an art unto itself, but nothing compared to the texture and flavor of Dad's fish that evening. Although I hadn't filleted it (I didn't know how nor had even heard of it) all of us could still take fairly large bites without coming in contact with any small bones, just a few large ones. Mom was an expert at cooking fish, but what she fried up that evening using only corn meal and Crisco in a heavy iron skillet over an open fire was the most succulent fish any of us had ever tasted, or have since.

A northern? In a word, no. In hindsight, I wish it had been released, but it was delicious; 1961 guilt-free delicious.

The bluegill was delicious too, except with our preoccupation with Dad's fish as Mom served it, not enough attention had been given to the greatest scavenger in the history of Aurora, Illinois. Yes, the bluegill had no doubt been delicious as well, but Scamp was the only one that knew for sure.

Chapter 5

E ven though I was fourteen and not as inclined to envision things as unrealistically as when I was eleven, our August, 1962 fishing trip had me doing it all over again. With the exception of the very lucky or very good, Wisconsin lakes are generally merciless on musky hunters that don't know much, if anything, about the waters they're fishing, and also have little or no understanding of their prey and its habits, instincts and preferences.

If you don't have at least a partial working knowledge of what, say, a musky guide has, you might as well just cast away and hope for the best as far as catching a musky is concerned. Since we had never hired a guide, and articles and stories in 1962 about musky fishing were scarce to say the least, we needed all the help we could get. That's why I became so excited when Dad announced our destination that year would be Canada.

Not only were we going to Canada, we were going a fair distance north after crossing the border, all the way to a place called Perrault Falls. We would also be meeting up with family friends, Burke and Mariam Burkhardt. Mr. Burkhardt taught in the same school district as Dad, but his true love was the outdoors, especially Northwoods wilderness areas; the more pristine the better. He was an expert fisherman whose freestanding freezer was always packed with a variety of freshwater fish. Whenever we visited their home I never failed to pester Mr. Burkhardt until he took me to the garage and opened the freezer. I always had questions, and even though my brothers left the pestering up to me, they always ended up standing right there staring with awe at the results of Mr. Burkhardt's fishing prowess.

There was one major drawback as far as our first Canadian fishing adventure was concerned - Don wasn't coming along. He would turn nineteen later that year and was going off to college. It wouldn't be the same fishing without him, just like it wasn't the same in our family when he finally left for school. You expect a family to change as time goes on, but when it actually happens it's as if you weren't prepared for it at all. I know I wasn't anyway.

***

Trips to northern Wisconsin seemed to take forever, sometimes eight hours or so. It hadn't occurred to me to ask Dad how long it would take to get to Perrault Falls until we were past Hayward, Wisconsin. He chuckled and said we'd be stopping for the night in another three hours somewhere in Minnesota, then added, to my dismay, by then we would be maybe half way there.

It was a long trip all right, but once we arrived it was worth it. It took me less than ten minutes after we had pulled into the campsite to put my fishing gear in order and head straight for the dock, but Dad had other ideas. We would unload and set up camp first, then I could cast.

As exciting as it was for me was exactly how boring it was for my brother Larry. He would be turning eighteen that coming November, and had lobbied arduously to stay home. His passion had turned to music. He was the best high school trombone player in Aurora and most other high schools in the area as well. That summer he was in a local drum and bugle corps, and the last thing he wanted to do was pass on that just to go to Canada with his parents, kid brother and sister - and the infamous Scamp. That was part of it anyway. It wasn't lost on Mom and Dad that he also wanted the house to himself for two weeks, and that prospect didn't exactly make for sleep-filled nights as far as our parents were concerned.

***

Predictably, Scamp managed to get in trouble right away. As soon as the car door opened after pulling in to our campsite, he was gone like a shot. It wasn't until we had just finished making camp before he showed up again, and believe me, it wasn't a pretty sight - or smell. He had located a mound of bear dung of monumental proportions and had apparently spent the better part of half an hour rolling in it until he had attained the perfect amount of alluring fragrance necessary to make him irresistible to any female dogs that might be in the area.

Mom insisted she didn't really want to shoot Scamp, but he was probably lucky she didn't own a gun. Personally, I thought he was a goner anyway, after Mom told Dad it was his responsibility to wash our four-legged Don Juan in the lake. Scamp somehow survived, but would spend most of his remaining time in Canada on a chain. Dad ended up feeling sorry for him though, what with the constant whimpering and all, but Scamp had no sooner regained his freedom than an awful commotion broke out two campsites over.

We weren't positive if the package of bacon Scamp had in his mouth as he hightailed it back to our campsite was the only thing that had upset our enraged fellow camper because the large, ruddy-faced man apparently only spoke French - at least that's what he was speaking - yelling more like it, when he showed up. Scamp must have done something else though, because when Dad offered to pay more than the bacon was worth for our miscreant mutt's behavior, the guy, probably yelling French swear words, barely acknowledged Dad's atonement at all.

All that guy wanted to do was kill Scamp near as we could tell, so Larry and I had to assume it had something to do with the perfectly trimmed, little white poodle that was standing behind her master, eyeballing Scamp with either fear or ardor; fear if she was smart. From the look of her, it was highly unlikely Scamp had gone there to pick a fight.

Although the guy couldn't or wouldn't speak English, Dad made it clear that harming Scamp wasn't an option, unless he rolled in bear dung again, which was none of the French guy's business to begin with. Maybe the guy didn't speak English, but from the look in Dad's eyes he understood that Coach McCabe had no intention of repeating himself. The guy made some overly dramatic gestures that may or may not have been obscene, then left. Once again, Scamp had somehow survived.

Scamp was capable of escaping his collar and chain; he must have accomplished that feat at least twice a day. That always created nervous time, because there was no telling where Scamp's wanderlust, among other things, would take him. As it turned out he had discovered something he must have been convinced would prove absolutely irresistible to any female dogs within a five-mile radius. Forget bear dung - that was for amateurs - Scamp had figured out a way to not only slip under the fish-cleaning house, but had located rancid fish guts as well. Scamp had never believed in half measures, and rolling in putrid fish guts until he was thick with it was no exception.

If Mom had wanted to shoot Scamp before, the fish guts residue from head to tail was a hanging offense as far as Dad was concerned. The only thing that saved that crazy mutt was Dad's love of animals in general, and the fact he wasn't, at heart, a violent man. That's the only thing I could figure out anyway. Even so, I was surprised Scamp survived the bath Dad administered in the lake. That was the only time I ever heard Dad use certain words he *never* would have uttered in front of Gramma...

***

Dad, Larry and I fished all the next day, but we only managed to land a few small northern. Once again, we apparently didn't have the expertise to catch the big ones, but that changed when the Burkhardt's arrived later that evening. Burke, as Dad called him, saw right away what we were doing wrong and corrected the situation. He also knew where, exactly, we should be fishing.

We spent all the next day trolling for walleye, using the spinner rigs Burke had given us. I insisted I was fishing for muskies and spent over half my time casting crankbaits, but it was fun catching walleye too. We all caught our limit by the time shore lunch rolled around, and were releasing the smallest walleye as soon as we landed a bigger one, which was happening on a regular basis. I also caught a few northern while casting, but no muskies were even sighted let alone caught.

Before long it was time for one of Mariam's famous shore lunches. They didn't just fry the fresh walleye; they deep-fried them using a beer based, spiced batter. There were plenty of standard side dishes that were excellent as well, but the deep-fried walleye, filleted and cooked within moments of their demise, may have been the best fish we had ever tasted, except for Dad's Carrol Lake musky and even that was debatable.

It didn't hurt to be surrounded by the unparalleled Northwoods ambiance of the Perrault Falls area either, on an island located miles into the Canadian wilderness. As peaceful and relaxing that our break for shore lunch had been, it was time to get back on the water. I wasn't overly bored catching walleye but I wanted more, and true to its promise Perrault Falls was about to deliver.

***

It was Dad's idea, although he didn't bring it up until we were supposedly done for the day and settled in at our campsite. Evening was approaching, but being that far north in August kept that a secret, and Dad wasn't wearing his watch; he never wore it once we arrived and wouldn't put it on again until it was time to head home. Even so, dark clouds had begun to gather, creating the illusion we were much farther south.

I was casting off the dock with a brown, jointed crankbait the size of Grampa's Pikie Minnow when Dad approached. The lure was nameless, except for the *JC Higgins* logo on its rear section spelled out in black cursive writing. I liked the way it looked in the water, the way it squiggled smoothly through the shallows like a small, naive perch without a care in its dangerous, watery world.

I thought Dad had showed up to ask me if I had seen Scamp, who had managed to slip out of his collar - again. Apparently, the French guy was looking for Scamp as well, or more likely his cute little female poodle that had also disappeared. For some reason, Dad must not have been too concerned about that French guy being able to find Scamp though.

"Let's head out to those lily pads across the lake," Dad suggested, pointing to a spot about half a mile away. No mention was made of Scamp. I figured Dad knew what our adventurous mutt was up to and wouldn't be back until he'd accomplished his mission anyway, so there was no sense worrying about it. "We can get in a good hour or two trolling that lure of yours along the edge of those pads. Might even find a musky," Dad said as he untied the rear of our boat after having climbed in. He didn't have to repeat himself, and before long we were on our way.

***

It hadn't begun to rain but it sure looked like it wanted to. A thick cloud cover had moved in from the northwest with varying shades of near black and deep purple. They appeared so pregnant with moisture we could smell, and almost taste it.

Dad lined up the boat along the north end of the long section of lily pads and began idling south at a slow, steady pace. I had my lure trailing about forty feet behind us, maybe three feet away from the thick patch of pads that had to have been a hundred feet from its outer edge to the shore and several hundred yards long.

I wasn't at all convinced we would find anything, and said so to Dad. After all, we traveled over who knew how many miles by water from our campsite to locate the walleye, so it didn't make sense to only go across the lake from where we were camped and expect any action. Dad just smiled as I continued to pontificate about my theory, then he told me something that embodied the essence of my father as much as anything I would ever come to know about the man.

"Remember Dowdie Lake?" He asked, knowing full well I did. It was in the Colorado Rockies, where we used to camp.

"One afternoon I took my pole and sat on a large boulder by the shore. Had a nightcrawler at the other end of my line, and a clear plastic bobber floating about twenty feet out. This old timer, a Colorado native, said I was wasting my time at that spot, but he wasn't surprised, me being a flatlander. He was a gruff old guy, and made it clear that he didn't have much use for folks in general and Easterners in particular."

"We're not Easterners, Dad." I felt compelled to interject, to my father's amusement.

"That's right, Mot, but when I told him I was from Illinois that was far enough east for him. He also didn't have any use for fishermen who went after rainbow trout with worms. Said there should be a law against it, and I don't think he was kidding. He tolerated my company enough to bum a smoke, and when he was done with it he flicked the butt towards my bobber, and said that part of the lake was only good to use as an ashtray, not that a flatlander would know the difference."

"I wish you would've punched him, Dad," I again interjected, more than a little irritated with an old man I had never even seen. "Didn't you say anything to him at all?"

"Didn't have to. That cigarette butt no sooner hit the water when my bobber disappeared. A few minutes later I netted a three-pound rainbow. I did ask him if he wanted another smoke, and if he wouldn't mind flicking the butt in the lake again, but I guess he had better things to do."

"Like what?" I wondered out loud.

"Oh, shuffle off grumbling about flatlanders I guess." Dad had a slight smile on his face as he savored that particular recollection. "Keep your eye on the end of your line, Mot. You never know."

I did as Dad instructed, but the here and now didn't hold the same promise for me as his past conquest did for him. That was about to change - about to change about fifty feet farther down the outer edge of those lily pads.

***

"Dad! *Dad!*" I screamed as the eruption of water shattered the peaceful evening's ambiance. Something had slammed into my lure with such force it seemed as if the whole lake had exploded right before my eyes. It happened so fast and with so much fury all I could do was hang on. Setting the hooks was a moot point, because whatever was on the other end of my line had taken care of that itself. Mr. Burkhardt had adjusted the drag on all our reels, and had explained why. I tried reeling in, but my line just kept whizzing off the spool as I helplessly cranked to no avail, as if the entire mechanism had become suddenly useless. It wasn't until I shoved my thumb against the line on the spool that I truly felt the power of what I was up against.

Thankfully the fish, or sea serpent, or whatever it was had taken off for the deep as opposed to shooting into the thick growth of lily pads. All of a sudden the line went slack, so I began to reel desperately as my heart sank into the pit of my stomach. Unlike small fish, however, when you're not sure if they're still on or not, this one informed me in no uncertain terms that the fight wasn't over. I managed five or six turns of the reel, bringing in line as fast as possible, when the water again exploded maybe twenty feet from the boat. What may have been a musky, I hoped, had leapt from beneath the waves and crashed down on its side with a resounding splash that sent water flying a good five feet in all directions. The line began to come off my reel again, but not as fast as the first time.

"He's tiring, Thomas, keep the line tight and keep reeling!" Dad sometimes called me Thomas when a situation required full concentration, whether it was a snowball fight I was losing to my older brothers, a foot race I was trying to win or now, with a large northern that I was, with sheer force of will, trying to change into a musky. The line went slack again, but this time we could see why. The fish was coming straight for the boat!

"Reel, Thomas, reel!" Dad and I were definitely on the same wavelength, at least as far as reeling was concerned.

"See Dad, it's a musky all right!" I yelled as I cranked, my hand a blur. "Muskies charge boats! I read that in Field and Stream!"

"We'll soon find out," Dad exclaimed as he grabbed the net, "just keep reeling!"

I managed to get all the line in just as the fish got to the boat, and in one shift motion Dad pulled the net through the water, scooped up my prey and deposited it on the floor of the boat with a resounding *thud!*

One look at the fish told us the Quest was still unfulfilled. Nice catch, but not a musky. We had nailed enough northern trolling for walleye or casting the past few days to realize that immediately, but at least it was the biggest northern any of us had ever landed. It weighed out at eight pounds, which to my fourteen-year-old eyes was massive. As excited as I felt I couldn't help but wonder what it must be like to land the ultimate fresh water fish, especially a huge one like Grampa's.

Still, catching that northern had felt great; the feeling was further amplified when Dad, a huge grin on his face, reached out his hand in my direction. It was the first time my father had offered to shake my hand man to man, at least under that type of circumstance. I had fought a big fish and won - a big fish others might have lost, indeed *had* lost over the years. Maybe not that one, but fish just like it. I took Dad's hand and shook it, returning his firm grip. I had heard never to let your hand go limp when shaking someone else's hand, and I wanted to make sure I didn't mess up our rite of passage.

We stayed out there until it was dark and managed to hook into several more northern, although none as big as the first one. I asked Dad why he wasn't fishing, why he was just driving the boat. I even offered him my lure, which by then had teeth marks all over it that in my mind elevated it to a warrior status of epic proportions. Dad wouldn't take it though, nor let out a lure of his own.

"How come, Dad?" I asked. "Don't you want to catch a few?"

"I have been," he said with his trademark smile. "I've been catchin' 'em all evening."

***

The rain was beating against the top and sides of our tent so hard it had awakened Larry, Suzie and me from a sound sleep. At least the old tent was waterproof, as long as you didn't touch its sides or the top. If you did, the canvas would allow the rainwater to bleed inside from the precise spot you touched, and before long things would get pretty messy if you kept doing it. It was a moderate wonderment, tame as far as real wonderments were concerned, yet difficult to resist since we liked to touch the side of the tent during a heavy rain just to watch it happen. I couldn't get away with it if Mom and Dad were in the tent, but that night they were sleeping in the old Plymouth station wagon.

Suzie was only six, and even though Larry or I should have accompanied her to the outhouse that night, neither of us felt like getting drenched. It was only forty or fifty feet away and besides, the well-worn path through the brush wasn't *that* hard to follow even if the rain hadn't let up all that much, as in not at all. Still, when nature's call took that step past simply calling and started screaming as it had with our kid sister, something had to give.

"You're the oldest," I reminded my brother after I had turned on our flashlight. "You should go with her."

"Yeah, well, you're closest to her age," was his response, which made no sense at all. Didn't matter though; he was the big brother and didn't have to make sense. Suzie just sat there looking at us, the flashlight casting an eerie pall as the storm raged, wearing an expression that had begun to show signs of urgency as opposed to mere impatience.

"I'm closer in age because you were born first, so you have to go." Suzie squirmed at my nonsensical remark. Her expression seemed to be asking if either of us dopes knew what we were talking about.

"You were born *second* so you go. I have seniority."

"No, *you* were born second, I was third, so you -" Suzie grabbed the flashlight from me and stood up, unzipped the tent flap and headed outside without so much as a word or a second glance at either of us. A clap of thunder followed a burst of lightning that illuminated the woods, brush, station wagon and the roof of the distant outhouse simultaneously - and Suzie – it illuminated her too as she trudged along the path with deliberate six-year-old steps.

"You should'a gone." I admonished Larry.

"*You* should'a. Zip the flap." He rolled over in his sleeping bag. The debate was over.

"Open up!" Suzie hollered. Larry and I went for the zipper at the same time. She hadn't been gone long, but for some reason it had seemed that way. She managed to get one foot into the tent when the pungent odor all but crossed our eyes as if we had inhaled from a vat of ammonia.

"Out! *Out!*" Larry commanded. "You need to wash up!" He was right. Suzie had been the recipient of a skunk's direct hit, and I mean *direct*. The invasive, pungent odor had already permeated the tent.

"Let me *in* you guys!"

"No!" I yelled, competing with the driving rain. "You need to see Mom! Go to the car!"

Neither of us derived any pleasure from having been forced to send our kid sister away in a driving thunderstorm, covered as she was with highly concentrated skunk stench, but such was the fate of the fallen. After all, we wouldn't have expected to be let back in if it had happened to either of us.

To her credit, Suzie didn't cry or whine. She had a few choice words for us, but spoke them only as she stomped away towards the station wagon, her flashlight illuminating the driving rain. It sure was coming down all right; Suzie could've been sitting in a convertible going through a carwash and not been any wetter. Larry and I felt more than a little ignoble, if not downright contemptible. The inevitable confrontation with Mom and Dad wasn't lost on us either.

"The boys won't let me in the tent because I stink!" Suzie announced to our groggy mother after Mom had unrolled the side window.

"Oh sweetie," Mom replied, half asleep, before she knew what was up, "you don't stink. Here, come inside…" Then the smell hit full force; it even awakened Dad.

The skunk had pretty much covered our kid sister, including a direct hit to her head. No amount of rainwater was about to remove all that from her hair. Mom had to throw Suzie's pajamas outside in the mud, not that it helped much. From his spot at my parent's feet only Scamp was intrigued – no big surprise there.

Larry and I went back to sleep, figuring we'd need our rest for the next day's inquisition with Mom and Dad. We had abandoned our kid sister in her hour of need, and probably deserved whatever fate awaited us. Not much happened though. Once Dad had fully awakened and got a whiff of his only daughter, he understood - maybe.

***

The following morning Suzie was washed down with tomato juice. It didn't help – not even close. More importantly the fishing remained good, and although we continued to catch a fair amount of northern and all the walleye we wanted, we never did see any muskies. They were out there though, and I refused to accept anything from anyone that suggested otherwise, at least as it pertained to us.

Most folks we ran into on our fishing vacations either acted politely condescending or not so polite when letting us know muskies, although not impossible to catch, might as well be. Stick to walleye, bass, panfish and of course northern if you want something that at least resembles a musky, they would sometimes advise. *The bobber and worm crowd*…Grampa's words - and especially his fish - I refused to forget those things. Most important, I refused to forget *him*.

Chapter 6

"*Iowa? For muskies?"* I was beyond skeptical as it pertained to what Dad was telling me. Near as I could tell, our 1963 fishing trip had evolved into a bad news / worst news scenario. Not that I had anything against the state of Iowa, far from it. Mom had been born and raised in Cedar Falls, where Grandfather Corbin still resided. My Aunt Zada Smith and Uncle Aub lived in Marshalltown along with my cousins Carolyn and Jim, and I always enjoyed our yearly visits to both places, but not because of the great fishing. Dad assured me there was a good musky lake near the Minnesota border and that's where we were headed after visiting our relatives. I didn't even know Iowa had any lakes, let alone any that held muskies.

At fifteen, masking my skepticism wasn't exactly my strong suit, nor was keeping my mouth shut about it. I also wasn't adept at putting two and two together. My parents had one son in college and another right behind him. Dad was putting in twelve hour days painting houses that summer to supplement his teacher's salary just to make ends meet, but that didn't register with me. It had been decided that combining our annual trip to Iowa along with some time on the water best served our financial situation, but that wasn't something my parents felt comfortable discussing with their children; I didn't know why.

My complaining must have been annoying but I guess they were used to it. The same couldn't be said about my Iowa grandfather, Robert Corbin. I didn't know him nearly as well as I had Grampa McCabe, simply because of geography. I used to see Grampa almost every Sunday and on holidays as well - my grandfather Corbin, once a year at most. He was, in his own right, a good storyteller, and when he picked up on my disappointment regarding Iowa musky lakes he set me straight - and in no uncertain terms.

"Get over here, young man, take a seat." He said as he sat in his large, upholstered rocking chair. He wasn't a man to be taken lightly so I immediately did as I was told, another rarity for my fifteen-year-old disposition.

He took a non-filtered Raleigh cigarette out of its pack, wetted the end he intended to put in his mouth and lit it. He was the only person I had ever seen do that to a cigarette, and I found it somewhat interesting, the way he could smoke an unfiltered cigarette after saturating the end without ending up with a mouthful of tobacco. He picked up a church key, opened a Grain Belt beer and started in with his story.

He could probably tell I was only half interested, with skepticism making up the other half. I seldom felt the urge to mask my feelings unless I was in trouble, let alone appreciate the immortal words of George Burns, the famous comedian and actor: "Sincerity is the key to success; once you can fake that you have it made."

"Wisconsin's a good place for muskies, Minnesota too, and certain parts of Canada shouldn't be overlooked or so I've heard, but neither should West Okoboji Lake right here in Iowa. Wish I was going with you, except not for the fishing. There's a lot of history up there and if you want to learn about it, have I got a book for you!" He got up and walked over to a bookshelf, pulled out a book and handed it to me. I looked at the cover then spoke, mostly to myself.

"*Spirit Lake,* by MacKinlay Kanter -"

"Kan*tor*," Grandfather Corbin said, correcting me. "Thing is," he continued, "I actually know the man, or used to more like it. Haven't spoken to him in years. He grew up not far from here, over Webster City way. His writing is some of the best you'll ever read. Even won the Pulitzer once. That's a true story you have in your hand, Tom, as far as historical fiction goes, and a good one too. Spirit Lake is connected to West Okoboji Lake. Has plenty of muskies, or at least enough. But that's not what the story is about. It's about an Indian massacre." That got my attention.

"An Indian massacre? In Iowa?"

"Hell yes, in Iowa!" He exclaimed, feigning indignation that I fell for completely. "Damn near forty souls were lost! If I were going where you get to go tomorrow, the first thing I'd do is go to the very spot where some of it happened, not far from the lake. The graves of the butchered settlers are there along with one of the original cabins where part of the massacre took place. Why, one of those Indians grabbed this baby by its heels, walked over to this huge oak tree and -"

"*Father.*" It was Mom.

"Well, just read the book," he said, one eye on his daughter. "You'll appreciate your trip a great deal more that way."

***

Grandfather Corbin was right. He was right about a lot of things. MacKinlay Kantor was an excellent writer, if mesmerizing a fifteen-year-old boy utilizing exceptional, descriptive story telling counted. I began reading it that evening and put it down only because several hours later my eyes refused to stay open. I was grateful when Grandfather Corbin told me to take it along, and I kept on reading all the way there. By the time of our arrival, the entire area had grown to mythical proportions in my mind. I was surprised how beautiful the area was, although Kantor's story had cast an unsettling pall over everything. There was an amusement park not far from the settlers' graves, and even that seemed haunted somehow, as if it had been built, irreverently, upon sacred ground.

It had been over a hundred years since the massacre, but since I had just read Kantor's chilling account, it might as well have occurred the day before we arrived - almost anyway. It seemed as if I was the only one in the whole area who appreciated the significance of the massacre. That changed after we visited the graves and the original cabin where much of the bloodshed had occurred, and I had explained to my family what was in the book.

There were quite a few old growth oak trees standing near one of the original cabins that had been preserved, and I couldn't help wonder if one of those trees had been used to smash that ill-fated baby's skull my grandfather had started to tell me about. MacKinlay Kantor had brought the story home full force, and it was disquieting to think we were standing right where it had happened. It wasn't until we made it to our campsite and I could look out over West Okoboji Lake that the disturbing images began to fade back into history. Even so, that night in the tent I had my hunting knife right under my pillow.

***

The morning sun was a welcome sight and again the beauty of the lake and surrounding area was impressive. All I had known about Iowa was corn and soybean fields, and although you didn't have to travel far to find them, we were camped amidst soaring, old growth oak and hickory trees. West Okoboji Lake was equally impressive; the locals even maintained it was the bluest lake in North America. That may have been a stretch, but it did look as good as any lake I had ever seen, for the most part. If I caught a big musky it would take first place hands down, and I wasted no time making my way to the shore for a few casts.

Dad had left to rent a boat, so with some ambivalence I tossed out a bobber and worm from shore, figuring to switch to a crank-bait once we were on the water. My big brother Don had made the trip, and the two of us were killing time until Dad's return, watching my bobber bounce on the waves. It began to dance, so I set the hook into what turned out to be an average sized bluegill.

"Mind if I cast that out?" Don asked. Sounded like a plan to me, so I said sure. He took off the bobber and let fly, placing the bluegill a good thirty feet or so from shore. We were talking, at least I was, about the Indian massacre as Don slowly reeled in the bluegill. With maybe ten feet to go before reaching shore, a sizable blur in the water shot out of nowhere and slammed into that bluegill before we knew what had happened. Don's reflexes were a thing of legend all right, and in an instant a four-pound northern was flopping around on the sandy shore. It hadn't even been hooked - just too ornery to let go of its meal. We were so dumbfounded by what had just occurred that all we did was stare at it, at least at first. That northern had a nose for the water however, and that's exactly what it was flopping towards - and fast.

Still dumbstruck, I just stood there like I had fallen out of the stupid tree and hit every branch on the way down, but not Don. After all, it was his fish. He was almost between that rapidly moving, determined northern and the lake when it first touched the water, and he made it nearly knee deep *in* the lake when that northern, straining off one more heroic flop, splashed down just to Don's left - big, big mistake. Don was left-handed.

The northern had righted itself in the shallows and was in the process of executing a tail thrust when Don, true to his reputation, shot his left hand down and knocked his prey sideways, disorienting it for the split second it took Don to grab on with both hands and fling it back on shore. After that it was no contest, and our evening's dinner was secured. A good thing, too, because after casting all day Don's northern was all we had to show for our efforts.

***

Funny thing about some people who love fishing, at least any number of novices; once a decent catch has been made on unfamiliar waters, the exact spot of that particular conquest looms so large it's as if the rest of the lake becomes a longshot, or at best questionable. That counterproductive mindset came full circle the following morning when Dad had to resort to using his coach's voice to get my brother and me away from shore and into the boat - the boat Dad had paid good money to rent. Again, no luck. Not even a follow.

Misery not only loves company, it seeks it out. A possible sign that you may be camping near other uneducated, or at least unlucky musky hunters, is when every one of them reports the same failure rate. Invariably, someone will claim to have had at least a follow, one that they "just caught out of the corner of my eye, but it was a whopper!" Those claims are almost always suspect, especially when they are delivered as an afterthought. A sure sign is when folks hover around a four-pound northern like Don's and someone wonders out loud if it might be at least a state record, or "darn close to it".

Sometimes, it's not until you go into a local bait shop that you're even convinced there are any fish of consequence in the area lakes at all. Skunked musky hunters, naturally skeptical to begin with, have even been known to question whether or not the brutes mounted on the wall represented the last big fish those lakes had to offer, assuming the mounts weren't purchased somewhere else to help sell lures.

Those types of irrational thought processes don't go away until you stumble across some lucky (or knowledgeable and lucky) person, face flushed with victory, holding onto a major catch. If they released it, you can usually tell by their excited demeanor whether or not they're telling the truth, unless they are exceptionally good liars - another natural trait, some insist, of musky hunters in general.

None of the above even begins to fade until you've landed a few big ones yourself, something that continued to elude the McCabe clan as the 1960's came to a close. The Quest remained unfulfilled, but not our desire. More importantly, our determination to fulfill it was intact as well.

Chapter 7

By the time 1971 rolled around Don and I were both married with children, Larry was traveling the world as a professional musician and Dad was in the home stretch heading towards retirement. Having survived her plunge into Lake Tomahawk and a skunk attack as well as growing up with three older brothers, our kid sister Suzie was sweet sixteen, and as of late answered to the name Sue. Mom was the director of the Wesley Methodist Church nursery school, and both of the females in our family no longer expressed much interest in camping, and even less in musky quests.

Not so for Dad, Don and me, and as it turned out that year, Larry as well. He would be back home for a short while that September and the four of us agreed it would be a great time to jump start the Quest, and what better place to do it than Pelican Lake?

To us it remained sacred waters and hallowed ground, consecrated decades ago by Grampa. Larry insisted Grampa still held sway over the area and he received no argument from the rest of us; not even a sideways glance. To do so would have been more than folly - it would have been a sacrilege. In a way, Grampa was there all right. You could feel him in the breeze as he eased your lure on target, or when the air was so still a down feather wouldn't sway an iota as it descended upon the mirror-like water so gently there wasn't a ring-wave to be seen. Every eagle perched on a tree only appeared detached and bored as it watched us throw cast after cast. Most of all, he was there when the lake was shrouded in mist and especially when the wind and rain held sway; Grampa's favorite musky weather.

I'm not saying we accepted anything, like Grampa was actually up there with the eagles for instance, maybe even one of them, but we enjoyed entertaining the possibility, whimsical or not. One thing was for sure; our desire to have him there when it finally happened, when the waters of Pelican Lake exploded and a fish like Grampa's had joined the fight.

I made sure to stop at the small country grocery store near the Old Hotel, as Grampa had always called it, where we were staying. I didn't need anything the store had to offer, at least nothing on the shelves. It was what I had spotted out front that had drawn me to the place. I doubted it was the same cooler Grampa had called me over to inspect way back in 1959, but my doubt left once I was in front of it. It was the same one all right, a little worse for wear, but not really. It was empty, but that was also a matter of perspective. Just because there was nothing in it didn't mean it was empty at all.

***

We were pounding the north shoreline of Antigo Island when it happened. We had been casting all morning with nothing to show for it, and I had become more involved with conversation and changing from one lure to the next than concentrating on the job at hand. I let fly for what felt like the millionth time that day. My bucktail eased its way right next to a large, fallen tree that appeared as if it had been in the water for years. I looked away to respond to something Don had said as I gave the reel a few turns. Suddenly the water just past the fallen tree erupted as if an outboard motor had roared to life. I felt the tug and immediately tried to set the hooks, but just as instantly as the turmoil had erupted, it disappeared.

First one, then another of my brothers' lures found the same spot as Dad maneuvered the boat for a better angle. I frantically took another few shots at the spot myself, then a few more, but I might as well have been casting into a retention pond. The fish that created all the excitement was somewhere in the lake, but it sure wasn't anywhere near that fallen tree any longer, unless it had decided to hang around to ridicule our futile attempts.

Another in a long line of lessons had been learned the hard way, which I was beginning to believe was the only way to truly appreciate anything worth learning; when you're fishing, *fish*. Don't gaze at the scenery or turn your attention away from your lure until it is back in the boat. There's plenty of time for that other stuff after you have completed your cast and retrieve. As it turned out that was the only strike of any significance, at least for me, on the whole trip. Muskies, it seemed, were only willing to offer one chance, at least on Pelican Lake. We had little reason to believe otherwise.

***

How many different ways are there to lose a musky? I'm not sure. I can't comprehend the concept of infinity or the lack thereof as it relates to the universe, either. Sharpen all your treble hooks except one, and that's the one the musky will find. Spend several hundred dollars on your fishing gear but in your haste or ignorance tie on a cheap leader, and that's what will malfunction when the big strike happens. If your drag is too tight, too loose, or if the angle of your retrieve is thrown off by the shifting of the boat, be ready for another big strike. I could go on, and probably will eventually, but it was Don who discovered a new way of losing a fish that hadn't occurred to any of us.

We were approaching what the locals called Town Bar, but we didn't know that at the time. I suppose they had depth finders in 1971 but of course we didn't have one. Don let fly at what looked like shallows stuck right in the middle of the lake, and not three turns of his reel later his lure disappeared so he set the hooks hard. Nothing happened, at least at first.

"Looks like you snagged a rock," I offered. We had been doing a lot of that lately, depending on the area.

"Well, yeah," Don responded, "except my line's going out pretty fast." He had a point.

What he didn't have was a whole lot of line on his reel. Not only that, but he had just picked up his backup pole and had cast with it, dry line and all. He tried reeling it in, but his drag acted as if he must have been joking. Looking down at his reel Don realized time was indeed working against him. Time, and whatever was swimming rapidly away with authority.

It's always a really bad sign when glimpses of the spool begin to appear as your line is whizzing away, and that time was no exception. To his credit, Don had purchased the heaviest test black Nylon line he could find, he just hadn't purchased enough. As desperation gave way to panic Don did the only thing that came to mind. The look in his eyes indicated more than a little pain was involved when he eased his thumb against what was left of his line – the dry as a bone line – with just enough pressure to slow it down. I had given myself a few friction burns throwing out the first cast of the day, having forgotten to wet my line before doing so. The last thirty feet or so of Don's line was anything but wet. I wouldn't have been all that surprised to see smoke appear.

Rather than ease up he applied enough pressure upon the spool to stop it. Before long his line grew as taut as piano wire, and his pole had more arch than a cobra eyeballing a cross-legged flute player. Slowly, the bow of the boat where Don was standing turned towards the retreating fish, or whale, or whatever it was Don had hooked. That's when Don did the one thing none of us had ever considered while in the process of losing a musky - he did nothing - except hold on.

One thing was certain; Cortland made strong black Nylon line. Remember the movie *Moby Dick?* Remember when those guys in the rowboats would harpoon a whale and then it took off, causing the rowboats to go flying across the water, skipping on top of the waves? Well, that's not what happened. We kind of inched along, but we were definitely moving, and at a steady pace. Actually, it was a little unnerving - just what *was* that thing, anyway? As you have probably surmised by now we never found out.

Cortland made strong black Nylon line all right, but everything has its breaking point. We just hadn't expected it to sound like the report of a distant rifle shot. Don was very agile, which may have been the only reason he didn't end up in the bottom of the boat. He didn't, but his heart did.

Another lesson learned, another dues payment made - with interest. Grampa's "thrill of thrills" would have to be put off another year. Or two. Or perhaps a decade or so. We weren't sure. We weren't sure, at least about that, but we were sure about one thing - the Quest was growing into mythical proportions, and we were growing (and learning) along with it.

Chapter 8

Don hadn't made the first trip to Canada in 1962, and had regretted it ever since after listening to our stories of having our limits of walleye before shore lunch and the lightning strikes from northern while trolling endless edges of lily pads at dusk, hunting for musky. As the years went by, those long-ago walleye catches became more plentiful and the northern, at least the ones that got away, flirted with near world record size. Don knew his kid brother was prone to exaggeration once in a while, but since Dad didn't dispute most of my stories there was no way Don was going to miss our 1972 expedition to Perrault Falls. He almost did, though.

Don was single again, and although Dad and I thought we had covered our departure time with him there had apparently been some miscommunication. When Dad and I arrived at Don's place around seven the morning of our departure, he had been in bed about an hour or so. At first, no amount of cajoling on my part had much affect. Don had spent the entire night and early morning hours with a few friends, including a young lady whose appearance had steadily improved as the ample supply of Budweiser in the refrigerator had just as steadily dwindled.

That would have been it for most guys I knew, but Don had always been able to function with little or no sleep regardless of circumstance. Still, his self-imposed paralysis that morning appeared to be insurmountable - until Dad weighed in. Actually, Dad didn't do much of anything. He just looked around Don's disheveled bachelor pad of an apartment and announced it was time to head for Canada – *all* of us. A half hour after that we were ten miles out of town with Don stoically propped up in the back seat - eyes glazed over but breathing steadily. He turned twenty-nine that year, so with relative youth on his side and a long nap (as in coma) he started to look human again about the time we made International Falls, Minnesota, right on the Canadian border.

***

I had been impressed with the Canadian wilderness on our first trip when I was fourteen, but at twenty-four it took on a new perspective. I had been married to my high school sweetheart five years already, and Peggy and I had two beautiful children. Although most folks warn against teenagers marrying, ours was working. Neither one of us had been mature or wise enough to know what we were getting into, so in some respects we had been blessed by sheer luck.

The trip to Canada that year was a perfect example. Peggy had seen me off with her sincere blessings with an understanding of how important family fishing adventures were to me. It wasn't only about putting a line in the water; she understood that, too.

The anticipation prior to a trip might not be half the fun, but it's a significant part of it. It's one thing to wander the aisles in some tackle shop the rest of the year, but when a special trip is imminent it takes on a whole new perspective. There's always at least a few new lures that have to be purchased, maybe even a new reel if the money is there. Every well-prepared musky hunter knows you need back-ups for your back-ups, including but not limited to another rod, extra line and leaders, quality reels, split rings and other hardware in general, maybe a new fillet knife even if you hadn't used the first one, and of course anything that's even remotely related to fishing that is new and innovative.

There was a tackle shop in International Falls we decided to visit. We marveled at the huge, freshwater fish that were mounted on the walls, especially the muskies. Seeing huge musk-ies mounted on a wall usually elicited one of two emotions; if were we beginning a musky hunt they offered hope with a tinge of envy. If we were on our way home, envy with a tinge of hope.

I was with Don looking at musky lures, trying to justify purchasing a few, when this older guy overheard our conversa-tion. We had been talking about muskies of course, but when he heard us mention our destination he took it upon himself to correct what he maintained was a misconception on our part. According to him, there were no muskies in any of the waters in the vicinity of Perrault Falls because that area was too far north for the king and especially queen of freshwater fish. He went on to tell us we were in luck, however. Lake of the Woods was not only much closer, but was also home to some of the finest musky fishing in the world.

Boy was that depressing. Suddenly, the vacation we had been planning for months was considerably diminished. I picked out some musky lures anyway, and wondered out loud as I approached the counter with Don if maybe we should try Lake of the Woods instead. The clerk overheard me then asked where we were going and why. I told him everything that had just happened, and he started to chuckle.

"That's not the first time that sneaky old codger has pulled that one," the clerk said, still snickering. "He's part owner of a resort on Lake of the Woods. He's right though; there are plenty of big muskies there. I'm surprised he didn't try to talk you into staying at his place. By the way, there's plenty of muskies in the Perrault Falls area too, believe me." Suddenly, the sun was shining again.

We hadn't bothered making reservations for a cabin, assuming we'd always be able to get a campsite and throw up Dad's large tent. When the twenty-two hour drive was over, however, we were informed that not only was a cabin available, it was right on the water with the main pier just to the south of it. It even had a screened-in front porch, and that's exactly where the three of us were lounging the following evening over a few Canadian brews.

***

Our first day on the water had been a major disappointment. Ten years had passed since our initial trip to Perrault Falls. Dad and I had not only forgotten the long and winding route through the connecting lakes that Mr. Burkhardt had shown us back then, but we also didn't know exactly how he had assembled our walleye rigs, or whether or not we had even purchased the correct type. We wanted to bring home our limits in walleye while still looking for muskies and had spent the day trolling in areas that looked good to us, but not one walleye took our minnows. Worse yet, not a single northern, let alone any musky, took one of the Pikie Minnows or Daredevils we kept throwing while trolling, even after nearly a dozen passes along the same edge of lily pads that had been so productive in 1962. Don knew his kid brother was susceptible to an occasional touch of poetic license from time to time, but as the day wore on his remarks started to redefine the word "snide".

It didn't help Don's mood any when a group of fishermen from Iowa, staying in the cabin next to us, just happened to return to the dock the same time as us. I don't suppose I'll ever forget the look on Don's face as one fisherman after another hoisted his heavy stringer of huge northern and slammed them upon the wooden dock with authority, and no small effort. No muskies though.

Don asked them where they had managed to catch so many big ones, and to their dubious credit they didn't just point and say "in the lake" – they hadn't said that because they were as creative as they were diabolical. According to them, we needed to find the heaviest weed growth possible, "a real jungle", and cast right into it. Oh, we "might" get snagged, perhaps lose a lure or two, but the casts that didn't get snagged stood a very good chance of ending up creating stringers like theirs, and perhaps a few muskies. Uh huh. We decided to stick to trolling, and casting *close* to the weed beds and lily pads. We were ignorant, not stupid - usually.

***

So there we were after our first day, looking out over the lake from our screened-in front porch a good twenty-two hours from home, pining for the good old days. What happened next was legendary, and would go down in McCabe family fishing lore. Don had returned from the kitchen with three ice-cold beers, and as he handed one to Dad then me, Dad made the following, fateful comment:

"Sure would be nice if Burke was here."

Don and I concurred, took a sip from the cold bottles as the three of us fell silent and gazed out over the magnificent body of water directly in front of our cabin. We were silently taking in the unspoiled Northwoods grandeur when our peripheral vision caught the image of a fisherman walking by, coming from our left. A number of such men had passed by during the past hour or so, all looking pretty much the same. The fisherman walked past our cabin, and with his hat on didn't look any different from the rest of the men in camp. Then Dad got a good look at the man's profile.

"Burke!" Dad hollered in his loudest coach's voice, and the man's head turned instantaneously. There we were, a million miles from nowhere, with who knows how many fishing camps between Aurora and where we were in northern Canada, and staring up at us with a smile on his rugged face was the one man we would have most wanted to see in the entire world.

By stupefying coincidence, perhaps fate, Burke and his wife Miriam had ended up at Perrault Falls the day after us. I was so excited I nearly tripped going down the three wooden steps of the porch to shake his hand. Don and Dad were right behind me, and before long the four of us were sharing stories from ten years ago, along with bottles of Canadian beer so cold it fairly hurt to hold them.

There's a few things about Burke you ought to know. His parents immigrated to America from Russia before the murder of the Czar and his family in 1917. Burke's parents ended up in the iron country of Minnesota where Burke gained a reputation as one tough high school football player. Those were the days when face masks were unheard of and even the wearing of helmets, at least in certain parts of northern Minnesota, was for some guys tantamount to pirouetting onto the field sporting ballerina shoes and lipstick; bright red lipstick.

Anyway, Dad had met him when they played football together at Iowa State Teacher's College, which later changed its name to the University of Northern Iowa. Burke had been there because Coach Starbeck had gone all the way up to northern Minnesota from Cedar Falls to recruit him.

According to Dad, Burke was one exceptionally tough hombre. For some reason, quite a few folks from the World War II generation didn't run off at the mouth much, so it was usually difficult getting that type of information out of them. Same was true with Burke, although others certainly took note of him. Reputations like his were almost impossible to suppress.

His Christen name was Wendelyn, but God help the poor soul who was foolish enough to address him so in his younger days. There were all sorts of stories about how he had made a living before attending college and his demeanor in general for that matter, but Dad had always liked and respected Burke, so that was enough for the rest of us.

Dad was an opinionated man who rarely shared his opinions without being coaxed, and had little use for those who didn't comprehend the concept of keeping their mouths shut when those around them wished for nothing greater. Actions didn't just speak louder than words as far as guys like Dad and Burke was concerned; a person's actions were generally *all* that mattered. I never saw them throw their weight around or try to intimidate others, but it was a safe bet giving them a hard time was probably a really bad idea.

When Dad had just finished basic training during World War II, his sergeant not only wouldn't give him a three-day pass to attend his grandfather's funeral in Naperville, but went out of his way to make sure the powers that be supported his decision. Dad wasn't very far away from Naperville; he was stationed at Camp Dodge outside of Des Moines, Iowa, but his sergeant apparently didn't want to miss the opportunity to further his reputation as a complete horse's ass. Dad's request was not only denied, but eventually done so in a loud and derisive manner in front of the whole squadron. Something about "Private McCabe can do his boo-hoo-hooing in his bunk tonight, because he sure as hell ain't gonna be doin' it on vacation at some damn funeral with a war going on."

Fast forward one year to 1944. Private 1st class Pete McCabe was in Italy with the 329th Field Artillery of General Mark Clark's Fifth Army. One day a "friendly" touch football game was in progress with none other than Dad's former sergeant at quarterback for the opposing team. He attempted a naked bootleg for the third time during a goal line stand that Dad easily saw coming. So much for "touch" football; the hit Dad put on Sergeant Loud Mouth not only rendered the man unconscious, but when he came around and uncrossed his eyes, his right leg was broken in two places. If Burke had been there it may well have been four places.

You would never know Dad and Burke were capable of such things by their usual demeanors; at least you probably wouldn't assume that was the case. In their younger days they weren't necessarily inclined to express a desire to draw first blood, but once it started flowing it was a safe bet all of it wasn't theirs. Like I said though, you'd never know it by hanging around a campsite with them. They were basically quiet, reliable men who worked hard at their jobs and in their spare time enjoyed being with family, especially if fishing in a wilderness setting was involved.

***

Burke, of course, remembered the exact route to the prime walleye waters Dad and I had been telling Don about for a decade. The slow journey the five of us set out upon in two rowboats powered by relatively small outboard motors, through some of the most unspoiled Northwoods Canadian wilderness you're ever likely to see, was itself worth the trip. For mile after mile there were no cabins, power lines or even primitive dirt roads to remind us we were in the twentieth century. If some variation of a science fiction time warp occurred and a few natives indigenous to the area a few thousand years ago suddenly found themselves in a canoe next to us, we would've been the only things out of place.

We passed an outcropping of a sheer granite cliff located on one side of a pine studded island that soared straight up two hundred feet or more, with the opposite end being a gently sloped, sandy beached shoreline you could easily step upon. I was torn between the desire to begin catching fish and trying to catch muskies, or in taking the time to hike to the pinnacle of that magnificent island and take in the majestic view. Or...

"What a great place for a shore lunch." I said to no one in particular as I stared at the top of the cliff. Dad was in the back of the boat manning the outboard; Don was sitting in the middle and I was at the bow.

"Might take a while to get there," Don observed as he followed my gaze upwards. He was right, of course. The half-mile long island was dense with trees and brush, and although it sloped gently to the sandy beach on the one end, the last third of the way towards the cliff went up at about a thirty-degree angle, unless you actually went there anyway; then it would have probably been closer to forty degrees; a pathless trek over boulders amidst the dense forest, fallen trees and through thick brush. Dragging all the shore lunch equipment and utensils along didn't seem too appealing either. Still...

"Maybe someday," I said, rationalizing away the enticing concept, at least for the time being. Even though I was only twenty-four, a mild, nagging doubt set in, if just for a moment, that questioned my reluctance to pursue the small adventure. Something inside asked just how many times in my life had I found myself in such a pristine Northwoods setting deep in the Canadian wilderness, or would again? Of course I would, I told myself. Today, decades later, my advice to all concerned would be to hike, climb or crawl if you have to, but take the time to get to the top of that cliff. I wish I had. Maybe someday...

***

The walleye fishing that morning was okay, but not like Dad and I remembered from ten summers ago - especially Dad. For some reason, maybe because he was sitting at the stern, he ended up getting skunked the first morning. Don had caught a few, and I was, for some reason, luckiest of all trolling from my position at the bow. So much so, Dad dubbed me King Neptune for the day, and suggested we rotate the bow position, which seemed fair enough. It always seems fair when you're behind in the count, and when you're ahead it's tempting to prove you can out-fish the loyal opposition from anywhere in the boat.

Shore lunch was, true to the Burkhardt's reputation, outstanding. Miriam started out by frying in a huge iron skillet freshly hand-grated, hash brown potatoes and diced onions in bacon and butter while at the same time heating up her homemade baked bean casserole, loaded with brown sugar, onion, bacon and some secret ingredients that made it a meal by itself. You had to be careful though; overdoing it was not only an easy thing to do, but with that many beans and onions, well, you get the picture.

The main course was definitely the star of the show; walleye so fresh they were flopping about on a slab of granite just seconds before Burke and Miriam transformed them into sizzling fillets. The Burkhardt's displayed remarkable efficiency, with Burke first slicing then tossing the fresh fillets to Miriam who proceeded to coat them in her special recipe beer batter then deep fry them in four inches of bubbling Crisco, then onto our plates. The entire process took less than five minutes, and we washed down our Northwoods feast with some of Miriam's homemade lemonade.

After the dishes were done and we had cleaned up our campsite, Dad proved he was still snake bit. I had captured a frog and Dad rigged it to his spinner bait then made a soft cast into the small bay where we had tied the boats. The frog kept moving and jerking about, but nothing happened. Finally (probably because Dad hadn't had the heart to actually put a hook into the little guy) the frog managed to slip out of the makeshift harness Dad had constructed. The frog didn't make it two feet before the top of the tranquil little bay exploded in a white-water frenzy just beneath the spot where the late Mr. Frog had been last sighted.

The frog was, not surprisingly, never seen again. For a moment, judging from the look on Dad's face, I thought the same might have been said about him. He looked as if he wanted to slowly walk into the water, step after stoic step, until the top of his head disappeared under the gentle waves forever. I felt sorry for my father. There's skunked, then there is *skunked*.

I guess Don and I could have been a little more considerate by not contemplating out loud the possibility, judging from the watery explosion, that a world class musky had just intruded upon our shore lunch and dined on frog ala carte, but true to form Dad took it in stride. He also managed to land three good-sized wall-eyes within an hour or so after shore lunch. Still, it was obvious the lunchtime commotion in that little bay was on Dad's mind. There's nothing wrong with walleye, but they're not muskies.

Burke had caught a glimpse of the fish, and later on that evening while the four of us were sitting in the screened porch of our cabin he said he was fairly certain it wasn't a musky; nope, probably just a thirty-pound northern, or maybe a fifteen-pound walleye. Dad shot Burke a look few others would have felt comfortable delivering, at least a second time. Burke just shrugged and helped himself to one of Don's cigarettes, keeping a watchful eye out for Miriam who had been led to believe her husband had quit smoking years ago. After all, a man can't be too careful.

***

The name of the Indian guide Burke somehow talked Dad into hiring, splitting the fee fifty-fifty, was Cecil. If he had a surname he never shared it with us, or much else that required using the Queen's English. Cecil spoke English but did so with a certain abruptness that bordered on distain, as if he wanted to get the annoying words out of his mouth quickly, using as few as possible.

He was somewhat crossed-eyed with a severely broken nose that had never been set properly, as in not at all. He was maybe five foot five and weighed 130 pounds at most, but he was surprisingly strong. On our first and only day out with Cecil, he lugged a Johnson outboard on his back over a mile to the secluded lake he had chosen. There were no roads, just an overgrown footpath that led to the water's edge. It was tough enough lugging all our gear through the bush on that warm day, but one look at Cecil plodding ahead of us with that hunk of iron on his back made me feel sheepish for complaining, even if it had been mostly to myself. He never stopped to rest either, not even once. Not only that, but when Dad, Burke, then Don and I offered to carry it at least part way, Cecil said no. Actually, he pretty much snorted his responses, his annoyance with our offers gaining momentum after each entreaty.

***

When we arrived at the shoreline there were two old, wooden rowboats. Cecil attached the motor to one of them. Burke hopped in with him then motioned for Miriam to step aboard after Dad had offered them to do so. Dad, Don and I got stuck with the boat that just had oars and no guide. No matter, Burke insisted. It was a small lake and they would go slow so we could keep up. Dad smiled and mumbled something about "that's Burke for you" and let it go at that.

In a way, it seemed as though Dad got a kick out of Burke's behavior, as if it reminded Dad of their old college days or something. Dad knew Burke would have taken the motor-less (and guide-less) rowboat instead, since rowing all day wasn't the sort of thing that bothered Burke at all. Even so, we were the ones who ended up doing so.

We managed to keep within forty or fifty feet of their boat until they took off for another spot, but it seemed like whenever Cecil would get to a new area one or both of the Burkhardt's would usually hook a good-sized walleye or northern before we could catch up. This went on all morning, with the three of us catching a decent amount of fish, but nothing compared to what the Burkhardt's were hauling in.

The mood in our boat grew somewhat darker with each howl of delight that danced across the waves from the Burkhardt's boat every time they landed another big one. It wasn't so much that we were getting out-fished (we were used to that with Burke) but it wasn't lost on Dad that he had agreed to pay 50% of the guide service only to have 90% of the advantages of hiring a guide sitting squarely in Burke's boat.

Dad grumbled that when it came time to actually pay Cecil, Burke might do one of his famous disappearing acts he had perfected during their college days when Burke would sometimes manage to be conveniently attending to nature's call or some similar ruse about the same time the tab arrived. Dad seemed to get a kick out of remembering their college days when they all had acted their age employing similar tactics; Burke certainly hadn't been alone in that regard, although Dad, not surprisingly, wouldn't go into details.

Men of the World War II generation, a lot of them anyway, had a habit of insisting upon single-handedly paying for everything from bar tabs in swank hotel lounges to hotdog vendors working Wrigley Field as a matter of honor. Sometimes they would grab for a bill before the waiter had a chance to place it on the table.

That would invariably be followed by verbal jousting coming from those with supposedly slower reflexes. Once the debate had finally been settled (Dad and Uncle Aub once spent over *half an hour* fighting it out in a restaurant in Marshalltown, Iowa) it was over and done with - usually.

Dad, from years of experience, realized no one was more acutely aware of that than Burke, who probably figured Dad would never approach him later for Burke's share of the guiding services, at least not without Dad losing face in front of Miriam and his two sons. I never could see why that was so important, but that generation had all sorts of stuff I found perplexing. The thing was, though, Burke wanted to joke around. He pretended to pull an old college ploy on Dad again by disappearing when it had been time to pay Cecil.

Prior to that, however, the more fish the Burkhardt's kept reeling in that morning, the more Dad's suspicions of Burke's possible, if not impending duplicity grew, even if Dad didn't actually artic-ulate his concerns. He didn't have to; all Don or I had to do was joke around about Mr. Burkhardt's unquestionable integrity and the inevitable grunt could be heard coming from Dad's spot in the boat. All of Dad's negative energy would have immediately dissipated if he had hooked into a genuine trophy, but by the time shore lunch rolled around that hadn't been the case. Still, things have a way of evening out, as we soon discovered.

***

Miriam, for obvious reasons, had taken a hike well into the brush of the island we were on, having rocked in a boat drink-ing coffee all morning. She happened to come up behind Burke just as he was putting the finishing touches on a story about the monumental struggle he had endured while landing the biggest walleye of the morning, if not the entire trip. It was an impressive brute Burke was holding up as he spoke, approaching eight pounds.

"Thought my line was gonna snap for sure before Cecil could get a net on it (at that point Cecil gave him an odd look) but I managed to ease up on the drag just in the nick of time before it could -"

"*Burke!*" Miriam exclaimed loud enough to scatter some gulls on a nearby rock. "You know darn good and well who caught that walleye, and don't you try to deny it!"

"That's *enough*, Miriam," a red-faced Burke growled, his head lowered and shoulders hunched as he stood up and basically crept away.

"*Honestly,* I do not for the *life* of me understand that man sometimes." Miriam went on to say. "Not only did I catch the largest walleye, I also caught the second largest as well, plus that big northern there, oh yes, and that other -"

"*That's enough,* Miriam!" Came from behind a large bush, where Burke was taking an inordinate amount of time answering nature's call. In a way, I was somewhat surprised he ever came out.

Cecil kept glancing about with nervous, quick eyes, keeping a safe distance from all of us as he expertly filleted enough fish for the lunch he was providing. I found it disappointing that after he opened the assorted cans of peas, baked beans and corn he tossed the empty cans upon a fairly large heap of similar trash that had obviously been collecting there for years, much of it no doubt his.

Some of the cans were so rusted they had nearly blended into the ground itself, but not in a natural way by Northwoods standards. It was more reminiscent of the garbage dumps back home where Dad would sometimes take trash rather than pay extra for the garbage man to haul it away. I used to tag along with Old Daisy and take pot shots at the rats, which were usually plentiful. To see something similar in such an otherwise unspoiled locale of Canadian wilderness seemed a sacrilege, and I couldn't understand why someone, especially of native descent, would treat such otherwise unspoiled beauty in such a disrespectful and damaging manner.

I asked Cecil why he didn't just bring the trash back with him after each trip, but all he did was shoot me a quick glare as he let out an even quicker snort of an answer:

"Not my damn island," was all he said.

***

Towards evening we were hanging around the fish house back at camp, watching Burke fillet his (arguably) day's catch when Cecil came stumbling in. I had been telling Burke about a walleye I had reeled in just after shore lunch.

I had it ten feet from the boat, about five feet down, when somehow it found an amazing amount of strength and swam rapidly away before I could get control of the line whizzing off my reel. I bulled it back to the side of the boat, but it was still a good ten feet down and not yet visible amidst the weeds. I reeled it straight up until I could first see the head of the walleye, then much to my surprise the *gigantic* head of an angry-eyed northern that had most of the decent size walleye's body easily inside its mouth. "Unless it was a musky." I wondered out loud.

Burke said it might have been a musky all right. The brute had given me a quick snarl or two just as Don had shoved the net deep into the water, only to have the rim smack the monster well above the tip of its tail. Suddenly, after another fierce glare, the biggest one third of a fish I had ever seen up close spit out what was left of the walleye and sped swiftly into the deep. I had lifted what was left of the mangled walleye out of the water. After I described the size of the northern's, or perhaps musky's head to Burke, he estimated the fish to be in the thirty-pound class.

"Not thirty no way, is like forty, may-maybe more is like it forty…" Cecil more or less babbled as he attempted to steady himself against the heavy wooden table used to clean fish. "Not no musky though. Not no muskies there."

We all fell silent and looked at him. His eyes were naturally crossed to begin with, but the Canadian whiskey he had managed to polish off since our arrival back at camp exaggerated his unfortunate condition. He was still holding the 750 mm bottle, which was almost empty. It appeared as if he could look at everyone at the same time, regardless of where we were standing in the fish house, even if he was likely seeing eight instead of four of us. Regardless, it was a good bet we were undoubtedly out of focus.

I felt sorry for Cecil, mainly because it wasn't likely his condition was an aberration. Later on, I found out that it wasn't, a fact made all the more depressing when we were told something we already knew, that Cecil was a highly knowledgeable guide and a very hard worker when he was sober or at least not drinking. I didn't know Cecil's past, all the whys and so forth, but I knew what a waste of talent it was.

Dad, Don and I had each taken turns trying to learn from Burke how to fillet our walleye, but it was obvious we still had a lot to master. As drunk and visually challenged as Cecil appeared to be, even he could see we didn't know what we were doing. He staggered over and took the fillet knife from me and proceeded to flat out butcher the first fish he had begun to slice.

"Gimme the knife." Burke said as he took it from an indignant Cecil.

"I, I love Kedney, Kenndy...Nixon bastard he killed him... sure killed Ken, Kenndahee...Nixon bastard..." After that bizarre little outburst Cecil staggered out of the fish house, his hands dripping with a generous amount of fresh fish slime as if nothing could be more natural.

***

Burke offered to fillet the rest of our fish so we could take a ride into Ear Falls for some supplies and supper. That was nice of him, and to a man we felt we had judged him too harshly earlier that day after he had continued to out-fish us - with Cecil still in *his* boat. That was us just making excuses because we were feeling sorry for ourselves - pouting about it all really. It didn't last long, not with Burke. He could out-fish us using barbless hooks and sewing thread. We appreciated that but still wanted to out-fish him. We never did.

To Burke's credit he eventually not only paid for Cecil, but included the tip and refused Dad's offer to cover even part of the expense. Later on, Dad said he had learned a lesson; just because you knew a certain person acted one way as a young man, especially a broke young college student, you would likely be making a mistake to assume he would still act that way decades later. That's what Dad said, but somewhere inside I had to believe Dad missed the younger Burke; and probably missed the younger Pete McCabe:

"The decades go by so fast it sometimes seems like just a few years have passed, if that." Dad said. "I guess that's it, and I suppose Burke remembers things about me from back then I'd just as soon keep in the past."

"What things, Dad?" I asked, hoping for a rare story of his younger, wilder days.

"Huh? Oh. Things that should be kept in the past."

Don and I knew that was where those things would remain, too.

***

The three of us were in Dad's 1970 Olds 88 preparing to depart when Cecil staggered up to the right side of the car. I was sitting in the rear right seat with the window down, having just lit a Players non-filter, an act that wasn't lost on our inebriated guide. He mumbled something incoherent, but it wasn't until he reached an unsteady hand through the open window and with surprising quickness snatched the pack of smokes from my shirt pocket before it became apparent what he wanted. After a couple of unsuccessful attempts, he finally managed to extract a cigarette from its box then tried to hand it back to me. I told him to keep them. For one thing, there were only a few left, and for another Cecil had managed to coat most of the box with a generous amount of coagulated fish slime which was anything but fresh. He kept thanking me over and over again as he stumbled around the front of the car, preventing Dad from pulling away.

"Where you going now?" Cecil asked Dad after lurching around to the driver's side window.

"Just into town," Dad replied as he shifted into drive.

"Hey, town! Okay then!" Before Dad could react, Cecil had swung open the rear left door and unceremoniously plopped down in the seat, weaving from side to side. He still had the cigarette he had bummed from me stuck in his mouth, and kept indicating he needed a light. I reluctantly handed him my matches and told him to keep those as well before he even pretended to give them back.

"Bastard damn Nixon, bastard damn killed Kenndanay... I love Kenndanay bastard damn Nixon..."

He went on like that halfway to Ear Falls before finally passing out. He crashed right against my shoulder, but I quickly rectified that situation by placing him in the opposite corner of the back seat. My hands, even my left shoulder smelled like I had just wrestled with the guy. None of that mattered to Cecil of course, who had dropped his cigarette on the floor without me seeing it happen. I stamped it out after smelling the smoldering carpet.

It was easy to view Cecil with disgust. He probably hadn't bathed in, well, weeks maybe? It was more than just a few days, anyway. His clothes looked and smelled as if he had put them on after buying them a year or so ago and hadn't quite gotten around to washing them yet, or even taking them off. His teeth may or may not have been rotten. Perhaps the thick, dull orange coating that covered them had protective properties of one kind or another. Whew.

There was, however, a sincerity to the man when he had attempted to express his feelings about the man I assumed was the late Senator Robert F. Kennedy who had been assassinated in June of 1968 while running for president. Cecil may have been referring to the assassination of President John F. Kennedy in 1963, Bobby Kennedy's older brother, but I didn't think so. I figured

Cecil's hatred of President Nixon probably stemmed from him becoming president not long after Bobby had been gunned down.

The subject hadn't come up until Cecil was drunk, but once it had he kept coming back to it until he passed out. His eyes were hopelessly crossed and bloodshot, but there had been nothing disingenuous in them, not even a little. Even though the Kennedy brothers had a worldwide following, I wondered why a United States politician would mean so much to Cecil. I was judging him because he was so drunk; perhaps a sober Cecil would have been able to explain himself better. I never got the chance to find out.

***

We spotted a likely looking place to eat as soon as we hit town. Judging from the appetite-whetting aroma of frying hamburgers coming from the outside vent above the tavern's grill, it seemed like the perfect place. Cecil was crumpled up and snoring away in the corner of the back seat he had commandeered, so we decided to leave him be - with all the windows rolled down. I even snatched away the matches I'd given him, just in case.

Unlike most Northwoods bars we had encountered over the years, this one was rather spacious. It even had a good-sized, hardwood dance floor with a jukebox blaring away from its opposite end. We had no sooner taken our seats at a table near the bar when Cecil wandered in and spotted us immediately. He maneuvered his way through the crowd with some difficulty and plopped down in a chair at our table, much to the apparent displeasure of virtually all the local patrons. The waitress who had been approaching us just as Cecil arrived seemed especially put out, as if she were approaching the very personification of putrefaction itself. Things went downhill from there.

Keeping what can only be described as the quintessential Evil Eye on our uninvited guest, she proceeded to reluctantly take our orders after we just as reluctantly acknowledged the exceedingly drunken fellow was indeed with us. Even though she had appeared to be genuinely cautious as it related to Cecil, she must have diverted her glance briefly as she was taking Don's order, and at the worst possible moment.

With amazing speed and agility considering his condition, Cecil managed to slide his hand under her dress. The shocked waitress, eyes bugged out of her head for the most part, let out a bloodcurdling howl that easily drowned out the jukebox, if just for a moment. It was as if her banshee wail had exploded from the very depths of her, which may well have put it in close proximity to Cecil's hand. Then things *really* went downhill.

The resounding wallop our waitress delivered with her order pad to the top of Cecil's skull had little effect, but the same probably wasn't going to be the case with the sawed-off baseball bat the bartender was clutching as he high-hurtled the bar. From the look of him, it was doubtful his intentions were to simply admonish our uninvited miscreant's abominable behavior.

For his part, it appeared Cecil had been to that rodeo before. He sprung to his feet and backed off a few steps, smiling and moving his hands in front of himself back and forth as if to say he didn't want any trouble.

"No no, Mr. Bartender. Just joking, see? Just joking!" Then Cecil made the miscalculation of trying to return to his seat.

"You get your scrawny ass outta here *now* or I swear I'll whop your fool head off!" The bartender bellowed as he continued to approach Cecil, whose face had lost its smile.

"Okay for you then!" Cecil yelled as he started to leave, the very picture of indignation. "No more business for you!" He swirled, put a foot down on the edge of the hardwood dance floor and proceeded to fall flat on his face. Not even his arms reacted in time to break his fall. Undeterred, he got to his feet and marched out of the place, nearly falling again just as he stepped off the dance floor near the bar's entrance.

Dad, Don and I just looked at each other then glanced towards the ceiling as it became painfully obvious the not-so-friendly stares from the local patrons were aimed directly at us. The arrival of our beers couldn't have been timed more perfectly. It gave us something to look at besides the ceiling and each other, and also afforded us the opportunity to apologize to the waitress.

"Well," she said, "it's not the first time he's acted up in here, but it's the first time he did it in front of his own fishing clients, which I suppose you are."

We assured her that he actually had been guiding some folks we were camping near, and we had just tagged along behind their boat. We admitted we gave him a ride to town, but we hadn't expected him to follow us into the bar. She seemed as if she understood, but made it clear not only to us but everyone else in the general vicinity that if he ever entered that establishment again, he'd be "leavin' on a stretcher!"

We hurried through our burgers and got out of there. We stopped at the local grocery store and loaded up on supplies, then started to head out of town. About a block from the bar, sitting hunched over on the curb was Cecil, so Dad pulled over and offered him a ride back to camp. He looked up, and at first it appeared he didn't even recognize us. Then something in his eyes indicated he did, but he just motioned for us to leave.

***

It sounded like a siren, but at five the next morning it seemed too out of place to register immediately, since we were sound asleep in a cabin in the Canadian wilderness. That's what it was though, screaming from the fire engine that had arrived to extinguish the blaze that had all but destroyed the small shack at the top of the hill near the entrance to the camp - Cecil's small shack. What happened next would no doubt be talked about for years; it's probably still remembered by a few old timers who have lived near Perrault Falls for the last four decades or so.

It was Cecil's shack all right, and it had caught fire with Cecil in it. I'll grant you there was nothing strange about that - it was a wonderment that it hadn't previously occurred. The part that left everyone who witnessed the aftermath with their collective jaws dropped was Cecil himself. He had not only survived, but wasn't even hurt. Drunk and passed out or not, something must have made him leave in time, although a few guys insisted Cecil had been passed out on his cot and the structure had burned down around him, and it must have been the concrete floor that saved him.

Whether it was God Almighty, Fate Almighty or a guardian angel named Bobby Kennedy, one thing was for sure - it wasn't Cecil's time. Other than smelling of burnt wood, there had been no damage done to Cecil at all; except to his pride. Even so, he berated the firemen for what he insisted was their slow response, and also insisted he had absolutely nothing to do with starting the fire. Since no one was hurt and it wouldn't take long to rebuild Cecil's shack, the volunteer firemen packed up their gear and headed home.

***

Three days later that's exactly what Dad, Don and I did as well. We continued to catch plenty of walleye and a fair share of northern, but if there were any muskies in those waters we never saw them. A few other minor misadventures occurred, like the time I went to cast a heavy sinker and jig combo and inadvertently smacked Don upside his head, driving the hook into his face just below his right eye.

Dad had to take him into town to get the hook removed and a tetanus shot. I stayed behind, contemplating the passage of time as it related to being his twelve-year-old kid brother who would have run the risk of swimming frantically to the nearest shore for doing something so asinine, as opposed to the twenty-four-year-old younger brother who Don justifiably made feel lower than sundown with just one withering glare.

Uncharacteristically, Dad managed to get walloped by the stupid stick as well, just as we arrived at the border crossing at International Falls. It didn't take much as far as the United States border guard was concerned. He wasn't as skinny as Barney Fife, but there all dissimilarities ended. From a dedication standpoint, he was a better man than me; no way would I have methodically gone through a week's worth of some fishermen's dirty laundry, including underwear, but that's what old Barney did. Maybe he would have anyway, but when Dad tried to lighten the mood when we had pulled up to the border by stating: "Good thing we didn't stop at that fireworks stand, boys!" our fate was sealed. It was all we could do to keep our suspicious friend from breaking the seals on our coolers. The thought of our dry ice evaporating before reaching Illinois must have appealed to the fisherman in him or something.

It was a long, sixteen-hour drive home from there. All three of us were fished out and glad to get back to our routines and loved ones, but in a certain sense something left a hollow feeling inside. We were slowly learning what to do as far as real fishing was concerned, but we still had a long way to go. In 1972 there simply wasn't an abundance of readily available "how to" information as it related to musky fishing unless you hired a guide, or if there was we hadn't found it. For the most part we were learning by trial and error.

Over the next few years we would again converge upon the scared waters of Pelican Lake, and in 1976 a member of the newest generation of our McCabe clan would be coming along - my seven-year-old son Danny would be taking up the Quest, and taking his place in our family's musky hunting history as well.

Chapter 9

Most folks didn't give our marriage much of a chance since Peggy and I were teenagers when we took our vows, and were still teenagers when our first born, Cari Ann, entered the world. We were only twenty when our son Danny was born. Peggy and I knew our children were the best part of us, or at least our greatest accomplishment on what was a work in progress.

There are families with brothers and sisters who have more of an age disparity than what exists between our two oldest children and us, which partially explained why I encouraged Cari Ann and Danny to do things before a lot of adults thought they were ready; like taking Danny musky fishing at age seven in northern Wisconsin, for instance, and it was his second trip. Danny and I had already been up to Pelican Lake the year before in 1975 with Don and his son Ricky, who was close to Danny's age.

Dad had come along that time as well. The boys' attention spans had been a little too short to appreciate extended time on the water, especially since their fathers didn't have any luck catching much, as in *nothing*. Even so, the boys had seemed eager to head out on the lake, as long as we didn't keep them out there all day.

True enough, Danny and Ricky were considerably more interested in the pool table back at the Old Hotel than spending hour after fruitless hour watching their fathers throw one cast after another with nothing to show for it. Don and I suspected we should have started them out with bluegill fishing, but to our discredit we rationalized that away. Our increasing obsession, our musky mania, was the culprit but we rationalized that away as well; if we hooked into a Pelican lake trophy musky, the boys would be hooked as well. The high skies remained clear the whole three days, and the most telling sign – hardly anyone else on the water - pretty much told us we were going to get skunked again.

By late afternoon on our last day we finally decided the boys had paid their dues. They more than agreed, especially when we promised them a handful of quarters for the pool table back at the hotel. Besides, the seven ounce drafts that cost only a nickel back at the Old Hotel bar were sounding better with each futile cast – it was time for Don and me, "the adults" to sit around and feel sorry for ourselves. At least the boys were happy, which ended the 1975 trip on a positive note.

***

In 1976 we gave Cari Ann and Danny the choice of going with me to Pelican, or going with Peggy to her aunt's and uncle's lakeside cottage on Diamond Lake near Cassopolis, Michigan. More specifically, musky fishing on Pelican Lake where swimming and other activities for eight-year-old girls were at a minimum, or Diamond Lake where the opposite was true – for Cari Ann it was, of course, no contest. Beverly Meagher, or Auntie Bev as Peggy and the kids called her, and Uncle Wayne always made us feel more than welcome, which was just as important as all the activities the kids enjoyed.

Uncle Wayne had built a steamboat christened the Diamond Belle from scratch, or at least the engine which was no small feat. The kids enjoyed riding in it, although Uncle Wayne's speedboat rides were the most exciting of all; that boat could really fly. I knew Danny loved Diamond Lake and choosing between the two options wasn't easy for him. Still, I really wanted him to spend time musky fishing with me and especially with his grandfather.

Dad, or Papa as the kids called him, would be going to Pelican as well, although Don couldn't make it. Despite the previous year's fishing failure, I regaled Danny with stories about successful angling adventures in order to peak his seven-year-old interest, as well as convince him he wasn't making a mistake by going to Pelican again instead of Diamond Lake. I even pulled out the heavy artillery - Grampa's picture - monster musky and all, and the story that went along with it.

I also had a snapshot of Dad in 1931, age eighteen, sitting on the hood of his Model A Ford that had been parked at the railroad depot under a sign that said Pelican Lake. Coincidentally, or maybe not, Dad had parked his car way back in 1931 on nearly the exact spot he had parked when we had been caught in that tree pulverizing storm during the summer of 1959. Danny's eyes, however, kept going back to the photo of his great grandfather hoisting up a very large fish.

I told Danny the 1931 story anyway, how Papa had made the trip with his older brother Don the summer of 1931 before Dad had left for his first year at college. Back then it was slow going most of the way from Naperville to the small hamlet of Pelican Lake over three hundred miles away. Most of the roads were dirt or gravel and better suited for horses than a Model A that had no doubt seen better days. It was a worthwhile adventure though, and gave the two oldest "Six Micks" McCabe boys the opportunity to see the Northwoods wilderness lake where their father had caught his famous musky. They found plenty of time to stop and appreciate the Northwoods splendor as well, because the farthest they ever made it without having to pull over and patch a blown tire wasn't even forty miles.

"…and that was Papa's first trip to Pelican, Danny. Danny?"

"That," he said as he pointed, "is a really big fish, Dad." I understood completely.

***

I did some research and found what turned out to be a great place to stay called Weaver's Resort. We rented a small cabin not far from the main house that itself was right on the water. There was an old mount on the wall in the office, a musky that had to have been in the forty-pound class, perhaps upper forties. The owner told us one of his old Indian guides caught it decades before off Weaver's point, not far from where the boat we had rented was docked.

Any thought Danny had about swimming off that particular dock was immediately dismissed. We tried to tell him every single fish in the lake was more frightened of him, including the muskies, but one look at the mean-eyed, needle-toothed predator on the wall told Danny everything he needed to know. He had ten fingers and ten toes, and intended to keep it that way.

I couldn't wait to get on the lake. It was a warm, humid late afternoon in August with the threat of rain lurking in the overcast sky with a chop building on the water. It looked perfect. I had splurged and purchased my first genuine musky rod and reel. I had a brand new five and a half foot Heddon Pal Musky Special rod and my most prized possession, a new ABU Garcia Ambassadeur 6000C reel, jet black and beautiful. Fifty-pound test braided Dacron line, too.

Actually, I didn't think I had gone overboard all that much, but since I had just started a new job in Chicago with the Spalding Sporting Goods Company after trying to make a go of it as a real estate agent and failing miserably, I could see where certain people might come to that conclusion. When it came to musky gear, however, I was beyond guilt trips regardless of how hard anyone tried to lay one on me. Anyone except Peggy, who never gave me a hard time about fishing to begin with, bless her heart.

I loved my new reel so much I suggested Don, Larry and I chip in and buy a 6000C as a Christmas present for Dad that year, which we did. I wish you could have seen the look on his face when he opened the present; it made up for all the other gifts we had given him over the years, especially when we had been kids. Back then we had been more interested in what we were going to get as opposed to having learned to appreciate the warm feeling that giving a loved one something worthwhile generates, not that we had much money to do so to begin with.

Dad had rarely spent much on himself and never would have bought himself a reel that nice. It sure made up for those 25 cent bottles of Vi-Jon rose-scented hair oil I had given him over the years, at least until I was eleven. That year, feeling exceptionally magnanimous, I threw in a plastic bag of army men that had cost me nearly half a buck.

My generosity apparently knew no bounds that year, because I made sure Larry, age fifteen at the time, received the same things. I figured he'd appreciate the hair oil, and especially impressed with the advertising slogan on the label: *Impress your friends, use Vi-Jon hair oil!* He wasn't impressed though, not even a little – go figure.

***

I had been reading what few articles I could find on musky fishing, but it seemed all of the major sports magazines in the early 1970's, when they did have an article about fishing, focused primarily on bass or walleye. I had nothing against those fish, but I had already caught enough of those. There was only one species of fish I was interested in reading about; but not as much as I wanted to catch one.

Dad wasn't keen on hiring a guide. He didn't believe in them, partly because he used to be one – sort of. He had just finished another year of college at the time. He and his younger brother Ben had hitchhiked from Naperville to some resort area in the state of Oregon to visit their Uncle Huck McCabe.

They needed to earn a few bucks for the trip home, so Dad hired on at a local lakeside resort splitting wood and doing other chores. It was the busy season and when the owner was short a guide or two he would send Dad out with the eager clients. One problem - Dad knew nothing about the lake, and very little about fishing aside from wetting a line in the DuPage River back home. Dad said even the so-called experienced guides on that lake seldom caught much more than the novices, so from then on, he questioned whether or not most of them were worth the money; he knew *he* hadn't been anyway.

If Dad had known anyone from the Pelican Lake area he trusted he might have felt differently, even if he was a pretty frugal guy. Part of it had to do with Dad's sense of competition; there was little else that gave him more pleasure than going up against the local experts and beating them at their own game, regardless of the contest. Unfortunately, we hadn't done that yet with a trophy musky, which would make it that much sweeter when it finally happened; an assumption at best, all things considered. Still, I couldn't help entertaining the notion of at least checking around for an experienced guide. *Maybe some day,* I thought.

***

I already knew some of the musky spots on Pelican, especially off Indian Point where Grampa had caught his fish of a lifetime. Dad said he wanted to take a nap after the long drive so Danny and I headed out; the first time just the two of us were on a real musky lake together. I didn't want to fish Indian Point without Dad, so I made a bee line west from Weaver's Point and ended up a few hundred yards or so southwest of Crescent Island. There were weeds everywhere, mostly submerged.

I almost switched to a Jitterbug but decided to stay with a natural bucktail even though it was getting hung up quite a bit. We stayed out for over an hour with nothing to show for it. At seven years of age I could tell Danny's attention span had approached its limit. Still, he was a good sport about it, and picked up on the art of casting quickly.

I started heading slowly back to Weaver's, casting once in a while as I went. The weeds were still fairly plentiful, but there was enough open area to usually keep out of them. I let fly with a long cast and started to slowly troll forward, letting the boat pull the bucktail. That was technically illegal, but I figured I'd only do it that one time or so. When that rationalization failed to kill my guilt, I cut the motor just as we entered another patch of musky cabbage. The wind moved us around so the stern faced east; the bow, of course, was pointed due west. That's where Danny was, on the bow, looking into the water as I reeled in the latest cast I had thrown due west, to the outside edge of some musky cabbage.

"Dad, look! Dad, *Dad!*" Danny yelled, his eyes wide as he jumped up and pointed to a spot just off the port bow.

I also jumped up and looked around as I kept reeling the final few turns before my lure was out of the water, but I didn't see anything. I hadn't learned to appreciate figure eights yet.

"Did you see that, Dad?" Danny asked after returning to his seat, his face flushed with excitement.

"Didn't see a thing. What did you see, a big fish?"

"Just part of one. It was moving really fast, going for your bucktail thing. It came from out there." Danny pointed again, to an area along a line of musky cabbage to the west of our boat.

"How much of it did you see, Danny?"

"Just the tail, not much more. It was kind of red. Kind of dull red." Danny said, as he looked into the lake again as I started casting like a madman. I beat the general area half to death, but I didn't see so much as a follow.

Later that evening in the cabin I started to question Danny again after he had told Dad what he had seen. I asked him how big the dull red tail had been; asked him to show me by parting his hands. I know I'm his father and prone to subjective evaluations, but no doubt thanks to his mother, Danny was a very bright boy and mature beyond his years. He considered my request as he slowly parted his hands until he was satisfied with the estimated distance he had created. Dad and I just looked at each other, then back at Danny's parted hands and innocent, seven-year-old face.

"Son," I said softly, "that looks as big as the tail on the fish hanging on the wall back in the office. Are you sure it was that big?" Danny looked me squarely in the eyes and answered without hesitation:

"It was bigger, Dad." He wasn't smiling, and didn't break eye contact.

***

Rain threatened all the next day, most of which the three of us spent on the water. If there were any muskies around, we didn't see them. I had a couple of strikes from what were probably small northern in Outlet Bay, but that was about it. I couldn't figure out why I hadn't been able to hook them. I had my new rod and reel, plus my equally new musky bucktail. Nope, I couldn't figure it out at all, until later that evening.

We were having supper in the dining room of the Old Hotel when a grizzled old timer at the next table overheard us talking about that very subject.

"None of my business, but with all else bein' equal, how often do you sharpen your hooks?" He was right about it being none of his business, but he seemed like a friendly enough guy. Besides, his question left me wondering.

"It's a brand new bucktail." I offered. "The hooks are sharp to begin with." I could tell by the look on his face that he had me pegged for a rank amateur, or worse. I couldn't have lost more credibility as a musky fisherman if I had been sitting there wearing an Easter bonnet.

"Why?" The man asked rhetorically. "Because they're sharp enough to poke a hole in your finger?" Actually, that was exactly why I hadn't given the subject any thought.

"Like I said it's none of my business, but a hook outta water's a damn sight more likely to poke a hole in your thumb than a submerged hook in a musky's mouth. Then there's the stretch in your line. You need all the help you can get, young fella. Better take a file to every hook in your tackle box." His food arrived about then, diverting his attention.

It wasn't that I disagreed with his advice; it was just that he had delivered it loud enough for at least half the dining room to hear.

"Does that answer your question, son?" I said to Danny.

"Nice try, Dad." Was all he said, speaking for everyone else who had been within earshot. I told you he was mature beyond his years.

***

The next day lightning and a series of heavy thunderstorms kept us off the water all morning. Then Danny came down with a case of the 24-hour stomach flu, so even when the weather did break we couldn't head out. Poor Danny; what a lousy time to come down with something as disagreeable as the flu, especially when you're seven years old and three hundred miles from home. Dad and I hung around the cabin and kept an eye on the little guy, who was stuck on a sofa bed in the living room.

I couldn't stop checking out the lake from time to time. Although there were a few low rumblings of thunder mixed in with the wind and rain, I didn't see any more lightning flashes. Heading outside for a little while, I did see several boats off of Meckanac Point and a few others in Treacherous Bay, and several more in Outlet Bay as well. I sure wanted to be on the water, and even though Dad told me he would stay back with Danny I couldn't bring myself to leave - well, almost.

***

We only managed to get up North once a year, and usually for just three or four days. It seemed a crime to be so close to the action but not be able to participate. Besides, it was a waste of money to rent a boat and motor, then leave them at the dock...

Things were tight financially to begin with. I had just started that new job with Spalding, working out of their Harlem Avenue office and warehouse in Chicago. It was a customer service entry-level position and the low pay was definitely entry level as well. Peggy and I had been blessed in 1975 with our third child, a beautiful baby girl we named Megan Mae. Now there were five of us to feed, clothe and shelter.

The thunder kept rumbling outside, but still no visible lightning so I decided to take Dad up on his offer. We both knew how inadvisable it was to be on the water with lightning around, but I rationalized that away. Okay fine, if there's thunder there has to be lightning somewhere, but none had flashed around Pelican, at least recently. Besides, there were at least half a dozen boats working the west side of the lake alone, and no doubt more on the rest of Pelican.

I threw on my raingear and grabbed my tackle, then looked around in the kitchen for my Zippo lighter. Dad was in there too, getting ready to make some toast. As innocent and everyday as that sounds, it turned out to be quite the opposite.

During World War Two, Dad had spent most of his combat time firing a 105mm Howitzer at Nazis, and had earned three battle ribbons. Although he rarely talked about his experience during the Italian Campaign (the first wedge into Hitler's "Fortress Europe", *Festung Europa*) I found out later he did write a little about them, including one reoccurring incident that had likely generated any number of nightmares for him over the years: *the short whistle and sharp crack that meant a Nazi bomb was too close.* Fast-forward thirty-three years:

It could not have been timed or staged more perfectly in a major motion picture. Even the antiquated electric toaster cooperated by no longer having the plastic switch in place to push down the toast - just a bare metal extension. Dad placed two pieces of bread in their respective slots and pushed the exposed, metal nub down with authority. When his finger hit the stopping point, and I mean at the *exact* split second it hit the stopping point, a crack - no, an *explosion* of thunder and lightning simultaneously erupted just above the roof of our cabin, and I mean *right* above it. The outside instantly lit up like a massive flash bulb, and the KA*BOOM!* that accompanied the blinding flash was so powerful it literally shook the windows and walls, even the *floor.* I fully expected a massive pine tree to come crashing through the place any second, or at least it would have made perfect sense.

Dad was a brave man, but not a stupid one. He hadn't survived World War Two by ignoring *"In coming!!"* He also hadn't lost so much as a step of his high school track star speed as he flew towards the living room, knees pumping high in the air, as if one of the exploding projectiles he had delivered to Hitler's minions so many years before was hot on his tail. He hollered "Yi!" that fit naturally with his wide-eyed expression as he high stepped it out of the kitchen, not stopping until he reached the living room. Danny, whose own initial response had been similar to Dad's, was suddenly overcome by hysterics after having witnessed the entire spectacle and fallen off his sofa bed onto the floor where he continued to howl with tears running down his cheeks. In one fell swoop, Dad had single-handedly cured Danny's stomach flu, or close to it.

I would like to tell you I was howling along with my son, but I had been in the kitchen with Dad and was still trying to uncross my own eyes. I felt compelled to go outside to see if we were on fire, but there was no way I was venturing anywhere near the Great Outdoors for awhile. It had taken all the courage I could muster to keep from diving under the kitchen table.

Any possibility of attacking Indian Point on the other side of the lake, or even the shore off Weaver's Point was suddenly out of the question. I remembered an old golf pro, a club professional from central Illinois telling me what had happened to some guy who had been struck by lightning while sitting in his golf cart. He had been a heavyset man, yet the direct hit had knocked him from his cart and onto the fairway. The grisly part happened after the paramedics arrived; portions of burnt flesh came off in their hands when they had tried to pick him up. They finally rolled his body onto a tarp then onto a stretcher;

it was a tragic, burnt mess. I wanted to catch a trophy musky more than almost anything all right, but I also wanted to live long enough to do it.

Later on, Dad's reaction had a more somber effect on me. Ever since I was a small child he jumped half out of his skin if touched while he was sleeping, and not just a little; if someone happened to shake Dad awake while he was napping on the couch to let him know supper was ready or something, they stood a fair chance of getting smacked or shoved before Dad had regained full consciousness. For some reason, if his feet were touched he really went off.

Years later I asked Uncle Ben if Dad had been like that growing up, assuming he had. Uncle Ben, himself having been awarded the Bronze Star during World War Two, said no, and wouldn't discuss it further. He mentioned a letter though, one Dad had sent to a former high school teacher of his, Angie Gale. She had requested some of her former students who had served overseas write of their war experience because she was writing a book.

"I don't know if Mrs. Gale ever wrote her book," Uncle Ben told me, "but I know Pete kept a copy of the letter he sent her. I don't know if he still has it, or if he'll let you read it even if he did keep it. I wouldn't be surprised if Pete threw it out."

I never asked Dad about it. The time never seemed right to do so. I was tempted to ask a few times, but I was afraid by doing so it would bring back memories Dad didn't want to revisit. Years later, after Dad died, I found it. He must have wanted others to read it or he wouldn't have written and sent it to his former teacher. That's what I choose to believe, but most of all I want others to get a glimpse, to better understand the essence of my father.

THE ITALIAN CAMPAIGN
Keith A. McCabe
Stateside, 1945

We dedicate this portion of the book to Bill Kelch who made the supreme sacrifice to his country and fellow men on the toughest of all beachheads – Anzio

The first wedge driven into Hitler's Fortress Europe was near Paestun on the Gulf of Salerno. H-hour D-day was 0330, 9 September 1943. From then until the cease firing order was given at 1200, 2 May 1945, the Italian campaign was underway.

Volturno, Rapidio, Cassino, Anzio, Rome, Bologna, Po and others that followed Salerno are more than just names to many Naperville boys and parents. Some of these places have a deep and lasting meaning.

It is not a difficult task to describe the Italian campaign in a few words. One short one covers it from start to finish – HELL. But as that so well describes all war, perhaps a word or two of explanation as to just why this campaign was more so, is in order.

Historically, it was the first time in all Roman and Italian history that Rome had been conquered from the south. It was an uphill battle all the way to the Alps, except for the plains around Rome, the narrow valley of the Arno, and the broad valley of the Po. It was a common expression along the 'boot' - "The Krauts are always looking down our throats." It was natural terrain for a defensive war, which in the final outcome made the victory a greater one. But along the way led many a G.I. to doubt the wisdom of such an offensive and wonder "If that next hill was really necessary."

In late spring of 1944 it was like old home week at the 24th replacement depot just north of Naples. Brother Bill, Dick Kluckholn, Otto Haido were the ones I met up with. No doubt other local boys were in that hole at one time or another. Bert Haas was there, but the day Dick and I were going to look him up the Army had other plans. The feeling of seeing someone from home when you are that far from it and no guarantee that you'll see it again is a feeling that is hard to describe. Along with mail calls, those were the more pleasant moments abroad.

*Getting back to the realities of war - we'll never forget the mud, mules and mountains. The outstretched hands along the Appain Way; the bucket brigades at the garbage pails; those odd night rides up Highway 65; or that sickish feeling on the way back when the tension was off and the nerves had started to unwind; Bed Check Charlie and his running mate Axis Sally; the vino and vermouth, or the quick way to forget – grappa; the short whistle and sharp crack which meant that one was too close; and last, but not least, that great feeling when we knew it was finally **over** over there.*

***

The thunder and lightning didn't let up for the rest of the day, but when the worst of it had finally passed through later that evening, we headed out until after dark. Danny continued on his road to recovery that had begun when "Papa" had made him laugh so hard. Danny also continued to break out in sporadic laughter without warning. I knew what had ignited his outbursts, and judging from the icy glare from Dad that fooled no one, so did he. If Dad was going to get pensive, or worse yet maudlin, it wasn't going to be because his recently ill seven-year-old grandson was laughing his way to better health.

I didn't know it at the time, and it didn't occur to me when I finally read Dad's letter, but later on when I was putting all of these memories in perspective it occurred to me that Dad was about as happy and grateful as a guy can be, as he sat there in a boat on Pelican Lake experiencing his grandson's laughter as opposed to those foxholes, and those short whistles and sharp cracks which meant one was too close.

The thing is, most of us can only imagine those emotions and attempt to appreciate them; my dad, and maybe yours, or perhaps your grandfather or even your great grandfather, didn't have to imagine a thing. They *knew* how fortunate they were to get a chance to experience, in a way many of us will never know, what it feels like to be on the water watching your child and grandchild fishing, laughing, enjoying life; the life my dad and so many others of his generation made sure all of us would be given the opportunity to enjoy. Dad never would have mentioned those things. Dad, and so many others, just went ahead and did what needed doing - to make damn sure most of us would be able to live our lives in relative peace for as long as possible.

***

We had a custom of calling our last cast at the end of any given trip. Don probably started it who knows when, because with his luck that's when he stood, in his mind, at least a fair chance of hooking a world's record. That's what Larry and I also believed as it pertained to Don, or were at least willing to acknowledge as a distinct possibility. Let me put it another way; if you're holding four of a kind, the last person you want across from you trying to fill an inside straight flush is Don. Anyway, after we docked the boat after another frustrating day with not so much as a musky follow, I announced my last cast from the dock off Weaver's Point.

Unfortunately, the water didn't explode like a volcano and a thirty-pound musky didn't break the surface. Danny had spotted the one chance I had on the very first day. True to form, those Pelican Lake muskies were willing to give us maybe one shot and one shot only, with no guarantee we would get even that much, at least not on every trip. I wasn't going to give up, however, and I knew Dad, Don and now Danny I hoped, felt the same way.

Life, however, shifted into high gear for Don and me. He remarried and immediately started a family, and I was promoted to what Spalding called a Territory Manager and transferred to Des Moines, Iowa. Territory Manager was a just another name for sales rep, which was the title most of us preferred to call it anyway. Whatever we were called, it kept me busy, as did our three growing children. The Quest was on hold, and would stay there for quite some time. I thought about musky fishing, especially in early fall, but building a successful territory selling golf equipment coupled with family responsibilities had devoured all of my time and money.

It finally happened though, during a phone conversation with Don in September of 1982. We were reminiscing about all the good times we used to have up North, and wouldn't it be great to jump-start the Quest. Then we both wondered out loud just how long had it been since we had been up North together… Good Lord, had seven long years gone by that fast? Well, that was going to change no matter what. Not only that, but this time around we were done *toying* around - the allure of the Quest was upon us once again, only this time failure was not an option – we hoped.

Chapter 10

On the shores of Upper Gresham,
In late fall of '82,"
We renewed again the Quest
That had ended once with you...
                              - D.C.M.

A strong sense of at least nostalgia had been permeating my psyche ever since we moved from our hometown of Aurora to Des Moines three and a half years earlier, especially when we returned home for the holidays or a few days in summer. I had turned thirty-three, and although I didn't feel old, whatever that meant, there was no escaping the reality that time seemed to be accelerating, just like the old folks had always said it would.

The significance of certain childhood memories however, priorities more like it, were impervious to the passage of time, like our long-ago family camping and fishing vacations in northern Wisconsin. Those remained as young, and more importantly as relevant, as ever. Nothing however, had prepared me for the intense emotion, the pure excitement that was generated when I thought about the upcoming trip Don and I were going to be making to northern Wisconsin.

The first thing we agreed upon was to skip Pelican Lake. I had been doing some research, and from what I could gather Vilas County appeared to be the musky capital of Wisconsin. We would discover later there were folks from other areas of Wisconsin who would hotly dispute that claim, not the least of which folks from the Hayward area, but Don and I still had a lot to learn about where, and how, to catch muskies. We still held Pelican Lake in high regard if for no other reason than our memories of Grampa, but rumors that Pelican was fished out that came from a few so-called experienced anglers both Don and I had met over the years made us decide we would better our chances elsewhere. Vilas County or bust! That was our war cry in the fall of 1982.

***

Another reason I was so excited about getting away had to do with my job. I *really* needed a vacation, one where I was truly away from it all. Along with off-course golf specialty shops, I had been calling on local club pros at various golf courses and country clubs throughout Iowa, central Illinois, Nebraska and South Dakota non-stop for close to four years. Most of them were good guys, but a few of them were prima donna snobs of the first order, and that was on their good days. The more "prestigious" the country club, the more affected they seemed to be, especially at two exclusive clubs in Des Moines for some reason.

Maybe because they had to kiss so many of their members' butts all day they had a natural tendency to take it out on others they considered beneath them, as in everyone else in their lives. Another theory difficult to dismiss was their inability to live with the overwhelming frustration of being the best golfers around, easily within in the upper 1% of all golfers everywhere, but not good enough to compete successfully with the players on the PGA Tour. In my opinion, lacking the ability and/or temperament to run with the big dogs on the PGA Tour drove some of them nuts, I swear it did. *Drive for show putt for dough* was an adage not lost on a number of those guys.

Anyway, it would be good to get away from it all for a while. Believe me, different trajectories of Top-Flite golf balls, the degrees of pitching wedge angles and the advantages of graphite shafts were the last things I wanted to think or talk about. As the big day of our departure drew near, I found I could concentrate on little else other than a Northwoods musky hunt. If I wasn't in the fishing tackle section of some retail outlet or reading whatever I could find about muskies, I intended to do so at my first opportunity.

***

Don and I were to head up North the second Thursday in October. I had read somewhere that later in the fall was when the biggest muskies went on a feeding frenzy in order to fatten up for the long winter months. Don had moved his family to the La Crosse, Wisconsin area near the small town of West Salem, so I decided to work the northeast part of my territory and end up in Dubuque, Iowa that Wednesday evening. I was so filled with anticipation it was all I could do to stop opening my two tackle boxes and fooling around with everything over and over again as I sat in my motel room waiting for Don to call.

He was a railroad engineer, and had been for years. He had signed off for some vacation time, and the way I had understood it he was due home around five that Wednesday afternoon. I was going nuts cooped up in my cramped Super 8 Motel room as five o'clock came and went, and since nothing will make a call arrive quicker than not being there when it arrives, I went out and grabbed some supper. I figured Don would leave a message at the front desk and I'd just call back.

"No," the front desk clerk informed me when I asked her to check again after my return from supper, "There's no messages for you."

"Are you *sure?*" I asked for the third time, causing her to bristle - again. It was apparent she didn't like her job very much, and one of the main reasons was standing directly in front of her.

"Sir, I would *know* if a call had arrived for you. I have been *right here* the whole time." Her level stare and tone told me the last thing I wanted to do was continue our conversation. The only thing she hadn't done to convince me of that was to have finished her last sentence with "dumb ass".

I gave her a tentative smile and headed directly to my room. This was getting serious. It was after six and no call from my otherwise dependable big brother. Good God, had there been a derailment? A train wreck? A car accident?? At least Don had always demonstrated the ability to take a punch, so if the worst had happened perhaps we could just tape him up and salvage our fishing trip. I decided to call.

***

Don's wife Linda was known far and wide for having a great deal of patience to match her heart of gold, all of which came in real handy when it came to raising three boys under seven with two of them being identical twins around four years old. I could tell she was having a day of it by her tone of voice when I called, but regardless, I wasn't prepared for what she told me.

"Don's not here. Not sure when he's due in. Why? What's going on?"

What's going on? What's going *on?* I basically yelled to myself as I stood in that dreary motel room that was growing drearier by the second. My heart had begun to pound like a slow-motion jackhammer, so I knew I had to choose my words carefully and speak in measured tones.

"Well, Don said he'd be home around five, and I just wanted to verify what time he wanted me there in the morning."

"Oh, are you coming by tomorrow?" Linda asked, her tone indicating in no uncertain terms it was the first she'd heard about it. Uh oh. The ice had gone from thin to transparently so. Unfortunately, I was caught wholly off guard, incapable of tap dancing my way around what was coming down.

"Well yeah, Linda, tomorrow morning is when Don and I are going on our fishing trip." Thump thump. Thump thump. Thump thump.

"Don's not going on any fishing trip tomorrow. I don't know where you got that idea!" Linda said, as if I was an idiot for doubting that foregone conclusion.

"Uh...uh....c-could you have Don call me as soon as he gets in please?"

I sounded pathetic. I must have, because that's how I felt. For whatever reason, logical or not, I had turned what should have been a pleasant three or four day fishing trip into an unbridled obsession that could no more be denied than breathing itself. I mumbled a "thanks" as I hung up and fell into the chair next to the small desk. I just stared at the phone dumbfounded, not wanting to accept what I had just heard, and realizing I had no choice but to accept it.

Maybe it was the couple extra glasses of wine I'd had with my steak at supper, but whatever it was I didn't know how much time had elapsed from hanging up with Linda and the shrill ringing of the motel phone not two feet from my ears as I sat there, still in a state of shock.

"Don't worry about it." Don informed me with all the confidence in the world. It hadn't occurred to him his kid brother would be naïve or forgetful enough to actually think his big brother didn't have the situation well in hand.

"You sure?" I asked, even though the sensation of relief was already washing over me like a tidal wave. "Because Linda said -"

"Just a minor misunderstanding. Tell you what, why don't you head up here tonight? You're not two hours away. We can go over our game plan, have a couple brews and head out first thing in the morning." I was packed and heading out of that gloomy motel room before I hung up almost.

***

"Miss?" If you wanted some cooperation, sometimes it seemed to help if you referred to women over thirty or so as "Miss". It usually helps more than calling them Ma'am, I can tell you that, especially if they think you are older than them.

The front desk clerk turned when she heard my voice, her standard customer service smile vanishing the moment she saw who was standing in front of her - *again*.

"I'm sorry Miss," I continued, "but I just received a call from home. Seems there's an emergency and I have to leave immediately. Any chance of me getting a refund on the room?" Like most places where I stayed, the Super 8 in Dubuque made you pay in advance, or at least processed your credit card so they could charge you at their convenience.

"I'm sorry, sir, but we have a "no refund" policy once you have actually checked into the room." She had me all right, and boy was she loving it.

"I understand Miss, but I didn't even use the bathroom, honest. The paper's still across the toilet seat. I haven't been in there two hours, couldn't I just -"

"I'm *so* sorry sir, but I don't make the rules." Boy did *that* make her evening.

"Of course, I understand, but for five bucks do think you could bend them little?"

She feigned major indignation over that one. Her only regret was she wasn't a cop who could lock me up for attempted bribery.

"Here's your receipt, *sir*. Have a *real* nice trip." She said, her voice as warm as dry ice.

"Thanks...*Ma'am.*" I couldn't get out of there fast enough.

All you can do when vacation time has arrived is place the added expenses in that timeworn category "miscellaneous" and keep on truckin' - I was already flying high before I pulled out of the parking lot. Less than two hours later I was indeed heading up the gravel driveway that led to my brother's place, a farmhouse in the country outside of La Crosse. We didn't know it yet, not for sure or even close, but a significant era regarding the Quest was about to unfold.

***

Don insisted we take his old pickup truck, mainly because it had a boat hitch for Don's flat bottom boat. My car didn't have one, and didn't have a cassette player either. Don had reached the conclusion the Quest needed musical accompaniment, and since there was no finer musky hunting music than The New Christy Minstrels, they became the musicians of choice, with the Kingston Trio coming in a close second. Actually, Don had been listening to those groups for years. I had always liked their music as a teenager, at least until the Beatles, Byrds and Stones got my attention. Still, I had to admit Don's choices were a much better fit for what we were doing. I couldn't feature casting away while humming *Paperback Writer* or *19th Nervous Breakdown*, although in a broader sense the latter did relate to musky fishing.

Don's truck was a real doozy. There wasn't too much rust and it ran pretty good, but I could have done without the two huge decals on both doors of some wombat doing a wheelie on what appeared to be a generic version of a Honda 50. The smiling idiot looked like he was straight out of a Clutch Cargo cartoon. At first I thought I had developed some sort of visible deformity or something, the way the motorists we passed kept staring - then I'd remember the goof on the door.

We waited until Merrill before making our first official tackle shop foray. It was a fairly well supplied establishment located in the downtown area, and the proprietor seemed like a decent enough guy. Don needed a new reel, but wasn't impressed with what was available. When I went to buy one of the biggest nets the guy had for sale, his eyes lit up.

"So, you fellas goin' for a hawg, eh? That's a lot of net!"

"Hopefully we'll get a chance to use it." I said as I put it against the side of the counter and dug into my pocket.

"You fellas lookin' for northerns, muskies or both?"

"We're going after musky," I said, "up in Vilas County."

Don was inspecting the large collection of lures about twenty feet away as I spoke. When he heard the conversation about muskies he started to work his way towards the counter.

"Vilas *County?* Why the hell ya wanna go all the way up there? Muskies are everywhere, not just that tourist trap," the guy said, sounding like a man of conviction. "There's a forty pounder been hangin' 'round my uncle's dock on Pesibic Lake, just outside of town. Been swimmin' 'round that dock for over two weeks now, seen 'em myself, and you can bet he ain't alone. If it's big muskies ya want, ya oughta save yourselves the drive and expense and rent out his cabin for a few days. I'll put in a word and get you a good deal. Sure wish I could take the time off. I'd go and catch one'a them hawgs myself!"

One rumor about sales reps that seems to have a life of its own is we are especially susceptible when it comes to being on the receiving end of a sales pitch. You'll hear sales reps deny it, maintaining "you can't kid a kidder" or some equally inane response, but that's not true; at least it wasn't for me. I stood there listening to that guy as if he'd just stepped off Mount Sinai cradling a set of stone tablets.

"No kidding? Wow. Hey Don, guess what!" I turned to my big brother, but he was already standing next to me with a look in his eyes that immediately made me feel like I had just been transformed into one of those gigantic suckers in a Warner Brothers cartoon.

"Uh…I'd better talk it over with my brother," I finally said to the guy as I paid for my new net. Don was almost out the door so I followed him. He hopped in the truck, I tossed my new net in the back, and we got out of there. We hadn't gone half a block when it was apparent Don could no longer contain himself.

"Just what is it about Merrill that makes you think we are anywhere *near* Vilas County?" He asked.

"Well, it's just that he seemed like…I don't know…I sensed that he…just forget it." We pressed on, ever northward. *Muskie…*

***

If the anticipation of an upcoming fishing trip is a large part of the excitement, rolling along pine studded Northwoods highways joking, pontificating, theorizing, plotting, planning, debating, joking some more and catching up on each other's lives with a brother or close friend you haven't seen for awhile ranks right up there as well. The closer you get to your destination the livelier things seem to become. Our only problem, not that we saw it as such at the time, was we didn't have a planned destination outside of our general strategy of making it to Vilas County in one piece. Once we were north of Minocqua on route 51 later that afternoon, however, it was time to find a rustic cabin on a musky lake.

We weren't in any huge hurry, but getting settled in had become somewhat of a priority, especially after we pulled into this one blacktopped driveway that led to a beautiful looking lodge overlooking an exceptionally awesome looking lake. Something, however, was amiss.

It had to do with the cars that were parked in the lot by the lodge. We were expecting Northwoods Rugged - mean, razor-toothed fish, wildlife such as bears, virgin forests surrounding unspoiled, natural lakes with unshaven fishermen casting away from dull hued boats. So what was up with all the late model Mercedes, Beemers and Audis? The place looked immaculate, too. Don's pickup could have backfired a couple times with a flat tire and not been more out of place.

I was almost reluctant to get out, like I was trespassing or something. The place may have been owned by some major corporation for private use by its executives, I didn't know. We didn't see a restaurant, which wasn't a good sign, or a bar, which was even worse. Funny thing - I hadn't noticed Don's muffler being so loud until we were sitting there idling in the paved parking lot without so much as an acorn out of place.

Finally, some guy a little too old to be called middle-aged stepped out of the lodge, but instead of coming over with a smile on his face and his hand held out, all he did was stare at us, or at least the truck and what was attached to it. Don's dirty brown, flat bottom boat appeared better suited for fishermen noodlin' for catfish on Mississippi backwaters as opposed to Northwoods musky hunts. I hadn't noticed the blue exhaust belching from the truck either... probably should've had those rings looked at...

Even from thirty feet it was obvious the guy took pride in his wardrobe. He looked as if he were modeling Northwoods attire for a catalog, but not any we had heard of, like L.L. Bean or something. He had the look of a guy who would be disappointed if guys in a truck like ours *did* recognize the names of his catalogs, let alone the labels on his plaid shirts and creased khaki trousers – worsted wool, of course. Still, maybe I was getting carried away so I decided to go over and introduce myself. I smiled, waved and took three, maybe four steps when he turned, sullen-faced, and went back inside, closing the door behind him with enough authority to keep me from wanting to knock on it. It was time to hit the road.

***

"Pull in here." I said to Don after I caught a glimpse of a lake through the trees of an area that also had a motel, bar, and rustic looking cabins close to the water. Don wheeled his trusty pickup into the gravel parking lot and stopped right in front of the log cabin bar. That was more like it, we assured each other – gravel, and cars made in Detroit. We walked past the bar to get a better look at the lake. There were small log cabins right on the water all right, maybe a hundred yards away from the road, surrounded by old growth pines. Perfect. We headed into the bar.

It looked great too. There was a big musky on the wall behind the knotty pine bar, a pool table and a general ambiance that said "welcome to the Northwoods". Even the bartender looked impressive; a strapping six foot four hulk of a guy with a blond crew cut. He wasn't smiling though, at least not really. Maybe it was because business was slow, since it was October and all. Except for a few guys hunched over their beers, we were the only ones in there.

"May I be of assistance?" He asked us as we stood there looking around, then at him. He sounded more like the maitre'd at a four-star Gold Coast restaurant than a Northwoods bartender.

"Hope so," I answered. "We're looking for a cabin on the water for a few days. This lake have good fishing?"

"And might I inquire what species of fish is of interest to you?" The bartender asked as he placed both his hands on the bar and looked down at me. His demeanor definitely didn't fit the stereotype, let me tell you.

You need to understand a couple of things about Don. Number one, he's a pretty imposing looking character in his own right. Before his knee operations he was close to six feet tall, and at the time of our trip weighed in around 230 stocky pounds or so with a full, dark beard. The other thing about him was his deportment when he was in a really good mood, like when he was all excited about a musky hunt. He'd get a little carried away sometimes. When that hulk of a bartender asked me 'what species of fish was of interest to us', Don immediately flew to the bar, slammed his fist down so hard it shook everything on it and yelled, *"MUSKY!!"* I mean he really yelled it, with a growl in his voice and a wild look in his eyes directed right at the bartender. Don being a total stranger, if not a total stranger ax murderer, definitely got the guy's attention.

"Well then! Yes, yes indeed!" The bartender, all six foot four of him, said as he stepped as far away as he could until he backed into the rear area of the bar, rattling a few bottles of liquor that were resting on their suddenly precarious glass shelves. "The muskellunge is indeed present in these waters, indeed they are, and in abundance I hasten to add!"

The poor guy was all wide-eyed as he rattled on, keeping a careful watch on Don, as if he were afraid a truth-extracting hunting knife of mythical proportions would appear at any second. Don didn't even *own* a hunting knife, mythical or otherwise. I had to act fast - a clean shaven, kid brother-sales-rep type of fast.

"I'm sorry, really, it's just that Don and I, he's my brother by the way, are really looking forward to spending some time on the water, uh, how about a couple drafts? Can I buy you one?

I'm sorry, what was your name?" The bartender, who appeared to be coming around but not quite, took a tentative step towards us. He finally served us anyway, which was a good sign, but he kept his eye on Don.

***

His name turned out to be Sid, and he was an okay guy even if he did get carried away from time to time after stepping onto his soapbox. He tried his best to talk us into renting one of his motel rooms that were next door. It turned out he didn't own the lakefront cabins - those belonged to another character, a label that described the yet to be met owner of the cabins perfectly.

We liked Van Jolin the minute we met him after he entered the bar. He had the weathered look of a man who had spent most of his fifty-plus years outside; a gray peppered beard, perpetual tan, lean and tough looking. He not only owned the cabins by the small lake and would rent us one right on the water for less than what Sid wanted for a motel room, but was a fishing guide as well. He used to own the entire section of land from the road to the west shoreline of Upper Gresham Lake, but had sold off the road frontage some years back. I asked him if he guided for muskies. He looked at me as if I were insane.

"Well hell *yes* I guide for muskies! Be glad to take you boys out except there's a tournament goin' on this weekend and I'm already booked. Since you're rentin' a cabin though, I'll give you a few pointers. I'll be spendin' most my time on a different lake, but there's some good-sized muskies right here in Upper Gresham. What kind'a lures you boys throwin'?"

We had what we believed was a fairly good assortment of musky lures. Mepps Musky Killers and Giant Killers, a few Suicks, large Rapalas, Cisco Kid Toppers and a couple good-sized Jitterbugs. I even had a huge Daredevil that some tackle shop owner guaranteed would catch big northern and probably even bigger muskies, too. I never had the confidence to stick with it long enough to find out though. Van Jolin listened for a while, then spoke up.

"Those are all good enough lures I suppose, but on Upper Gresham you need to be throwin' Eddie Baits. Damn good jerk bait. Works like a Suick, but they're made from hardwood and go deeper, especially after they're broke in and a little water logged. I got a friend up the road that sells 'em. Make sure you tell 'em I sent you."

After Don and I secured our cabin and unpacked, we headed over to the tackle shop Van Jolin had told us about. By using his name, we hoped the owner would take good care of us. He took care of us all right, especially Don.

***

I sold wholesale golf equipment for a living, but inventory is inventory regardless of what it is, and I was well aware of what it meant to a shop owner to be overstocked. We bought some of the many Eddie Baits the owner had in stock which was fine; they're a good lure. Still, I should have paid more attention to why the owner, his shop empty except for us, kept extolling the virtues of certain products that, coincidentally, just happened to be items he had in abundance; and in October with his prime selling season well behind him. He didn't do it all the time, but his efforts increased once he found out we weren't exactly the most knowledgeable musky men ever to walk through his door. Like when Don mentioned he needed a new reel.

"Well hell's bells!" The owner said, a gleam in his eye. "Have I got the reel for you!" He reached under his glass case and pulled out a blue and silver box, one of about a dozen or so identical boxes that were sitting there.

"This beauty is state of the art. You need a high-speed retrieve to get a musky's attention, and this baby's got it! 5.18 to 1!" With that, the owner slowly placed a steel blue, 4 HM Daiwa Millionaire on the glass in front of Don as if he were caressing the Hope Diamond.

"So," Don said as his eyes wandered back under the glass counter in search of the more famous Swedish Ambassadeurs, "this is the latest and greatest, huh? Kind'a had an eye out for a good deal on a Garcia 6000C like my brother's got."

"Too slow!" The owner exclaimed. "3 to 1 ratio won't cut the mustard with the muskies 'round here. No *way* Jose'! If you wanna out-fish your brother, here's the baby ya need! Hell, I hardly carry Ambassadeurs anymore. Damned relics is what they are. Anymore outdated they'd have dinosaur dung on 'em!"

"Hmm...how much?" Don asked.

"Well, I normally charge ninety bucks, but since Van Jolin sent you, eighty will do. I'll even throw in the tax."

Don thought it over then went for it. Back at the cabin that evening he marveled at his new toy, reading the small pamphlet that came with it. That's when he noticed the 4 HM model was a bass reel. He rationalized that away due to the high retrieve ratio. A few months later he found the same reel in K-Mart for

$39.95. Later on, he became further unhinged when the thing started making this annoying screeching sound on every cast. It was almost as annoying as my complaining about it on an equally regular basis.

Not to be outdone in the tackle shop that day, I allowed myself to be talked into buying a wooden "musky" club. It looked liked a sawed-off Pee Wee League baseball bat, but the owner assured me it was specifically designed for muskies and extremely large northern. One well-placed wallop between the eyes and our trophy would be secured - the trophy we would no doubt hook in the fertile waters of Upper Gresham with our dozen Eddie Baits of various colors, Don's new reel, the new line the owner insisted we both needed and of course my new musky club. The owner maintained (with a straight face no less) "you'll need this club in late fall because bigger muskies become more aggressive this time of year." I bought the club (and the owner's b.s.) then Don and I headed for the door.

"You boys need a good net?" The owner said as he stood behind the cash register counting what used to be our money. "I got about thirty real nice ones!" I told him thanks anyway, but I had bought a new one earlier that day.

"Hope it's not one'a them new fangled jobs with that rubber netting," he warned. "That stuff deteriorates in nothing flat. The nylon kind I have is what ya need!"

Much to the owner's disappointment I assured him that was exactly what I had just purchased, but reluctantly thanked him anyway as the uneasy sensation the entire experience had created continued to grow inside me. We were learning though, even if some of the things were obvious to begin with, or should have been.

***

I liked Don's new boat. Well, it wasn't new, exactly; Don had bought it off a guy from Savanna, Illinois who used to take it out on the Mississippi. It was a flat bottom with a 35 horse Johnson, and I liked the way we could maneuver inside of it. I also liked the flat bow area where I could stand and cast. Don had even managed to acquire a trolling motor, a first for us. Yep, we were good to go all right, and we couldn't wait to get on the water the following morning.

My excuse was we had always rented boats that were already in the water, so how was I supposed to know? Don's excuse? He had been driving the truck as he backed his boat into the lake, and since I was back there directing, I should have noticed it right off, especially since I had unhooked everything and had pushed the boat into the water. Regardless, we discovered boats sure seem to take on water a lot quicker than expel it when that stopper in the rear isn't plugged in. Good thing we were next to a dock, or at least sort of close to one.

Kneeling on the dock, I managed to grab the edge of the port side near the stern just before the boat floated out of reach. Good thing, too, because it had already taken on over six inches of water and more was flooding in - fast. In no time the stern had maybe another six inches to go before it was low enough for half of Upper Gresham to come rushing in. I got a hold of the fore rope as well, and managed to work the bow a little ways towards the boat hitch the same time Don arrived. We pulled (extra water makes a difference, eh?) the bow onto the hitch and hooked things up. Don jumped in his pickup, nearly popped the clutch and lurched forward. Like I said, it seemed to take a lot longer for all that water to drain.

We thought that was going to be our last screw up, and it would have been, at least for a while, if the wind hadn't picked up so much once we were on the water. We had been searching out submerged weed beds like Van Jolin had recommended we do, but the wind was up enough to render the trolling motor pretty much useless, especially since it wasn't very powerful and we were just learning how to use it. We would no sooner get to a good spot to cast and in nothing flat we were past it, back in open water. We were lucky to get off two casts each. It was getting pretty chilly, too; fifty degrees tops, not counting wind chill.

Don didn't start out with one of our new Eddie Baits, but an old, tried and true black Suick, not that either of us had ever caught anything with one. We were again being blown off course just as Don had made his way to the bow for a quick cast, only that time the wind shoved the boat sideways, with a little help from my errant operation of the trolling motor. Don was as agile as they came, with reflexes to match, and at that precise moment he needed every iota of those qualities to remain in the boat, and I mean literally.

He dropped like a rock to all fours right on the bow with a resounding thud, as his large body yawed towards the abyss. He was *that* close to going in, as in inches; maybe just one inch, and I'm not kidding. Although he managed to barely stay in the boat, the same couldn't be said of his rod, new reel and black Suick. There were no buoyant rods in our boat, and that mostly metal Daiwa Millionaire wasn't about to float either. Worse yet, in all the confusion the howling wind was pushing us straight out to God knew where, and at an alarming clip. We were too far out in the lake to ascertain our previous location with landmarks on shore, so I figured Don was pretty much screwed as far as ever seeing his gear again. Don had never been, however, the quitting type, although some might define it as mule-head stubborn.

He shot to the back and revved up the engine (miracle of miracles, it started on the first try) and goosed it back to where we *may* have been. We looked around, but all we saw were white caps churning over gray water. At least that's all I saw, but Don must have been especially motivated (and lucky) because just as we were again being blown to somewhere in the next county he somehow spotted a black thing that was suspended about twelve inches under the waves. He horsed the boat to the spot and sure enough, there was his Suick, still attached to the line and the line to the reel and the reel to the rod. In hindsight, with decades of time on the water in-between, a dollar would get you a thousand for a successful repeat under similar conditions.

***

We stayed out there all day, beating the outside edges of weed beds above and below the water. I kept at it with an Eddie Bait. I was getting the hang of it for one thing, and for another I liked the way it looked in the water. What I didn't understand was why the muskies, or at least a few northern didn't feel the same way. Instead of them having to try and run down some darting bait fish, all they had to do was come after what appeared to be, to me anyway, a crippled, tasty target.

Don had abandoned his Suick and was tossing a bucktail. He had also been throwing an old, wooden Pikie Minnow for a while, in honor of Grampa; that, and because in our entire family that had been the only lure to catch a trophy musky going on sixty years. Don never went on a musky hunt without throwing one of those, for a little while anyway.

Another lesson had been learned before we finally admitted defeat for the day; Don had been wearing a T-shirt with a light jacket close by if needed. I had a T-shirt and hooded sweatshirt. Both outfits had been ideal when we had gone to breakfast that morning; before the October wind had started to howl and the temperature dropped twenty degrees, or at least felt like it. It was bad enough we had been skunked without seeing so much as a follow, although come to think of it, we had *never* seen a follow, just heard about them.

On top of that we were beginning to hallucinate from hypothermia. I thought I was anyway, judging by the eerie music that kept coming and going with the wind as I sat there shivering. Don said he didn't hear anything until we were nearly back to the public landing area. Someone had left the door to their cabin open, and along with a set of wind chimes on their porch, the radio had played a few tricks with my head, as if Stephen King was hiding behind a tree giggling his ass off.

October weather in northern Wisconsin is the ultimate crapshoot, and with our blue lips and numb fingers we felt as if we had just rolled snake eyes. As it turned out, the weather on our first day was downright balmy compared to what was in store for us. We, of course, didn't know that and couldn't wait to dock the boat and regroup. We were getting dangerously low on money, but a road trip to the nearest Northwoods clothing store was our next stop, and after that, the warmth of Sid's bar in front of Upper Gresham.

***

"What took you fellas so damned long to get here?" Van Jolin asked as he sat at the bar with a drink in hand when Don and I entered. "Days like this I get off the water by two, and don't go back on until ten the next morning! Unless I got an idiot client from Chicago or someplace that figures he *has* to be out in that crap all day."

I couldn't tell if he was kidding, not for sure anyway. Turned out he wasn't. He had arrived just after two that afternoon, according to the two rather attractive young gals sitting to his left at the bar. He had apparently been flirting with them the better part of the past few hours. Not only that, but their husbands were still out on the water.

He didn't display the demeanor of a guy who would allow such minor details, like women wearing wedding rings, to alter his behavior. One of the gals, a pretty brunette right next to him who looked like she had put a great deal of effort in choosing her wardrobe (tight jeans, thin plaid blouse and high heeled boots) questioned whether a man Van Jolin's age could back up his amorous bravado. She had been smiling when she mentioned it, but that was about to change.

Without the slightest hesitation, he placed a hand behind her neck, pulled her to him and planted one right on her mouth. I thought she was going to slap him for sure, but she didn't. Not only that, but even after the hoots and hollering from the patrons died down, those two were *still* going at it. When she did back off and started giggling with her girlfriend, Van Jolin turned to us and started talking about musky fishing as if nothing out of the ordinary had happened.

"Looks like rain and probably some snow will get here by tomorrow, so get ready. Along with all this wind that should stir things up. Hit those submerged weed beds and rock reefs. You fellas got a depth finder?"

"No." We said in unison.

"Well hell, just stick to the weed beds and pound the shore around the peninsula. Good luck!" Then he went back to the girls, who agreed to take a personal tour of Van Jolin's property, including some of the vacant cabins he owned down by the water...

***

We were out after lunch the following day, having spent time that morning in a canoe with some guy we had met the previous night in the bar. His credibility had been easier to accept the night before, although even then it had been suspect. He maintained he almost always caught muskies from his canoe on this river by his little cabin, and if nothing else, promised we would raise at least one lunker. That had been enough for us.

We were in trouble right off. For one thing, he didn't know much about handling a canoe. For another, the "river" he took us to wasn't any bigger than an average sized stream back home. We never did see any muskies, and with a stream that small we doubted he had either, as in never, much less caught any from there.

Not only had the guy lied to us, but it turned out he had done so in order to get us to consider buying his small cabin. It was surrounded by brush, perhaps fifty yards from the stream, and according to our host "not too far" from a small lake that held *plenty* of big muskies. The tiny lake was such a well-kept secret, he maintained, it didn't even have an official name.

He showed us the inside of his cabin, reminding us several times how much he hated to sell it, but the monthly payments were just that - monthly, and through no fault of his own he hadn't been able to make any payments for the past several months or so.

"Cut you guys a real sweet deal!" He said, also several times, while trying to get us to mention a price first.

"How much are you asking?" I asked at one point, ending up on the receiving end of another of Don's glares.

"Got me near three acres here, too!" Was his response. "Sure hate to let it go, but times are rough. You make me an offer, odds are I'll take it!" And so forth until we left.

After lunch Don and I were glad to be on Upper Gresham all right, and took turns admonishing each other for having been duped into wasting an entire morning. If we were in the market for Northwoods real estate, it wasn't going to be on that trip, or decade for that matter.

Still, I had spotted a number of cottages and larger homes on the water that really got my attention, and wondered out loud what places like that cost. Whatever they cost, I had a lot more golf balls to sell before I could afford one. Still, I wondered what it must be like to step out of your own front door any time you felt like it and throw a few casts into waters teeming with muskies. Maybe someday...

***

We had followed some of Van Jolin's advice and purchased brown cotton gloves that went on before the rubber dishwashing gloves that we had also purchased. He said that was the best way to keep our hands from freezing. Good thing too, because there had been ice on the dock that morning when we had checked on the boat, and things hadn't exactly warmed up since. The glove combination worked pretty well that afternoon, until the rubber gloves ripped from constant casting and the ice water soaked the cotton gloves. Frozen hands are the only thing that can take your mind off frozen feet, although just barely and not completely. All we had were tennis shoes, having been more concerned about traction than our feet freezing. Before long our toes were to the point where we could've stuck a fork in them and they probably wouldn't have even bled. It was fifty-fifty we would have felt the prongs actually break the skin; that's how it seemed anyway.

The wind and rain started up, with the flattened drops coming in sideways. It wasn't three in the afternoon, and I was half dead. The only way to keep going was to cast, cast, cast. We beat the shores, worked what weed beds we could find and even managed to locate a rock reef or two, at least we thought maybe we had. No muskies though - not even a follow. The rain finally let up, but not the wind and cold. Cast, cast, cast...

I had quit smoking a year and a half ago, but for some reason being on vacation, especially a Northwoods vacation, created a desire for tobacco. Even so, there was no way I was about to smoke cigarettes or even cigars. I compromised, rationalizing my foolish decision by purchasing a bag of Redman chewing tobacco. That was foolish all right, especially since I had never even tried smokeless tobacco of any kind. There's a first time for everything, but sitting in a boat being rocked by waves wasn't exactly the ideal time to shove a wad of tobacco the size of a golf ball in my mouth.

Worse yet, I had put a half pint of Christian Bros. brandy in my tackle box, allegedly to ward off the chill. At first the sweet flavor of chaw, not unlike licorice, was almost appealing. The brandy not so much, even though I tried to convince myself it wasn't half bad. You guessed it. Less than ten minutes later I made sure all the brandy and chewing tobacco had been hurled over the side, except not all of it had come from a small brown bottle and a bag of Redman.

We were about to try a spot we had hit earlier along the east shore when Don first spotted it - a football floating on the waves, maybe a football field or so away. I wondered out loud if it was a high-quality Spalding football as opposed to an inferior Wilson ball.

"Has to be a Spalding," I insisted, "a Wilson ball would have come apart by now."

"If Wilson footballs suck so bad how come they use them in the NFL?" Don asked.

"Because money talks and bull - hey, that thing's moving towards the peninsula *against* the wind..."

Don took another look, then turned the boat and headed towards whatever it was.

"So, Spalding has started putting antlers on their balls." Don said as we closed in on the young buck. "No wonder the NFL uses Wilson."

Sure enough, we were closing in on a young buck all right, and from the wide-eyed terror on his face he could have done without our arrival. He had a good fifty yards to go before he made shore at the peninsula he had decided to visit, but to him it must have felt like five hundred. We stayed along side of him until he managed to gain his footing as he neared shore, and we were flat out awed by the amazing speed and strength he displayed when he catapulted through the shallow water and disappeared into the woods as if he had been launched from an aircraft carrier.

Even though we ended our second day without seeing any fish, let alone a musky, it had been worth it to watch that deer go from the uncertainty of navigating through the water with a boatload of bizarre creatures just a few feet away, to the absolute certainty of solid ground as it had shot through the woods. Well, not entirely worth it, but it was worth watching from such a close vantage point. I thought Scamp could really fly in his younger days, before arthritis and finally the mange had done him in when he was fifteen, but it had been nothing compared to what we saw that day. Nothing personal, Scamp...you are missed, and will never have an equal.

***

Later that evening in the bar Don and I mentioned what we had seen. The guy from that morning could not believe, in a pontificating tone of voice, why we hadn't smacked the deer over the head with an oar, towed it to shore and gutted it.

I had already taken a dislike to the guy on general principles. He rarely opened his mouth unless he was bragging, or maintaining everything anyone had ever done was similar but inferior to something he had done or at least witnessed. He did it in a loud voice as well, fueled by beer as he interrupted you, all the while staring at you with this phony sincerity until you pretended to acknowledge his vainglorious feat; it was either that or he'd never shut up, which he never did anyway. I did that three times before I realized what a dope I was for standing there, getting what little intelligence I had insulted by that guy.

Beating a swimming deer over the head with an oar finally tore it. It wasn't so much that someone would do something like that, although that bothered me too, it was that I strongly suspected that guy was too much of a lazy goof ("been lookin' for work over six months now, ain't nothin' out there though") to go to the trouble of killing, towing, gutting and dressing a chipmunk, let alone a deer. Oh, he'd stand around drinking free beer and watch someone else do it all right, then beg for the best cuts, but actually do the work himself? Fat chance.

By the way, he insisted he not only made the best deer-meat sausage you ever tasted, but it won second place at the Wisconsin State Fair two years running as well. "Dang nephew of one'a them judges won first". After dropping that load of crap on us, our local hero insisted he was poised for a third sausage-king run, too. "Don't give a hoot'n hell if that danged nephew *does* show! No sir. I do not!" Again with the look; eyes wide, as if that alone would convince you that even if he was an imbecile, he was a sincere imbecile.

After he laid that last little gem on me I finally lost it, as his beery eyes took on a look of especially phony sincerity and his head bobbed up and down like one of those little toy dogs in the rear window of somebody's car, as he waited impatiently for my acknowledgement of his sausage making prowess. That much, at least, I was prepared to deliver.

"Bullshit."

"Huh? What'd you say?" He didn't look too shocked - he probably heard that or something like it on a daily basis.

"Bullshit." I repeated.

Over the years, Don had grown used to his kid brother losing his patience in similar situations. Those encounters had rarely amounted to much, mainly because Don would usually defuse the situation with humor or on rare occasions its antithesis. That time, however, Don had a better plan.

"C'mon," he said to me, "those two guys shooting pool wanna play us for drinks." I gave the deer sausage king a quick *adios* and headed to the pool table with Don.

***

I shot average pool, at least on my good nights. Don didn't care. For one thing, he wanted me away from that guy who had already corralled another poor sap, and besides, it didn't matter that I wasn't much of a pool player; Don was, and then some.

The guys we were up against were none other than the husbands of the two gals that Van Jolin had entertained the day before. They were not only from Chicago but for some reason wanted us to be well aware of it, including their specific neighborhood, or so it appeared since they managed to mention it on several occasions before the first game of eight ball was over. A game we won by the way - well, Don won.

They grudgingly asked what we were drinking. What they really meant was "what brand of draft beer" were we drinking. Don said Old Style then they glanced at me.

"Courvoisier, XO if they have it." I replied, as if I ordered that sort of thing everyday. One of the Chicago guys glanced at my empty pilsner glass, then followed his buddy to the bar, mumbling something I couldn't make out. He brought back a snifter of Courvoisier, but he wasn't happy about it.

"Sorry," he said, looking anything but sorry or amused, "they're fresh out of XO."

He racked them up, and again they lost. And again. If Don wasn't running the table every time it was his turn, it must have seemed like it to those two. At first, they acted as if they were setting us up by losing on purpose, like they had watched Paul Newman in *The Hustler* once too often. After their fourth loss in a row, however, that face-saving device had worn thin; or they really *had* set us up. Apparently, that had been their plan.

"Tell ya what," the bigger of the two said as he again put a quarter in to retrieve the balls. "To hell with the drinks. One time, twenty bucks a man. That's how we do it in the city. You cool with that?"

Don glanced at me as he stood there chalking his cue, but he wasn't overly assured with what he saw. A few Courvoisiers on top of a number of beers had taken their toll, he noticed, as I stood there weaving and smiling at nothing in particular. Don agreed anyway.

Don broke, but nothing dropped. Bad sign. The next guy dropped in four before missing, then I flubbed an easy one. We went back and forth for a while, until only the eight ball was left. It was directly in front of the far right pocket; a quarter inch closer, if that, and it would have already fallen in. The cue ball was at the extreme other end, flush against the bumper near the left pocket. Worse yet, it was my shot. There was no way I would be able to use english on the shot, not that I was any good at it anyway. Without it, the cue ball would follow the eight ball right into the pocket and we'd of course lose the game. Barely grazing the bumper close to the eight ball might have been an option for some guys, but not for me.

"C'mon Ioway boy, just keep shootin' your regular game!" The bigger one said, a smile on his face that didn't even pretend to mirror the tone in his voice.

Don just stood stock still, both hands holding his cue with the butt on the floor as he stared intently at the table. I took a deep breath and lined up my shot. I was aiming for a spot on the eight ball as opposed to looking at the pocket I'd just called, like Don had tried to teach me years ago, to no avail. He knew there was no way I could make that shot. He knew *he* couldn't anyway, nor had he ever seen anyone else do it either, and Don had seen a lot of amazing pool shots in his day. I decided to barely tap the cue ball; it was our only hope. It seemed to take about five minutes for it to even reach the eight ball, but when it did a miracle occurred. The eight ball dropped in and the cue ball somehow did not, by about a billionth of an inch; it sure wanted to though. I swear, if someone had sneezed on it from five feet away it would have dropped. I was in shock. Don put the twenty dollar bill he had already pulled out back in his pocket. I've received some dirty looks in my life, but those two guys redefined the entire concept. Don asked them if they wanted to go double or nothing and received two endearing glares of his own.

Minnesota Fats and Fast Eddie had seen enough. Then they realized their wives had the rest of their money and suffered further when they had to tell them why they needed it. The gals informed their husbands it was time to leave, but also invited Don and me to join the four of them for a nightcap back at their cabin. Those two guys weren't exactly thrilled when they heard that, let me tell you.

Don and I stuck around for a while, long enough to get Sid the bartender's goat although that hadn't been our intention. All we wanted to do was have him take our picture holding a musky. What seemed to unsettle Sid was that we wanted to hold the one he had on the wall behind the bar, a thirty-pound beauty.

"No self-respecting sportsman would lower himself to that level." Sid pontificated, and he was right. Except Don and I were just doing it for laughs; we weren't going to maintain we had actually caught it. Sid, however, was less than convinced and no less disgusted.

We reminded him it certainly wasn't a hanging offense, like beating a deer to death with an oar when it wasn't even deer season - well, we assumed it wasn't deer season, at least not oar whacking deer season. Sid finally came around to our point of view, or just wanted to shut us up. At any rate, to this day Don and I each have the photograph Sid took of us, and he did a great job, bless his soul. Nine summers later I happened by that bar with Peggy, and asked about Sid. He had died; died way too young. Bless his soul indeed.

***

Don and I shared a laugh as we walked towards the cabin of our new Chicago friends. All the lights went off as we approached the place, no doubt after one or both of those guys saw (or heard) us coming. We had to go by their place anyway, and felt pretty good about things in general as we continued to butcher our rendition of the New Christy Minstrels' song *Corn Whiskey!* as we walked by, both of us waving twenty dollar bills. You might say it was our way of making them feel relieved they hadn't invited us in - more so if a pool table was in there.

We felt pretty good all right. So much so, we decided to make a courageous, midnight sneak musky attack - maybe, just maybe, we could catch those needle-toothed predators off guard and beat them at their own game. Our determination took a detour once we were standing on the dock; the ice and snow covered dock. The wind was howling and the white caps seemed to be daring us to get in the boat. High wind or not, we could easily see our breath, intermingled with snowflakes racing through it - racing sideways.

It is never a good idea to head out on the water after drinking, especially at night, and *especially* when you are already freezing half to death regardless of how much cognac and beer you have consumed. Besides, by morning maybe the mid-October weather would improve. You know - mid-October *Northwoods* weather – weather that is trying to reach polar vortex status and nearly succeeding. Discretion being the better part of valor might be debatable, but it wasn't to us – not that night. Half an hour later we were snoring away in the cabin.

***

The hangover didn't bother me half as much as the thought of how I would feel when it started to wear off, with the two of us in the middle of Upper Gresham on what had become the ugliest day from a weather perspective so far that year in northern Wisconsin. The long underwear and rain gear we had purchased helped, or so we insisted, in a vain attempt to delude ourselves into feeling better. But on that day, our last one on the water until next year, we realized why avid outdoor enthusiasts spared virtually no expense when it came to top quality bad weather clothing.

We weren't surprised by the ice on the dock, or on the boat for that matter. Even the snow drifts in certain areas on the floor of the boat didn't get to us so much, but it got our attention when we had to keep dipping our reels in the lake to help knock the ice off of them. Still, it was either deal with it all or call it quits.

All the armchair musky experts we had run into back at the bar, the *warm cozy* bar, insisted we were in the right place at the right time with the right weather, and all of them maintained they had either caught huge trophy muskies under similar conditions or knew someone who had, and usually more than one.

By God, that's all Don and I had needed to hear. We headed out around eight that morning in Don's flat bottom and beat the daylights out of Upper Gresham; whitecaps and all. It was hovering in the mid to low thirties with gusts up to forty miles an hour, with the wind never dropping below twenty mph or so. The snow never stopped, except in its intensity from time to time, and the stinging ice intermingled with it all was especially endearing. We also came to realize a flat bottom boat under those conditions wasn't merely an inconvenience, but life threatening. We kept casting.

At one point, when I thought I was hearing that music again even though we were on the other side of the lake from where we had heard it before, Don glared wild-eyed at me from underneath the hood of his wet sweat shirt; his entire beard, even his eye brows, encased in crusty, white ice. He hollered at me in order to be heard above the howling wind:

"Hey! It just don't get no better than this!"

True enough, he had borrowed his observation from an Old Milwaukee beer commercial but the irony of his words, or at least the point he was making, were dead on, especially when all the other misadventures of the 1982 trip were taken into consideration. I had never, and have never since, heard that particular phrase uttered under a more appropriate circumstance if restating Don's intent was the reason for repeating the phrase. It put things in perspective to such a degree it was time to stop feeling sorry for ourselves and continue to beat the daylights out of Upper Gresham. Grampa had made a similar sacrifice in 1925, hadn't he? What if maybe, just maybe, he was watching us now?

We continued through the day, taking an hour for lunch before assaulting that stingy lake all afternoon. Eddie Baits, bucktails of various colors and sizes, Suicks and Pikie Minnows. We threw them all, anywhere and everywhere we could. This was our year, we insisted, this was *our time!* We certainly had no competition; we had the lake to ourselves. No other boats anywhere - no misguided, weekend idealists like us, and no locals...no locals? We refused to accept anything other than they must be jaded, spoiled really, and didn't bother venturing out unless the weather was perfect. Except "perfect" was suppose to have been the weather we were sitting in, if a huge musky was our goal - or theirs.

So where were the muskies? We didn't know, and certainly didn't want to let it mess with our heads. Even so, four o'clock turned to five, and a little before six we conceded defeat. Again. No muskies, no follows - not even a lousy northern.

Still, our 1982 trip to Upper Gresham remains a classic, if for no other reason than it renewed the Quest - *steeled our resolve* - in a way only abject failure can produce so thoroughly for the truly motivated. The prize we were after had become all the more priceless, an elusive dream whose degree of difficulty enhanced our obsession. There would be no more seven year hiatuses; no muskies were hooked, but we were.

***

For a finishing touch Don's truck broke down on the way home, although that didn't really surprise us very much. It sputtered to the base of some hill where we should have been going sixty, but the best it could muster was maybe twenty mph. We made it to the nearest town though, and after the last of our money was invested along with the help of a credit card, we were on the road four hours later.

Next year, I vowed, would be different. I would spend the winter, spring and summer researching Vilas County until I had located the *perfect* musky hunting grounds. And despite Dad's misgivings, maybe it was time to seriously consider the guide option as well, even if that would strain our budget. It was high time we stopped worrying so much about such things, however. We had a Quest to fulfill, and we intended to do just that.

> *Thru bodies chilled and numb to the bone*
> *We made to you this pledge,*
> *Across generations etched in stone,*
> *A fish like yours we'd catch.*
>
> *So they sent us out in snow and rain*
> *To fish a place that had no fish.*
> *We numbly laughed at cold and pain,*
> *"Hey! It just don't get no better than this!"*
> *- DCM*

Chapter 11

"**F**ence Lake, on the Lac Du Flambeau Chain." I told Don over the phone in July of 1983. "From what I've been able to gather, there could be a world's record in there. Forty and fifty pound muskies are sighted every year, but are hard to catch because the lake is so deep."

"Where'd you hear all that?" Don asked.

"From a few guys I ran into at the local Muskies Inc. chapter here in Des Moines. Thought I'd call around up there and find us a cabin on the water, maybe try to locate a guide. What do you think?" Don was all for it, as long as we didn't go in mid to late October. I heard *that* all right. I swear, my fingers still felt a little numb.

I contacted the chamber of commerce offices in all the towns of any consequence in both Vilas and Sawyer Counties, and before long my mailbox filled up with pamphlets and brochures from a variety of places. I finally narrowed our choices down to a place on Fence Lake that not only had cabins right on the water (what's the sense of driving all the way to a beautiful lake and not being on it?) but also offered guide services from the camp owner *himself* as part of an all-inclusive package.

Perfect, I surmised. We would be on a premier body of prime musky waters in the heart of Wisconsin's Northwoods, in Vilas County no less, and have an experienced guide to not only show us around, but show us the error of our ways as well. We were also going to be there the weekend after Labor Day, when most of the motor boaters and jet skiers would hopefully be gone for the season. Yes, it seemed perfect all right. Too perfect, and by then we should have known better.

***

Don asked Dad if he wanted to go, but Mom and Dad had moved to Rodgers, Arkansas, supposedly enjoying their retirement. Dad just wasn't up for the seventeen hour, one-way drive. Brother Larry said he could make it though, so for the first time ever Pete McCabe's three sons would be on their own together in the Northwoods.

As usual, I couldn't wait to get started. More and more "how to" musky fishing articles were appearing in both national and regional sport magazines, and I read as many as I could find. Everyone seemed to have an angle, or their own way of going about things to a certain degree, but one thing that seemed to remain constant was the importance of high quality tackle. I loved reading things like that; it justified my love of browsing through tackle shops and fishing equipment sections of the larger chains, at least if they catered in some degree to those of us who were obsessed with catching a trophy musky.

I had to temper my enthusiasm in order to keep within certain budget restraints, but thankfully the fishing industry's equipment manufacturers offered options besides new boats, electronic gizmos and other expensive products. Not that I wouldn't have enjoyed acquiring all of those things, but being married with three young children created an atmosphere that required restraint - an atmosphere which didn't necessarily exclude buying a new musky rod and reel, and definitely didn't exclude buying new lures and a larger tackle box to accommodate them.

I especially enjoyed this one tackle shop south of West Okoboji Lake in Iowa called Oh Shucks. I liked traveling in that part of my territory to begin with, mainly because the northwest section of Iowa was the only part of my territory that had any musky lakes I had heard about anyway. I rarely had time to actually fish when I was there, but the Oh Shucks tackle shop made up for it, especially if we were only weeks, or better yet mere days, from heading up North. It seemed as if the whole world brightened at such times, and life in general became more worthwhile during the one or two weeks before a foray into the Northwoods. Since our trip to Fence Lake was only a few days away, I was especially excited.

Disagreeable customers, even the occasional prima donna horse's ass I called on only because I couldn't avoid him seemed less aggravating somehow, bordering upon tolerable. The long miles through Iowa, Nebraska and South Dakota whizzed by, where even the most monotonous landscape took on a variety of interesting qualities, displaying certain nuances I hadn't noticed before, or at least hadn't appreciated. The tackle shop, however, topped everything.

***

West Okoboji, East Okoboji and Spirit Lake made up the main lakes of the chain. Although they were good-sized bodies of water and had a very active tourist season as well as quite a few locals willing to spend money, Oh Shucks was the one tackle shop of any consequence that I ever found in the area, at least for musky hunters. I remembered the place from years ago, when Dad had taken us to that area on vacation, and it was pretty cool back then as well.

The folks who worked in Oh Shucks, including the owner, were friendly too. If I bought enough lures they always gave me a discount. Actually, that was because I *always* bought enough lures, and then some. The place was a throw back that had everything from live bait wells with a large variety of different types and sizes of bait fish and other fish-enticing critters to the latest bucktails, crank and jerk baits as well as musky surface lures. If it was something I had heard of, they always had it, plus quite a few I hadn't heard of at all; oh well, you have to spend your money on something…

The place had the opposite effect on me during my spring run. I still enjoyed going in there, but it wasn't the same when I had at least four or five months before my next fishing trip. With just a few days to go before our Fence Lake trip, however, that wasn't worth dwelling upon except to savor the reality that those four or five months were now behind me.

I rolled into Oh Shucks around noon on my last day before heading home and bought enough lures, braided Dacron line and top quality leaders to start my own tackle shop almost, then high-balled it straight to Des Moines. In less than 48 hours Don, Larry and I would be casting away on Fence Lake with an experienced musky guide to point the way.

I could almost smell the old growth pines as I flew along the highways that led home, even if I rarely passed anything that wasn't a corn or soybean field. They looked beautiful though, with autumn poised to crowd summer out of the way. That was going to be even more widespread in Vilas County, I just knew it. Maybe the leaves had already turned on hard maples, and on the sumac shrubbery that turned sunset red with such ease. I hoped so anyway. Fall was my favorite season, and it never arrived soon enough or outstayed its welcome no matter how long it hung around.

***

Our anticipation continued to build as Don and I made the turn off Route 47 to another highway that led to a gravel road that in turn led to our destination on the shores of Fence Lake. So far it had turned out to be everything we had hoped for. The rental cabins were spread under an umbrella of large pine trees, with ours located right on the water, just like the owner had promised. It was a great looking place that conjured up postcard quality images of what we had hoped to find in a Northwoods setting. The lake was beautiful and much larger than Upper Gresham, which came as no surprise. I swore I could almost smell the muskies! I couldn't wait to get out there, and didn't. I was casting from the dock before I had even brought my gear into the cabin.

The owner's name was Abner, a jovial enough fellow who appeared to enjoy life in general, especially his situation. He and his wife lived in the main house right at the resort. Abner was a retired mailman from Ohio, although he didn't look old enough to be retired; how he ended up with that impressive piece of property was anyone's guess. Perhaps he had lucked out with an inheritance, unless the federal government had a pension plan that was on par with what mid-level executives from General Motors received or something.

"Well, you *are* anxious to hook into a big one!" Abner said in the form of a greeting as he approached me at the end of the dock, his ample weight making it shake as he approached. He had definitely enjoyed way too many Happy Meals over the years, although it looked natural on him.

"Four days goes by pretty quick," I said with a smile on my face as I shook his hand. "Maybe the next cast is the one, right?"

"If you say so!" He responded with a smile as he shrugged his shoulders.

Somehow, his words and tone of voice resembled a bell striving for perfect pitch, but not quite making it. *Nah,* I thought to myself. *We've just been burned too many times, that's all. Get a grip, McCabe.*

"So," I continued, "when do you want to get started in the morning?"

"Oh, golly, I don't know about that yet, but we could go out later this afternoon and catch a mess of perch."

"Perch?" I inquired, stopping my retrieve in mid-crank and looking at Abner. *Oh no...*

"Golly yes, perch! Great musky bait, good for walleyes too. I love walleyes, they're my favorite!" *Okay...* I sighed to myself, unable to dismiss my growing apprehension.

"You're the guide." I eventually responded with a weak smile. "If perch works, let's do it."

"You and your brother be ready in an hour, I'll meet you here at the dock! Bye bye now!" *Hmm...*

***

Don and I spent the time unpacking and settling in. It was a nice cabin with three bedrooms, a good-sized kitchen, and a living room with a picture window that overlooked the lake. We congratulated ourselves on finally getting it right, assuming everything else worked out.

I didn't mention my initial impression of Abner to Don. I had probably read the guy incorrectly, although my doubts lingered. I was in my fifth year of being on the road as a sales rep and reading people had, to a degree, become second nature. Many times, I had learned more by what wasn't said, or by paying attention to the *way* things came out when words were spoken. A person's eyes could be dead giveaways, same with reading body language - do it enough, like casting and not catching anything, and eventually it becomes automatic.

I was unpacking my suitcase in my bedroom when I found it. Peggy had placed it on top of my clothes. It was a pamphlet that had been distributed by the St. Croix Corporation called "Ten Tips to a Trophy Musky" written by Bill Resman, a St. Croix field specialist. I wasn't sure what that meant, but it sure sounded like a cool job to me.

I was about to place it on the dresser when I noticed Peggy had written something on the top of the outside cover: "Grampa's watching you!" She wrote. She printed it actually, and seeing her hand caused me to feel a pang just then, a connection between my grandfather and a heartfelt appreciation for Peggy's acknowledgement of how important Grampa and the Quest had been, and was, to me. She knew it was about more than fish, a lot more, and that endeared her to me more than ever. I again glanced at her words, and felt thankful I was married to someone who encouraged my well-earned musky trips as opposed to those poor souls who experienced the opposite reaction from their mates. In some respects, I figured that was the difference between a mate and a soul mate. It made me feel like a lucky guy, because I was one. I even went out and showed Don what Peggy had done.

"Hey, that's great." He said. "Let's get to the dock." I understood completely.

***

We made it down to the dock with time to spare, but Abner wasn't there yet. Actually, he showed up half an hour late, eating a sandwich. For reasons that were unclear, he wanted us to follow him while he took his boat, rather than the three of us going in just one. We finally got under way after Abner took another ten minutes or so to get his boat started. It was a dumpy little craft; I couldn't even find a name on it. It was doubtful all three of us would have fit in it anyway, especially with all our gear.

Abner took us to a spot where you could catch dozens of perch in a matter of minutes; no doubt about it. Abner kept jigging and jigging, but for some reason, one that escaped our learned guide, he wasn't able to get a single bite.

"Golly, I just don't understand it." He said as he reached under his oily baseball cap and scratched his head.

Don and I were anchored about twenty feet away in our boat, watching him in silence. He had told us not to bother rigging up our gear to help catch the perch, because he would catch plenty on his own in no time. So, all we did was sit there with a beer dangling in our hands and kept watching. About twenty minutes later he still hadn't caught anything, but judging by his constant stares, our brews must have looked pretty inviting to him.

"Care for a beer, Abner?" Don asked.

"Golly yes! A fellow could die of thirst waitin' for these little bait stealers to bite!" Don tossed him one, and Abner had it opened and chugged before Don had the lid back on the cooler almost.

"Maybe we should try another spot," I suggested.

Rather than actually answering me in English, Abner made a noise that may have meant "well, maybe". He avoided eye contact when he uttered the noise, and continued to jig off the side of his boat with increased resolve, looking more like a confused novice than a serious, let alone knowledgeable fisherman. Finally, he pulled in his line (he wasn't using a rod and reel) and just stared at the water, not unlike some clueless soul on the shoulder of a highway with their hood propped up staring blankly at the engine, as if by itself that would cure the problem.

"Don't perch run in schools?" Don finally asked.

"Probably." Abner offered, looking into our boat. "Anything left in your cooler?" There was. Don and I had planned to have only a couple, while we were on the water anyway.

After Abner downed another beer, he decided it was indeed time to try another spot. Before another hour had passed, we tried that spot and two others, and had exactly one perch to show for it; a very small perch that was already dead, since Abner had found it floating on the water.

"Must be farther out in deeper waters." Abner deduced. "This is a big lake, ya know!" Yes, we knew.

***

Abner maintained that was indeed the problem, and insisted he had wasted enough of our time, then told us to follow him to a marina some distance away. There was a decent bait and tackle shop there, so I figured at least that would be worth checking out. We followed Abner up the dock and into the shop, where he intended to buy some baitfish - well, almost. His intention was to pick them out, and have Don and me buy the baitfish.

There were several locals inside, along with a guy who appeared to be the owner. Abner said hello to everyone, but only one of them acknowledged Abner, and all he did was grunt a reply, making brief eye contact – really brief. Since we were obviously with Abner, we were on the receiving end of a few looks ourselves, ones that swayed between pity and what may have been distain, if not outright disgust. Finally, when Abner was out of earshot, the guy who I thought owned the place looked at me.

"You stayin' at his place?" He asked.

"Yeah. He's our guide, too. It's an all-inclusive package." The owner inhaled and rolled his eyes before commenting.

"Says all you need to know about your guide when he has to give it away to find work. Well, good luck," he added, an odd look in his eyes that appeared to be a cross between sadness and contempt when he saw Abner lumbering to the counter with a handful of candy bars and a family size bag of Fritos.

***

We were on our way back when Abner cut his engine and stopped at the first spot he had taken us to that day. He just couldn't accept the fact that he hadn't caught any perch from there, telling us that had *never* happened to him before, no way no how, and could he please have another beer because the Fritos (which were gone) had made him thirsty. He jigged some more while he shook his head, perplexed or pretending to be for our benefit. Finally, when he noticed he really was wasting our time, he packed up to go - except his boat wouldn't start. Ten minutes turned into twenty; then half an hour went by.

"Don't suppose you fellas got a long rope," he inquired. Thankfully, Don did. It was slow going though, especially since we had over three miles to cover. Every now and then Abner would wave and go "yoo hoo!" which meant he wanted another beer. Apparently, the candy bars had made him thirsty as well.

Whether he could guide or not was questionable at best, but he was quite adept at catching the beers Don tossed him from one boat to the other. Don and I had put a twelver on ice, figuring it would easily last into the evening if not all night. Well, we had been out there close to three hours, and Don and I had consumed two beers each. After Don's last throw, there weren't any left.

***

We expected Larry to come rolling in the next day before noon, but when Don and I made it back after our first morning on the water around 12:30 he hadn't arrived yet. Speaking of not arriving, Abner never made it out that morning to guide us either, not that Don and I had made a great effort to look him up. Actually, we hadn't made any effort at all. Not only that, but we were about as quiet as Death when we prepared to depart, until we finally did. Don goosed his 35 hp as soon as I pushed us away from the dock, with neither of us looking back in the general direction until we were so far away we could barely see our cabin.

Later on, we were throwing together a few ham sandwiches for lunch when we heard the door open. Since no one had knocked, we assumed it was our brother.

"Hey, bro, that you?" I called out.

"Golly no, just me!" Abner called back as he barged right in. "You boys do any good so far?"

"Not yet." I replied.

"Sorry I didn't make it this morning, fellas, at least as early as you. By the time I got to the dock you were gone," Abner said, as if it may or may not have been our fault.

"Well," Don pointed out, "we didn't take off until 8:30 or so. What time do you usually get started, Abner?"

"Golly, not that early! You fellas sure got the fever! By the way," Abner added as he lowered his voice to create the full effect of the condescending comment he was about to lay on us, "it's a waste of time to fish for muskies that early in the morning, at least around here. You fellas gonna eat all those sandwiches yourself?"

I told our distinguished host that was indeed the plan then asked whether or not he would be able to guide us that afternoon. I only asked on the outside chance he had some knowledge about certain weed beds or other structure we could take advantage of later, but when I got a load of the withering glare my big brother had directed towards me I wished I had kept my mouth shut. Although not his intention, Abner saved the day.

"Golly, sure wish I could take you fellas out," he said as he opened the refrigerator looking for a beer, "but my boat's still on the fritz. Maybe we could go walleye fishing from my pontoon this evening though. I'll have to get back to you on that." Then he was gone as fast as he had appeared, but not before he gave one last, longing look at the sandwiches we had made.

"So why can't we catch muskies from a pontoon?" I felt compelled, for some unfathomable reason, to ask Don.

"Because they're with Abner's perch." Don observed, getting no argument from me.

**

That first morning had been a learning experience for us, although we weren't certain how much of it was worthwhile. At over 3,500 surface acres, Fence is a large lake, and without any type of depth or fish finder equipment on Don's boat, we were reduced to casting towards obvious areas like surface weed beds and other visible structure. The water was fairly clear, but too deep in many places to make locating underwater bars or deeply submerged weeds possible, at least most of the time. We threw mostly bucktails but didn't manage to catch anything or even get a follow.

It was frustrating to look out over that great big, beautiful lake knowing there were muskies allegedly over fifty pounds swimming around, and us not having any idea which specific areas were best suited to raise such fish, or fish even half that size. I had understood we would have a guide, that it was part of a package deal. Unfortunately, it appeared that if Abner went out with us we wouldn't be any better off than if he stayed home, unless supplying him with a continuous flow of beer was our intention.

Still, we were on an awesome lake, casting away on a beautiful day in the heart of Vilas County. Who knew, really knew, when and where a monster musky would strike? Even the best guides in Wisconsin don't offer money back guarantees for something like that, we reminded ourselves. It wasn't like we were floating somewhere in the middle of the lake just casting for the fun of it. We knew enough to look for likely spots and what they looked like, and there was the tried and true tactic of taking note of certain areas other boats visited on a frequent basis, assuming the folks in those boats were casting and not just sitting there jigging or staring at a bobber. So who knew? We weren't going to catch anything whining about not having a decent guide or quality electronic gear, but we might catch something if we kept casting. And casting. And casting.

***

Before we headed out after lunch Don happened to notice Abner cleaning out a retired school bus he obviously owned. I had noticed it earlier, mainly because it reminded me of something from the 1960's that a bunch of flower children with bloodshot eyes had assaulted with paint brushes while saying "far out, man" to each other way too often. Not that I had anything against red-eyed flower children, it was just in hindsight I couldn't see Abner fitting in with them, not even a little. He cleared the mystery up for us though, right after I asked him what was up with the bus.

"Oh, I use it a lot in the summer. We get families with *lots* of cute kids packed in here pretty good, especially in July and August. The kids love it when I put on my clown suit and make-up and take them for rides in Mr. Wheelie Wheels. Why, even some of the parents like to come along! Everyone has their favorite songs, and *lots* of snacks. Time to put Mr. Wheelie Wheels up for the season I'm afraid. Well, good luck this afternoon, fellas! Maybe we can go out later for those walleyes!"

We just stood there in silence as we watched Abner lumber back to his bus, his second tenor voice in rare form as it echoed through the far reaches of the towering pines: "Bi ya kum ba, Kumba*yaa!*"

"Jesus Mary and Joseph." Don muttered under his breath as we made our way towards the dock. "Next year *I'm* choosing the place."

***

We stayed out for another four hours, and although we remained optimistic it wasn't because of all the muskies that had followed and then struck our lures. Regardless, why shouldn't we feel optimistic? We still had three whole days to go. Between marking visual spots and noting the spots other fishermen had worked, and the lake map we kept referring to with depths listed, we had to believe it was going to happen.

We even went to the marina where Abner (who by then we had dubbed Bo Bo the Clown) had taken us and inquired about the availability of a good guide. The guy who spoke to me before said he sure felt sorry for us all right, but as far as he knew, all the reliable guides were booked.

"I can give you a list of good guides for future reference," he said, "but on this short a notice there's nobody I'd feel comfortable recommending, at least not for the money they'd charge."

We thanked him for being up front with us. Just before we left he pointed out several spots on our map that he said were worth a try, and we thanked him again. Don got a laugh out of the guy when he asked him if he wouldn't mind closing up the marina so we could hire him to guide us, except it turned out he wasn't the owner after all.

"Well, as tempting as that sounds, boys, I kind'a like this job!" He said, making it sound like he really would get fired and probably deserved to be as well. He was a good guy.

***

When we made it back to the cabin Larry still hadn't arrived. We weren't worried though; he was always late. We hadn't seen much of him over the past years and were looking forward to catching up, joking around, and basically acting the way brothers do when they're on their own. Realizing he might show up any minute or maybe hours later, Don and I decided to head over to Woodruff for supper. We had spotted this really cool look-ing Northwoods steakhouse on our way in and thought we'd give it a try. We had developed strict criteria when it came to Northwoods steakhouses, and fortunately there are restaurant proprietors throughout northern Wisconsin who know exactly what attracts folks to their establishments.

We could usually tell just by driving past a place whether or not it had potential. It would be, but not limited to, a one-story structure made from logs or something that in some way paid tribute to its Northwoods environment. A quality sign out front was a good omen, although not necessary as long as it wasn't really cheap looking, such as a beat up, faded yellow or white plastic sign that had been donated by a beer company or some-thing before the outbreak of World War Two. Still, curb appeal can be deceiving.

The real test came upon entering the place. The food, of course, was the most important thing, but most places that serve outstanding food also take pride in their décor as well. There's a special aroma in places that serve great food; a mixture of smells that make you want to devour the air itself. Even a roadside hamburger joint usually smells good, but the best Northwoods steakhouses and their equivalent usually have an aroma that is especially enticing.

We preferred a place that wasn't too bright inside and had dark wood and leather booths, or their equivalent. A well stocked, good-sized bar with an honest pour was a plus, if for no other reason it gave you a comfortable place to wait for a table or booth, which you would probably have to do if the place was a great joint to begin with. I hate having to stand or sit in some crowded waiting area with nothing better to do but avoid eye contact with strangers. Owners and employees who treat you the way they would want to be treated is very important, as is responding in kind.

Ultimately, it has to have great food or most of the other stuff becomes meaningless. It doesn't have to be inexpensive as long as it's priced fair. If they're going to serve an awesome 24 oz. T-bone steak or an honest 16 oz. filet, I would expect to pay plenty for it, but it better be good. We also appreciated a decent variety on the menu, especially when it came to steaks, seafood and fowl. A good wine list didn't mean it had to be a long wine list, and the proprietors who understand that have increased in number over the years.

The place we spotted was called the Norwood Pines Supper Club and turned out to be a great place. On our way back to the cabin we agreed it had become our official steakhouse for that area, even if it sure wasn't the cheapest place around. It gave us what we paid for though, and that's part of what a successful vacation is all about.

To top things off that evening, Larry's car was parked outside our cabin when we pulled in. Although he was almost always late and we weren't overly worried he had been in a wreck or anything, it was still a mild relief to see his car. It was great to see him again, and the three of us talked and joked around well into the night.

***

Come morning it was time to do some serious musky hunting and it looked as if the weather planned on cooperating. They had been calling for a major storm front to come through later that afternoon. Judging from the increasing wind and thick, undulating cloud cover, it appeared as if it was coming sooner - fine by us.

Conventional thought on the subject, whether in magazine articles or word of mouth, insisted we were situated in the middle of the best weather scenario possible. We envisaged the lake being stirred like a hearty stew, churning everything up for all the hungry muskies that would instead come after our lures. Don and I had extra tackle for Larry, including Don's Millionaire reel from last year. God help us.

It sure wasn't Diawa's fault because they had been considerate enough to include maintenance instructions, but since none of us had a doctorate in engineering (or the proper tools) the annoying *screech* on every cast had become worse; funny how we could forget something for nearly an entire year that had been such an annoyance. Like I said though, it wasn't Diawa's fault:

Advanced engineering degree or not, all Don needed to do was follow their simple instructions: Using a Diawa needle-nosed oiler that wasn't supplied with the reel Don had purchased, he just needed to dismantle the entire reel and lightly oil the line guide worm-track, the ends of the spool shaft, the moving parts inside the set-plate assembly, the handle knob shafts, the bushings (ah yes, the bushings) and the all-important cog wheel gears. Of course, all that effort could possibly be for naught if he failed to rub all the leather drag washers with Teflon grease on a regular basis (*leather* washers? No wonder the Japanese lost the war) not to mention using Diawa's "superior" *Space Age Grease* on all the gears inside the reel body and the anti-reverse claw. Oh yeah, on the ratchet assembly directly under the master gear as well. Right. At least they offered a good warranty, bless their hearts.

The potentially scary part was, I had one of those reels myself, although I had left it at home. When I saw them in K-Mart for $39.95 (the sporting goods manager even threw in a Mepp's Musky Killer for half price if I promised not to bring the reel back) I couldn't resist. Mine didn't make that awful sound though, probably because I never used it. I had evolved from owning backups for my first line equipment to having backups for my backups, and then some, depending on what specific article of tackle I needed to justify buying.

***

The important thing was that we were on the water, casting away. Fence Lake was considered prime musky waters, the weather was supposedly perfect or almost so, and the three McCabe brothers were going after those razor-toothed brutes with one thing in mind; fulfilling the Quest. Except for Larry. He had been a vegetarian for almost ten years. He didn't screw around with it either, like people who *say* they're vegetarians, as long as it's okay if they eat fish, eggs, or anything else they don't feel like giving up. Not Larry though. When he gave something up, it was as if it had never been on planet Earth to begin with, and I'm not kidding.

I could go into detailed explanations about all the stuff he wouldn't touch, including a wide variety of things containing certain enzymes, but it's enough to know his heart wasn't into casting for muskies or any other aquatic creature that could possibly end up with a hook in its mouth. It could be argued he had nothing to worry about being in our boat, even if Don and I had invested a not-so-small fortune in our tackle.

The fishing equipment industry maintained or at least implied, or so we insisted, it was normal not to catch trophy muskies *if* you hadn't bought enough tackle and other related items, because, obviously, the musky fanatics who are prepared for all possible contingencies increase their odds. We almost stopped believing that, but not quite and never for long.

Shopping for and especially buying fishing stuff was too much fun. Besides, what if you were in the right place at the right time and threw the wrong colored bucktail or something? Nope, better to have all your bases covered, and the entire color spectrum in the known Universe in your tackle box (okay, boxes) even if some blasphemers maintain fish can't see as many colors as humans, much less distinguish one color from another. As with so many things we humans need to believe, it is, at the very least, annoying to be confused and especially thwarted by the scientific facts. Don and I refused to abandon our unwavering faith regardless of the alleged facts, despite what Grampa's favorite author, Mark Twain, had to say on the subject: *Faith is believing what you know ain't so.*

Even if we would occasionally allow our faith to waver as it pertained to buying more tackle (at least when we were broke) we refused to do so as far as Grampa's advice was concerned: *...when it happens though, when you finally hook into one, you'll be a cut above the bobber and worm crowd. They'll never know the thrill of thrills because they gave up*...how that particular phrase justified buying more lures and tackle may have been open to debate, but not for us; *faith is believing what you know ain't so* – we could fit round pegs of delusion into square holes of facts with the best of them, and marvel at the perfect fit.

We pounded away all day, going from one spot to another, never really sure if we were onto a potentially good area or not. We figured we were close because of the map, but whether or not we were casting to the exact spots we needed to be nailing, or at the right depth, was mere guesswork.

As the day wore on and the rain moved in without so much as a follow to show for our efforts, an all too familiar, grim frustration set in. Where were they? How can we throw so many casts, using the correct (?) tackle with such an array of lures, and not even *see* a musky? We didn't know; not even close.

After the rain really started coming down around five that afternoon, we decided to bag it. A warm cabin, dry clothes and a trip to the Norwood Pines Supper Club for a few drinks and their thick steaks sounded perfect about then. Perfect, and what for decades would be recalled whenever we felt like laughing as if we were kids again; the kind of hysterics that included tears, snorting, and all.

***

Larry ordered the biggest salad they offered, plus whatever else he could find on the menu that hadn't needed to replenish its blood with oxygen. After I finally convinced Don that a great steak dinner deserved a great bottle of wine, he finally relented, even though the French Bordeaux I had found on the wine list cost almost as much as our meals - combined.

I had begun to collect wine as a hobby, mainly because I had developed a taste for the stuff and also because you would be hard pressed in 1983 to find a wider selection of quality import and California wines, at a better price anyway, than in Iowa. Yes, Iowa. All liquor sales back then were made from state owned stores, and the ones in the larger towns and cities had great selections. There was a state sanctioned and funded "wine advisory board" that traveled all over the world to sample and buy really good wines. With the buying power of the State of Iowa behind them and since they were able to purchase in such large quantities, there were some great deals to be had, especially French and Italian wines, although really good California selections were in abundance as well.

The best wines in a quality restaurant were always expensive, but since we were on vacation Don gave in. Larry didn't drink, so I didn't have to persuade him to fork over any dough. After devouring his steak and washing it down with a few glasses of quality Bordeaux, I never had to talk Don into ordering wine again. If anything, a second bottle would usually appear.

***

The food that evening wasn't what created the problem for Don. Later on, we agreed it must have been the food we had stocked up on at a local grocery to cover breakfast, lunch, and hunger attacks while playing poker well into the night. That, and the musky hunter's nightly allotment of beer Don had been consuming. It was all that gut churning, worthless crap that caused the problem, the kind that tastes great and is really bad for you; all the stuff difficult to resist while on a musky hunt with your brothers. Fishing trips, like most vacations, demand that you overload on all the garbage you didn't consume all that much during the rest of the year, at least guilt free. There can be a price to pay, and believe me, you can thank your own definition of divine grace you weren't sitting at the same table with the two couples a little downwind from us that evening.

Remember the older guy at that swanky, private resort I told you about who looked like he modeled for exclusive outdoor clothing catalogs? You know, the guy who wouldn't even talk to us the year before because Don's pickup truck and boat weren't, at the very least, socially acceptable? Actually, he may have had a point there. Well, guess who was sitting not six feet away from us, at a table with three other people who looked just as impressed with themselves as he. I like to think I usually maintain a "live and let live" philosophy, but those four folks sure put my beliefs to the test that evening.

We were three brothers in our thirties who didn't see each other very often; three brothers who got along well. We were reminiscing, laughing and having a great time. We weren't all that loud or using foul language, and we weren't drunk, although Don and I had enough wine in us to suggest otherwise, and to ensure that Larry would be driving that night. They kept shooting us these looks as if we were a minor annoyance - at first. Don had his back to the foursome, so he couldn't see them, but Larry and I could. They took a great deal of pride in their appearance which was fine, even if all the multiple carat rocks the ladies had dangling from their fingers, wrists and necks may have been a little over the top. They were all pushing seventy, but looked great when they weren't frowning so it was hard to tell.

I began to eavesdrop, and it occurred to me the main thing they were really upset about was that we were genuinely having a good time; that we were *happy*. In a way, they appeared disappointed our behavior wasn't *more* rowdy, so they would really have had something to complain about. It was a safe bet they had arrived in a fully loaded, late model BMW or its equivalent, and it was sparkling clean; and when the guy at the carwash finished wiping it down the owner probably tipped him a whole quarter.

"Aren't there backwoods bars they would prefer?" I heard one of the women say, trying to be humorous, fooling no one. It was obvious she wanted to be heard by more folks than her dining partners.

"They'll probably hightail it when they see the prices, or get the check." The guy across from her replied, causing the other three to giggle in a reserved manner, followed by collective sighs.

Don hadn't done it on purpose, honest. He had been too busy having fun to have even heard those people and besides, he was deaf in one ear. If anything, it was his uncontrollable laughter because of Larry's reaction to the salad he had been served that caused the eruption to escape from Don with such alarming authority. It was similar to when we were kids in church with Mom and Dad. We would lose control over something ridiculous because it was the worst possible time to do so, especially if Mom was at the ready with her rapier-sharp elbows. We tried desperately to contain our outbursts at such times, biting our lips, tongue, drawing blood even, *anything* to stop the madness.

The Norwood Pines Supper Club wasn't noticeably drafty, but apparently, anything airborne wafted in a northeasterly direction, at least if you were sitting near our table. That spelled double doom for the two couples we had annoyed, since their food had arrived at the same time as Don's initial assault. I could clearly see their reactions, a convoluted mixture of disgust, horror, and what was approaching sheer panic, despite their attempt to maintain their composure - especially the women, bless their hearts. The one who had made the "backwoods bars" comment looked as if her plate of steaming linguini possessed all the culinary allure of steamed rat tails.

The stench even staggered the waitress, causing a small portion of buttered, diced carrots to end up on the lap of the elderly gentleman next to her. It was obvious she blamed him for the noxious odor, because instead of apologizing, she hurried back to the plates of food still upon the serving stand and in so doing, temporarily at least, managed to stay out of harm's way. That's the way it seemed anyway, since she didn't appear to be in any hurry to go back to those folks, that's for sure, and when she did she took a deep breath first.

For his part, Don was still in the throes of uninhibited hysterics. It had started when our waitress had served Larry his large salad.

"Bacon Bits? *Bacon Bits!?*" Larry exclaimed, very put out. "I can't eat this! I specifically requested no animal products!" He was very put out all right – boy, was he touchy about stuff like that, no kidding. The waitress looked at him as if he were nuts.

"It's just a little bacon," she said, somewhat defensively. That tore it.

"Just a little bacon? Don't you mean just a little slaughtered *pig?*" Larry was generally mild mannered, but not when it came to that issue.

"What*ever*." The waitress replied as she grabbed the offending salad. "I'll have them brush the Bacon – oops - I mean slaughtered *pig* off immediately, *sir.*" Then she was gone, just like that. Larry started in about animal residue on the lettuce, but she just kept going.

Don was beside himself. He always cracked up when Larry lost his cool over something like that. He continued to laugh so hard that salvo number two erupted with a Vesuvian fury unrivaled in the annals of northern Wisconsin and points beyond. Those poor people. Those poor, poor people. They were snobs of the first order, people who were disgusted by those beneath them and envious of those above, but Holy Mother of *God* they didn't deserve the fate my big brother had visited upon them - again.

I thought for sure the "backwoods bars" lady, as she gasped frantically for air, was going to career right out of her chair. She even had a cloth napkin plastered to her face. You should have seen her husband. He had been instantly transformed from a handsome, white-haired gentleman with fashionable clothes and designer glasses to a man blubbering for life as he had once known it.

To his credit, the other guy at their table maintained a stoic demeanor reminiscent of the captain on the Titanic towards the end of the movie *A Night To Remember*. You know, just before the windows on the bridge imploded, and about a billion gallons of the North Atlantic rushed in on the poor bastard.

The rest of them didn't demonstrate anywhere near as much class. By then they had also covered their faces with their cloth napkins, muttering all sorts of unintelligible things. Right about then Don unleashed salvo number three. They may have been unparalleled snobs, but they weren't stupid. When they heard a rumbling that resembled distant thunder coming from our table, it was as if they had been launched from the starting gate at Hialeah. They took their parting shots though.

"No shame, absolutely no shame!" One lady said.

"Elegant dining *indeed!*" The other lady said as she passed by, shooting us an especially endearing glare.

"You should see a specialist." One of the gentleman mumbled as he made a hasty retreat.

The captain of the Titanic maintained his stoic demeanor as he marched bravely away, head held high, without so much as a word. He dressed, acted and quite possibly lived his entire life as a snob, but during a crisis he was definitely the type of officer I would want next to me during a battle at sea. I wish you could have seen him as he walked away - *Oh Britannia, Britannia rules the waves!*

My brothers had made me lose all sense of propriety in the past, but with the possible exception of a particular midnight candle service one Christmas Eve as a child, nothing topped that evening. It was the look on Don's face as much as anything. He hadn't realized until salvo number two had found its target what was actually happening, and even then he couldn't bring himself to turn around and face his victims. So, he looked directly at me. He could easily tell from my reaction what was going down. His look was a cross between a bemused, curious grin and a plea for me to cover his back in case one of the walking wounded descended upon him with a steak knife or something.

Larry had definitely forgotten about the Bacon Bits. Tears and hysterics, hysterics and tears were the order of the evening. The instant we regained our composure, one of us would let out a quick snort and it would start all over again. My diaphragm and Adam's apple ached from the stress. We were kids again, and displayed the same level of maturity, or lack thereof. I'm not so sure that wasn't the best part. Actually, I'm sure it was.

At first I wondered if maybe we would get asked to leave, especially after I spotted our former dining companions conversing with perhaps the owner. They were talking with their hands as much as their mouths and pointing our way, but it wasn't likely they were ordering us after dinner drinks. No one asked us to leave though. As it turned out, no one else had apparently been offended by our laughter or broadsided by Don's salvos. Besides, ours wasn't the only table where folks were having a good time.

Even our waitress warmed up to us. The salad Larry ended up with was excellent, and he told her so. He thanked her, too. Don got her laughing with his typical banter, and later on she told us the two couples we had offended were always complaining about something or another, and she took extra pains to inform us they were terrible tippers. We left out the part about *why* they had bolted in such a hurry, hoping she still held one of them responsible. Regardless, we left her a large, well earned tip.

***

We were in a really good mood all the way back to our cabin, and well into the night. The only genuine downer actually had the opposite effect on my brothers. It happened during our nightly poker game, right in the middle of a rousing hand of in-between. There was over twenty bucks in the pot, which was huge considering we only played nickel-dime with an occasional quarter bet.

In case you're unfamiliar with in-between, you get two cards face up and bet on whether the third card from the deck will be in-between the first two. If it is you win whatever you bet, like a quarter, a buck, or if you really feel lucky, the whole pot; the downside is if you lose you have to ante up whatever you bet. I was dealt an ace, which I called low (you can call high or low on an ace before you see the second card) and then I was dealt another ace that was automatically high. Wow, I thought, I can't miss! Only another ace can beat me and along with the previous hand a total of three had already been dealt!

"Pot!" I yelled, my greedy eyeballs having turned into dollar signs. You guessed it. I always lost at in-between, but up until then never that bad. Worse yet, most of the money in the pot was mine.

The dumbfounded look of utter shock on my face when that fourth ace showed up struck Don as being so hilarious he literally fell off his chair. Larry lost it too. I was in shock as I sat there slack-jawed, my eyes half crossed, unable to blink even. Don insisted he wasn't laughing because I'd lost well over twenty bucks and potentially twice that much, but because of the look on my face when it happened. It didn't hurt his mood any or help mine when a few minutes later he calmly said "pot" while staring at a queen/six and won. I told you he was lucky.

Maybe I had used up all of my bad luck in one fell swoop I rationalized, and the next day I would be the one who finally landed a trophy musky. One thing was certain. I sure couldn't wait for tomorrow to arrive. Screw in-between. I still hate that game, and not surprisingly, I still lose at it.

***

The wind was howling, driving the rain sideways when we awoke the next morning. If it had been just a storm we would have gone out anyway, but with some gusts at nearly fifty mph the thought of being in Don's flat bottom boat didn't appeal to us at all. The white-capped waves were huge and moving fast. It was so bad that if someone had their boat improperly tied to the wrong side of a dock it was already underwater.

It was very frustrating. Like too many times before, we had only three or four days a year on prime musky waters, and to lose a whole morning and perhaps the entire day was catastrophic from a musky hunting perspective. It was really getting on my nerves, too. Talk about cabin fever; I couldn't stop pacing to save my life, constantly glaring out the windows as if that alone would calm the storm.

On top of that, every now and then Don would burst out in laughter. I knew what he was laughing about. He kept telling the story over and over again, describing the less than intelligent expression on my dumbfounded face when that fourth ace had shown up. I real knee slapper. I had gone from barely tolerating the episode to cringing every time it came up. Worse yet, no one could ignore or forget Don's infamous laugh once they heard it, especially if it was directed at them, and *especially* if you were his kid brother.

Don was sitting on the toilet, on the *toilet*, when he started howling yet again with wave after wave of spontaneous hysterics. It was impossible to miss, even with the bathroom door closed, the radio turned up and me pacing in the other room. The rain and wind were pounding away, Don was cracking up big time, and I was going slowly out of my mind. That's when this *noise* started outside. Howling storm or no howling storm, everyone within a mile or so must have been able to hear it.

In Don's defense, the boat horn had been added before he bought his flat bottom. I had never been a big fan of replacing a car horn with some goofy tune, or a boat horn for that matter, especially one as loud as Don's. I swear, that thing was blasting out *La Marseillaise* at about a gazillion decibels. I had always liked the French national anthem, especially in the movie *Casablanca,* but when it kept blaring over and over again, as if some deranged sadist had got his hands on a kazoo and a rock-star-grade amplifier, all that changed forever.

We had tied Don's boat away from the dock onto a mooring post to keep it from getting battered as well as keeping it from sinking. Even so, the wind, driving rain and large waves were giving it quite a pounding, enough to have somehow caused that high pitched, God awful horn to begin blaring away *Dee Dee Deet Deet Dee Dee, Dee Da Deet!* Over and over again, with nothing to stop the insanity until the battery died which wasn't going to happen anytime soon.

I tried to ignore it, but that became impossible. It was even getting on Larry's nerves, and he was usually pretty calm about everything except Bacon Bits. There's loud, and then there is *loud.* It wouldn't have surprised me one bit to hear the roar of someone's full choke 12 gauge blasting away, several of them even, until Don's boat was on the bottom, and I wasn't so sure I wouldn't have supplied the shells. There was indeed a strong storm blowing outside, all the doors and windows were of course closed and we had the radio on as well, but all you seemed to be able to hear was *Dee Dee Deet Deet Dee Dee, Dee Da Deet!* blaring away nonstop as if an electrified banshee from the Nether Regions was wailing from within the bowels of Don's boat.

"Just what the hell's *wrong* with that thing, Don?" I hollered as I stood in front of the bathroom door, pounding on it for all I was worth. "How do you turn it *off?!*"

"Don't know," he yelled back. "Never happened before. Sure is loud! Maybe you ought'a go see if you can figure something out. I'm gonna be busy for a while."

Perfect. Take the motor-less, rain-filled rowboat that came with the cabin and somehow fight my way through the howling wind and heaving waves, then figure out a way to get in Don's boat without losing the rowboat – or perhaps falling in and being swept halfway to the state line. Even if I was successful in tying the two boats together, I knew nothing about the electronic workings of the horn or anything else electronic for that matter. However, there was no way I could stand listening to that blasphemous rendition of *La Marseillaise* anymore. If any French citizens had been anywhere near that boat, they probably *would* have opened fire.

By the time I had rowed halfway to Don's boat my poncho had blown across my face and I was soaked, but still determined. I somehow lashed the boats together and stumbled into Don's heaving flat bottom and staggered my way to the front. Sure enough, no amount of switch clicking or button pushing had any effect at all. Worse yet, that lousy horn kept blasting away maybe a foot from my left ear. I swear, the horn of a diesel locomotive couldn't have been as loud.

Out of sheer desperation with absolutely no regard for the consequences of my actions, I reached under the dashboard, grabbed several multicolored wires that may or may not have been attached to something significant, and ripped them out. The insane, bleating horn fell silent immediately. I just stood there for a moment spitting broken raindrops, my chest heaving as the sideways rain stung every inch of exposed skin. I felt the wild-eyed exhilaration of a triumphant lunatic as I stood there shaking my fist at the suddenly silent horn.

"Take *that* you son of a bitch! Take th -" it finally dawned on me the entire electrical system had, in all probability, just been destroyed - my big brother *Don's* entire electrical system. And Dad was all the way down in Arkansas. Not good. Not good at all.

"So, how'd you get it to stop?" Don asked when I made my way back to the cabin.

"Oh, just flipped a few switches. Not much to it, really." That would have to be my story until I came up with a better one, which wasn't likely.

If the weather remained hopelessly inclement I might have been able to delay the inevitable, at least until things settled down, with me back in Iowa and Don in Illinois. I figured it would be better to send him a nice letter from a safe distance, asking him to send me the bill for repairs. Naturally, of course, the traitorous storm abated and we were in Don's boat in less than an hour. Miracles of miracles, he turned the key and it started right up. The horn didn't work though, and never did again.

When Don wasn't around I explained everything to Larry, figuring confession was good for the soul. Regardless, he concluded I had ruined any chance of landing a musky, at least on that trip. Grampa had no doubt intervened, and been forced to use up all my good karma on Don's boat in order to save me from drowning or worse, the same good karma that no doubt had been originally slated for a musky of mythic proportions. I had learned a long time ago not to automatically dismiss Larry's prognostications out of hand, but that wasn't a reason to stop casting. I didn't stop, and neither did Don; all the rest of the day and into the evening. Judging from all the muskies we caught or even saw that day, it appeared that mine wasn't the only good karma used up that day.

***

Our last day was upon us. We waited all year for our fishing vacations to arrive; reading, planning and plotting how to catch a musky, and just like that we had only one more shot at it for at least another twelve months or so. Larry had to head out that morning, which also put a damper on things. Over the years, the three of us had learned precisely which buttons to push, whether we were looking to infuriate each other or generate laughter. When we were kids it was a toss-up; dependant upon mood swings and levels of adolescent boredom.

However, as three brothers in our thirties on a musky expedition in the Northwoods, it was non-stop joking around - the more irreverent the better, since that made it more likely to create the desired effect; laughing our stupid asses off. It didn't have to be hopelessly juvenile bathroom humor or its intellectual equivalent, but that sure didn't hurt, either.

That mindset was best avoided if you were trying to impress an important client, or allay the skepticism of an elderly relative who suspected you were still an immature buffoon. Even so, none of that was of any importance, not when the three of us were together on a fishing trip where hardly anyone knew our names. If an M-80 with a delayed fuse going off in the pit of an outhouse with a rotund camp director squatting directly above it was funny when we were kids, it was still funny recalling the episode twenty years later.

Don and I would no doubt have a good time that final day, but Larry would be missed. He was the creative one of the family, whether it was playing musical instruments, drawing or painting, carving Halloween pumpkins for his nieces and nephews or imitating everything from people to ducks. Once, after an especially bumbling attempt on my part to throw an accurate cast that created a backlash followed by snagging a rock, a duck was heard in the distance, as if on cue. Larry mimicked the duck perfectly, as if it were mocking my obvious ineptitude with derisive duck laughter. "Quack, quack quack quack quack!" That may not strike you as particularly humorous, but with Larry's Mel Blanc caliber delivery it took on a life of its own. To this day, I can't get it out of my head whenever I hear a duck. The next time you're on the water casting away, frustrated because the muskies or whatever you're chasing aren't playing fair, listen for a duck. Just listen, and imagine that duck is on to you - maybe it is.

***

Don and I had a warm, sunny day on our hands with large, lazy clouds overhead. There was a pretty good breeze and a decent chop on the water, too. We were going over many of the same areas we had been attacking since the first day, but after a while we decided to do some exploring.

We came upon this channel that led into a somewhat manicured area, like a state park really, with towering pines and an old wooden, ornate walking bridge arched over the channel. It appeared to be there for esthetic purposes more than any practical reason. The grounds, privately owned no doubt, were very impressive as well. We slowly entered the increasingly idyllic setting, gliding just above idle. That's when we spotted an old, stately mansion across a large expanse of lawn. It sure hadn't been built by folks short on cash, that's for sure. We pulled right up to the shore for a better look. A man appeared some distance away, up by the mansion itself. He had his eye on us in a way, along with his body language, that said "May I help you now that you have trespassed all the way to my private shore?" so we just waved and headed back out. He waved back, seemly unconcerned but no doubt aware of our every move.

When we returned to the cabin for lunch Abner told us the man was caretaker for the estate, a guy who lived there year-round for the owners who never showed up anymore. He said the Mars family had built it decades ago, the same folks who sold all those candy bars, but their descendants had no interest in what Fence Lake or the area in general had to offer. Abner said they had so much money it didn't matter the place just sat there, or that a full-time caretaker was being paid to maintain and live on the grounds. The taxes were no doubt high but the place was also increasing in value, as do many lake front properties in Wisconsin and elsewhere.

Abner kept talking dollars, but all I kept thinking about was that guy's *job*. How did he fall into that sweet setup? The way Abner explained it, the fellow's number one priority was to just hang around that awesome place and make sure no one messed with it. That, and to make sure everything was maintained properly.

The property looked to be several acres but it could have been larger. The inside of the main house must have really been something too. It was the kind of place most folks wouldn't be able to touch in a million years unless they won a lottery or something - a *big* lottery. That guy basically got to call the place home. It wasn't like even once a year he had to make himself scarce when the owners showed up either, because according to Abner no one could remember the last time any of them had even been there, let alone stayed. There was always the possibility they could sell the place and the caretaker would be out of "work", but talk about a resume' with references to match – wow.

I wasn't thinking I wanted to raise my kids under those circumstances, but after kids leave home there's usually a lot of years left to go. You would be on a prime musky lake in one of the best resort areas in the Northwoods with plenty of time on your hands, living in a mansion and getting *paid* for it. Maybe that doesn't appeal to a lot folks, but if the Hershey family has a place on the water and they're looking for someone to stay there, give me a call, as long as it's a musky lake. Give me a call anyway. Speaking of muskies…

***

It was down to it after lunch. We had about another five or six hours left on the water to hook into something, or it was "wait 'til next year" again. We didn't look at it that way though, or tried not to anyway. We told ourselves we had already thrown so many casts that, if nothing else, the law of averages would mandate a strike.

It was a beautiful day to be out there, even if it wasn't wet and cloudy. Besides, we had heard plenty of muskies had been caught on sunny days. It sure made for a pleasant afternoon as we kept pounding away, one cast after another.

I had switched to a Mepps Giant Killer black bucktail with a silver blade, and decided to stick with it for the rest of the day. There were more and more colors being made available, and I sure wasn't shy about buying them either, but I had heard nothing had ever out-produced black and silver. Maybe that was because it was thrown more than all the others, but I wasn't about to debate the equivalent of the chicken or egg argument with only six hours to go.

Don had been working a large Rapala that looked really good in the water, so with the obvious variation in lure presentations we were hopeful something would happen. We hit several submerged weed beds, pounded a few points and some shorelines then headed south of Smelt Bay. We beat that area up for a while then decided to take a slow trip across the lake as the late afternoon gave way to dusk. Before long we found ourselves casting around Strawberry Point. We decided to pound that entire area really hard before calling it a day – and sadly, a trip. We hadn't been there ten minutes when I thought I spotted a flash in the water just as Don was finishing a retrieve with his Rapala. The lure had been pretty far down, so I couldn't be sure just what I had seen even if Fence is a fairly clear lake.

"You see that?" I asked.

"What?"

"That flash. Something was after your Rapala or at least checking it out."

"Damn. I was watching your bucktail." Don said as he let fly to the same spot as before. I waited until he was about a third of the way in and let fly in that general direction myself. We were both watching the water like hawks, especially right behind our lures.

It always took a while to spot Don's Rapala because it ran much deeper than my bucktail. It wasn't until he was near the end of his retrieve before the lure showed itself, with no fish in sight. Don was doing figure eights about the time I had another twenty feet to go on my retrieve. We were watching Don's lure by the side of the boat, then looked out at my incoming bucktail that was a foot or so beneath the clear water.

It started out as an indistinct movement coming from the left, like a self-propelled log. It only appeared that way for a moment, however, because it was traveling so fast. In nothing flat it went from something that resembled a log to exactly what it really was - an exceptionally huge musky that was careening directly towards my bucktail!

"Look at that! Look at that!" We both called out in unison, or something like it.

"Nail it! Come on, nail it!" I yelled at the fish.

Whoosh! Just like that, the monster was gone. It had homed in on my bucktail, probably after it had again inspected Don's Rapala during its retrieve, but for whatever reason it had not struck either lure. It had flown by like a shot, and we didn't know why.

"What happened to it?" Don asked as he threw his lure in the direction it had been heading.

"I don't know, it was shooting for my lure then it just took off. I slowed my retrieve to give it a clean shot," I said, as I threw out my lure like a man possessed, having forgotten Grampa's long ago advice in all the excitement:

Bring it in faster, Tommy boy, you can't reel faster than a musky can swim, no one can...

"He's gotta be around here *some*where!" Don called out. "How big was that thing?"

"I don't know, but it was huge. Bigger than most the mounts we've seen anyway."

Recharged with enough adrenalin between us to launch a small spacecraft, Don and I pounded away at Strawberry Point and everything adjacent to it as well. We never saw that fish again. We hadn't even realized it had grown dark, not really. Finally, we grudgingly accepted the fact our monster musky had made other plans, and they didn't include us.

It was dark, well past sunset. We both called "last cast" and let fly, putting our traditional, final touch on another musky hunting adventure. I looked around after reeling in, wishing we could have spent a few more days on such a beautiful lake. After reeling in and with a heavy sigh, Don put down his rod, took a seat and started up the motor. Then he went to switch on the running lights and spotlight. Oops. He tried the switches again. Nope.

"Funny, never had a problem with the lights before," he said, a concerned expression on his face.

I sat there silent as Death, and every bit as still as the dead as we slowly made our way across the lake in near total darkness. I was in no hurry to join the dearly departed. I was in no hurry all right, but it took a Herculean effort on my part to keep from humming a little ditty the French seem rather fond of...

***

Abner seemed genuinely disappointed the next morning while we were checking out when we told him about the one that got away. He apologized (again) for not having been there to guide us, as in for the entire four days. We told him not to worry about it though, recalling our first and only experience with him on the water. Then he told me something that indicted he knew more than we had been led to believe. Something similar to what Grampa had told me.

"You what?" He responded when I recalled the musky coming after my bucktail. "You slowed your retrieve? Never do that. Always keep it coming. If your lure gets to the boat before the musky strikes, then jam your pole into the water and do wide, deliberate figure eights. If it's in the mood, it'll strike about then. But *never* slow a retrieve! Golly, no wonder it took off on you."

Ouch. And it came from a guy I would have sworn knew less about musky fishing than the perch he was so fond of chasing.

Well, another lesson learned the hard way, not that we believed there was any *other* way when it came to muskies. I suppose if we had all season or at least a few weeks at a time we would learn a lot faster. That concept made for good excuses anyway. I would go back to Iowa and sell golf equipment, Don would return to his home in Savanna, Illinois and run locomotives, and the both of us would begin dreaming, scheming and planning for next year - so far away, yet so filled with promise.

***

Before spring arrived in 1984 I had found it - found the lake that convinced me (as always) it would finally happen. Several musky men I talked to agreed that if they were forced to choose just one lake in all of Wisconsin, it would be the one they would choose. Yep, the Quest would be fulfilled on Lake Tomahawk; could there be any doubt?

"No doubt at all," I told Don over the phone on a cold February night in 1984.

Those in the know had enlightened us, and they have directed us back to our roots! Well, close to our roots, anyway. It had to be fate or a variation of it, and if either of us questioned that, our doubts were erased when we received word that our parents were leaving Arkansas and moving back to Aurora. That meant Dad would be coming to Lake Tomahawk in 1984 as well and that had to mean, or at least portend, just one thing - the Quest would be fulfilled; our time was at hand.

Chapter 12

Our time wasn't at hand after all. The 1984 trip to Lake Tomahawk was so uneventful I won't even bother you with it. It wasn't the lake's fault or anyone else's either, or so we insisted. It was just another year of getting totally skunked and not realizing why; it was probably the weather's fault - even successful musky hunters found solace in that excuse if they ended up skunked. It didn't bolster their (or our) excuse if others had actually *landed* muskies on the same lake at the same time, but come on, those folks had simply been lucky, right? Sure. Why not. Let's go with lucky.

***

By the mid 1980's Lake Tomahawk hadn't changed much, far as we could tell, from 1960 when our family had vacationed there, but by 1985 we had changed a great deal as far as becoming musky fishermen was concerned. We liked to think so, anyway. We not only had an array of quality tackle that would make most musky hunters proud, but in 1985 I had come across a book that offered so much inside information I felt I was qualified to be a musky guide myself. Almost. I figured it would probably be prudent to actually catch a few first. I was confident that would come to pass once I had the chance to implement all of the new information I had discovered.

Bucktail Fishing For Muskies was the book's title, written by a northern Wisconsin guide named Joe Bucher. I was getting over the natural mistrust I had been taught or at least absorbed over the years regarding guides, but not completely. Two years before, our old pal Abner hadn't exactly been a confidence builder. With that in mind, I had adopted a "prove it to me" attitude as far as Mr. Bucher was concerned; incertitude built upon years of skepticism, fueled by defeat.

My mindset began to change the minute I thumbed through Joe Bucher's book. Not only were there pictures of him holding onto almost more lunkers than I had seen hanging on countless walls in Northwoods taverns and lodges, but in all those photos over the years the guy hadn't aged; not much anyway. What I mean is, to have caught all those muskies, plus guided all those folks to dozens more, I figured he should have been pushing the hundred year mark in the final photographs.

The other thing that was apparent once I began to read his book was he actually gave specific instructions, as opposed to offering just vague advice while trying to sell his lures. Oh, he mentioned his lures all right, I don't mean that, and even recommended them in specific situations, but what he said made sense to me as opposed to being a load of hype. I had been in sales for years, so right or wrong I felt qualified to distinguish between hype and fact as it pertained to products in general.

Not only did it appear that Bucher's book was fact, I wondered if maybe he hadn't revealed too much of his musky hunting knowledge. Then I thought better of it. It's one thing to know what to do, and quite another to know where, exactly, to do it. It was a safe bet his guiding business wouldn't suffer due to folks reading his book. Besides, I didn't believe for a second he hadn't kept a few aces up his sleeve, and I didn't blame him. I also concluded it was okay with him if you did happen to buy a few of his lures, or a few hundred; I didn't blame him for that, either.

We didn't know what a guide charged, let alone a top-notch guide like Joe Bucher. Even though the good ones were probably worth it, it was a luxury we felt we couldn't afford, especially since none of them, to our knowledge, would guarantee a trophy musky. That last point was one Dad usually told us to consider. Regardless, we had Bucher's book and at least a limited understanding, in a way, of where to look for muskies on a given lake. Since we were going to be on the prime musky waters of Lake Tomahawk for the second time in as many years, we had to believe all of those factors would put us in a position to finally fulfill the Quest.

***

We booked a September arrival, again waiting until the Labor Day weekend was behind us. We had really liked the cabin we had stayed in during our 1984 trip. I scoured all the pamphlets again anyway, but nothing appeared as if it would be an improvement so I booked the same cabin at a place called Cox's Resort.

It was an exceptional cabin all right; more like an older bungalow with an abundance of Northwoods ambiance, and reasonably priced, too. It had been very well maintained, and boasted a living room with a stone fireplace and a picture window with a western exposure that gave us a panoramic view of the lake. We would have our own bedrooms, even when we received the good news that Larry was going to be able to make it.

There was also a formal dining room ideal for poker and Trivial Pursuit, or Dad's favorite, Parcheesi. It sounds like a simple game and I'll grant you it isn't chess, but once Dad had you in his sights you were usually a goner. It didn't hurt that the man had an uncanny way with dice, either. Same with poker; on Dad's return voyage from Italy after World War Two, he had won over five hundred bucks playing both of those games. That was an awful lot of money back then, and for a lot of us it still is, especially if we win that much, and even more so if we lose it.

I had driven from Des Moines to Aurora so I could pick up Dad. Don was scheduled to meet us at the lake later that same day, with Larry arriving the following day. When Dad and I arrived around two that first afternoon, the weather was perfect, at least for musky fishing. It had begun to cloud over, and for the past couple of hours the weather reports had maintained some storms were coming in from the southwest later that evening.

We couldn't wait. After settling into our cottage and setting up our gear we fired up the small, 8.5 hp Johnson on the rowboat that came with the place and headed out. With any luck (okay, a lot of it) we would hook into a huge musky before Don even arrived. Wouldn't he be surprised! Well, there was going to be a surprise all right.

***

Dad and I had been casting near the west shore of Daniel's Point, due east of Roman's Point. The wind had picked up as the clouds begun to roil. The temperature continued to drop as well, and it hadn't been very warm to begin with. Somehow, I could smell the fish, I swear I could. Ever have one of those days casting when you just know you're wasting your time? Well, it felt just the opposite that afternoon. We hadn't brought up a fish yet, but I just knew, with each cast, we were getting closer. Then it happened.

"You see that fish?" Dad said, pointing to a spot in the water just ahead of him. "Came after my Pikie Minnow."

I was just finishing my retrieve, so I kept my bucktail coming about a foot underwater then made some wide figure eights without slowing down.

"There it is again!" Dad hollered as he pointed with the tip of his rod. That time I saw it, coming right towards my lure. It wasn't huge, but it was a musky and sure looked big enough to garner some bragging rights. It shot past my bucktail, went under the boat, and we never saw it again. Even so, we hadn't been on the water two hours and already experienced as much musky action as any McCabe had in the past two years, and then some. There may have been a number of reasons why we never saw that musky again, but perhaps the main one was just a few miles away, closing fast.

Don had arrived about an hour after Dad and I had already headed out, but rather than put his boat in the water he decided to take it easy and wait for our return. The owner of Cox's had told him we had gone out in the rowboat, so Don just lounged about in front of the large picture window with a cold beer and watched for us. At least that's what he did at first. After a while, he also noticed what was coming from the west, but it was the radio report that really grabbed his attention. Earlier, on a lake not far away, the same storm system that was bearing down on Tomahawk had produced a lightning strike that had killed a young man and his uncle while they were in a boat. The young man's father was in critical condition...

The huge, dark purple and darker gray thunderheads were bearing down on us fast, but we hadn't even noticed them yet. By then we were looking and casting east, in the other direction, concentrating all our attention on the water just behind our lures. That needle-toothed s.o.b. was out there somewhere, I just knew it, if *only* it would - ***KABOOM!!***

We were done fishing for the day. One look over my shoulder in the direction of the blinding flash and explosion of thunder was all it took for me to frantically yank on the cord of that Johnson motor; all 8.5 hp of it. I glanced again at the advancing storm as both of us quickly threw on our raingear. The nearly black clouds, as dark and angry as any I had ever seen, were tumbling towards us, not unlike a slow-motion avalanche.

The small engine sputtered to life so we beat it out of there just as the powerful winds begin to churn up Lake Tomahawk with ease. The waves reached two, then three feet before we made it a hundred yards. By the time we were approaching the tip of Daniel's point they were higher still, roiling and shoving into each other like lurching, drunken sailors; *large* drunken sailors.

The storm caught up to us as if we were barely moving and kept rumbling furiously across the lake. The slashing rain was so intense I was surprised it didn't sting more when it slammed into exposed skin, then realized the drops were too big to sting that much, even if that didn't make any sense – I was too panic-stricken to realize much of anything other than we needed to get the hell out of there. Lightning was shooting out of the black and purple cloud mass in all directions; sideways, straight down and every direction in-between. For the first time in my life I was genuinely terrified to be in a boat, especially one as small as ours.

As much as the lightning got my attention, it was the ever-increasing size of the waves that really freaked me out. Once we passed Daniel's Point we were even more exposed and vulnerable. Things really grew tense at that moment, not that they weren't before; we couldn't see the shoreline, not even an outline.

I fully expected the next huge wave, or the one after that, to swamp us. The way they were churning and slamming into one another, it was just a matter of time before the exact, deadly combination came together with us in the middle. That's when a gut-wrenching thought tore through me - what about Dad? He was up front, holding on, his useless yellow poncho flapping rapidly in the high winds. We had the cushions, but I didn't believe for a second they would be of much use to a heavily clothed, 72-year-old man once he was in the water, assuming Dad got a hold of one to begin with. Worse yet, we hadn't made it a hundred yards east of Daniel's Point, not that we could see it anymore as the storm continued to gain strength. I fought the waves as we continued east, but there was no safe haven at all, unless we could make it across the wide traverse. I yelled for Dad to grab one of the cushions, having to repeat myself several times for him to hear me. He finally nodded as he pointed to the one he was sitting on.

If we swamped, which I was convinced could easily happen at any moment, what could I do? I had a wife and three children back home, the youngest, Megan, having just turned ten. If I tried my hardest, I might be able to save myself, but how could

I leave my father behind, even if I would have been virtually powerless to save him? I couldn't just leave him, and I knew it.

"Dad! Dad!" I again yelled above the howling storm. "Grab two cushions and hold them to your chest!"

"You just keep in a straight line, Thomas. You're doing fine." He called back over his shoulder. Always the quintessential coach; he wouldn't even consider doing anything I might construe as a lack of confidence on his part. *Right Dad,* I thought, *we'll get there sooner or later...***KABOOM!!** *Okay, that was a close one...*

We began to make out the eastern shoreline, but I had no idea where our dock was located. We were headed in the general direction, but we could have been off by a hundred yards or so either way, and the last thing I wanted to do was travel parallel to the eastern shore while contending with a howling west wind.

Even with the rain pelting against his glasses, Dad spotted him first. There Don was all right, standing ramrod straight with his arms crossed in the blinding rain at the end of the dock as if he were telling the storm to go to back to whatever level of hell it had come from. Big brothers. You gotta love 'em.

I was never so glad to be back indoors before in my life. Dad knew we had been in a tight one too, and was glad to be on solid ground although he maintained a stoic demeanor. Don had a good fire going, but before Dad and I could enjoy it we had to get out of our not just wet, but drenched clothes. We literally could not have been more soaked if we had jumped overboard. That tore it. My next budget straining purchase would be the absolute best raingear Cabela's had to offer; and the same thing for Dad, too. We had survived, and deserved at least that much. No, we deserved more. We deserved that needle toothed predator that had messed with us earlier that day, and we were determined to find him.

***

When Larry showed up the next day, Don, Dad and I had already put in a full morning on the water. The high, cloudless skies and lack of any discernible wind was again the excuse we used for having nothing to show for our efforts. Larry didn't care one way or the other, not really anyway. He would have been glad if one of us had landed a big one, especially if Dad had done it, but it wasn't a priority for Larry; Don and I understood our brother's sentiment – sort of.

He was there because he wanted to be with his dad and brothers; we understood that much anyway. As usual he didn't own any fishing gear, and again as usual wasn't interested in borrowing any from us. He enjoyed going along, and liked to cast a few every now and then, but he didn't want to actually hook anything. We weren't aware of the barbless hooks some folks were using, which is what Larry would have preferred. He was into catch and release before most of us had even heard of it, but if catching them meant damaging them he wasn't interested. He appreciated the sport or at least the challenge, but not if one of the competitors had to die or was injured. He loved the wilderness, but remained a strict vegetarian - and held an abiding concern for all living things.

Personally, I didn't know how Larry did it. With four kids to feed, my parents couldn't afford to serve steak very often. If sirloin was on sale though, once in a while Mom would bring home two or three big ones and cook them up on the broiler part of our old Roper oven. Dad had to referee, or else Don, Larry and I would pretty much devour them before Mom had a chance to sit down. It didn't take long for Suzie to catch on, either. Dad's eagle eye or not, we learned how to eat fast. Those steaks were delicious, and Larry had loved them as much as any of us. How he could just sit there, twenty years later in a Northwoods steakhouse and not even flinch when Don, Dad and I were served our thick, juicy steaks was beyond me.

He blamed what happened to me later that night on the fact I had consumed a 24-ounce T-bone with all the trimmings for supper. He maintained, tongue possibly in cheek, that my gluttony had either diminished my reflexes or was the cycle of karma coming around on me. Whatever it was, I knew I would never forget it.

***

The four of us had decided to do some night fishing after getting back from supper that evening. Don's boat had its lights in working order again which was a good thing (I didn't ask) even if we were just heading across the bay east of Daniel's Point. Part of its shoreline had some impressive weed cover, and there were a number of areas where submerged musky cabbage was abundant. Sure was dark though.

All four of us were out there and even though Larry wasn't fishing, the rest of us had to be extra careful with our casting. Don and I managed to tangle our lures together twice, each of us silently blaming the other for his ineptitude. Dad had resorted to jigging off his side of the boat. I had these large, maroon musky jigs with weighted heads, and Dad liked the way they looked in the water, even if he couldn't see them. He had used them earlier that day, so he was working from memory.

We had been out there about an hour, slowly working our way up and down the shore then out to deeper water where more of the musky cabbage was located. The clouds started to break up then disappeared.

"I swear, the stars are brighter up North," I said to no one in particular.

I had just finished reeling in my last cast as I spoke, gazing at the magnificent night sky, momentarily mistaking portions of the Milky Way for thin, high altitude clouds. Rather than throw another cast right away, I kept looking up, searching the heavens for constellations or if I was lucky, a shooting star. I started splashing my bucktail in and out of the water in an absent-minded manner, continuing to look up as I did so.

Ker-splash! Suddenly the water directly in front of me exploded, and I don't mean a little. It happened so fast I was caught off guard, at least at first. Whatever it was, it had a hold of my Musky Killer Mepps and didn't appear to be in any hurry to give it back. The water looked as if someone was actually next to the boat thrashing for their life, spraying all four of us in the process. I could feel the pressure so assumed the hooks had been set, even though my rod tip had been pretty high up to begin with when I had tried setting the hooks; at least I thought I'd tried.

I held on for a moment then did something exceptionally stupid, even for me. Later on, a seasoned angler told me I had been ignorant, not stupid, which may or may not have been intended to make me feel better. Another of Grampa's favorite humorists, Will Rodgers, once said: *You know, everybody's ignorant, just on different subjects.* Well, I wasn't an expert musky hunter, but I knew enough about the subject to remember what I had been told about keeping a taut line. Too bad I was too big of a dope not to recall it at that precise moment, the moment I pushed the spool release button, on *purpose* no less. In my frenzied state and for a reason that still leaves me somewhat disquieted, I thought it best to let the fish make a run or two in order to tire it out.

It made a run all right - after easily spitting the lure when the line went slack, the same lure that apparently hadn't even been set to begin with. At that moment, I came to the conclusion I didn't deserve to catch a musky, something I obviously couldn't do anyway, not even when they came to *me*. At least, instead of losing a large musky and learning another lesson (it must've been a musky; I just knew it) I was fortunate enough to have actually learned two – make that three - if you want to count "always be prepared for the unexpected". The other two lessons? Never let slack develop and don't hit the release button until the fish is in the net.

We kept casting, but my heart wasn't in it. I'd had my chance, and I had blown it - again. Still, at least we were having some action. There was that seemingly aggressive follow just before the storm had arrived, and a genuine strike at night. Maybe, just maybe, our time had arrived; well, someone's anyway.

***

Don and I went out the following morning after Dad decided to wait until afternoon. There were a few clouds around, accenting the brilliant blue sky. Larry had his sights set on an extensive hike into the woods to do a little hunting with his new camera. It was September, some of the leaves had turned, and an early frost had cut down the bug population; a perfect time to be in the woods.

We headed over to the spot where Dad raised the musky the day before and started working the shoreline. There was a tall, brick chimney for a landmark, a spot the owner of Cox's had told us about. It was set back well into the trees, part of a building not visible from the water. It looked out of place, an intrusion really, but I was glad it was there. We didn't know the lake very well and needed all the help we could get.

I was throwing the same bucktail I had used the day before, a Mepps Musky Killer with natural hair and a gold blade. I couldn't cast it quite as far as a Giant Killer, but it had a way of moving in the water all its own. Although I almost always used a leader, I didn't have one on that morning. I thought I had brought plenty of good ones along, but I must have put them in a different tackle box. I only had older ones with crimped sleeves. I had read in Joe Bucher's book those could fail when it came to large fish, but a quality wire leader, one wrapped instead of crimped held up better, and like all leaders they were essential because of bite offs. I decided to take my chances with a bite off rather than use a cheap leader. Besides, the lure seemed to move better without the leader. In a word, it looked *convincing.*

From Grampa's tale of his monumental struggle with his musky, told to his wide-eyed grandchildren, and all the accounts by others of their fierce battles with the ultimate freshwater fish, one constant always shone through - *it was the fight of a lifetime.* No other freshwater species matched it, period.

I was watching my lure as it cruised towards me in the water, once again impressed with how good its movement looked. It was ten, maybe twelve feet from the side of the boat when, not "all of a sudden" or "like a crazed predator", but more like it was half asleep, a musky showed up. Lake Tomahawk is usually clear, and our angle gave Don and me a perfect view of my lure and the musky that was following it.

It wasn't a big musky. It looked to be legal – perhaps over thirty inches, but not much more, if at all. I had heard that smaller muskies were even more insane than their older brethren; sometimes attacking and fighting with such fury that hooking them actually caused some of them to die from heart failure. How that specific conclusion could be reached escaped me, but it didn't matter - the one approaching my lure appeared to be about as excited as a tollbooth collector at the start of his Monday morning shift. It was following the bucktail all right, but it appeared as if it were moving in a slow line to renew its driver's license.

Somehow, none of that registered until later. At the time, all I could see was this beautiful fish, this *musky*, right behind my lure. After all those years, all those casts, there it was! Not a lunker, but there nonetheless. The lure was at the side of the boat, the musky was right there eyeballing the thing, so I prepared to begin a figure eight. First, however, I decided to pull the bucktail across the water as far to my right as possible. The musky didn't seem to care one way or the other. It stayed directly behind the bucktail, but instead of appearing like it wanted to rip it to shreds, it looked like it wanted to ask it for directions or something.

Just before I started to do a figure eight, the musky opened wide and gently placed the bucktail in its mouth and began to glide slowly away. None of what was happening made any sense at all. If anything, it was almost a surreal contradiction of everything I had expected. I set the hook anyway, and I didn't screw around with it either. That got its attention. It was only four or five feet from the boat, so landing it wasn't a problem.

Don had netted it then proceeded to demonstrate why he was considerably better at most anything other than picking up a fish, at least one around thirty inches or bigger with sharp teeth, a fish Don just *knew* wanted to remove a finger or two. In Don's defense, he had grown up with Scamp, and although a fish isn't a dog, deep-seated psychological trauma coupled with a few scars on your hands is difficult to ignore, especially during a crisis situation. I finally had to grab it and remove the hooks. I wasn't braver than my big brother, but Scamp had only drawn blood from me once.

I thought maybe the musky was sick, but from all outward appearances it not only looked healthy, but beautifully marked as well. Don took a couple of quick snapshots and I let it go. The limit was 30 inches, and this one, my first musky, was only 29. It swam away faster than it had arrived, which we took as an encouraging sign. If my account of catching my first musky sounds anti-climatic, that's because it was. The entire experience was the antithesis of everything I had expected. I concluded it must have been sick after all; *I* was anyway, or at least disappointed.

Later that day a fisherman who said Tomahawk was his favorite lake told me I wasn't using my head by letting it go. He said he would have loaned me his "fish stretcher" if all I needed was another inch. Maybe the guy was just taking a jab at being clever. Still, it didn't set right. I had spent too many years getting skunked on Wisconsin lakes, and one of the reasons *why* just happened to be standing directly in front of me.

"Problem with those fish stretchers is they cut the odds for honest fishermen to catch trophy muskies." I said, perhaps in jest except I wasn't smiling much.

He smiled though, and started to chuckle until my words and demeanor registered. He wasn't smiling anymore, not even a little. I thought of my musky, my *first ever* musky swimming away faster than it had arrived after it had been released. The image made me feel good inside, and glad that guy hadn't been the one who had caught it.

Later that evening I told Dad and my brothers I wasn't against someone keeping their first legal musky. For most of us, a whole lot of time and frustration goes into that momentous occasion long before it ever happens. I vowed to keep a musky myself someday, have it mounted even, since at the time they hadn't started making mounts from photos; at least we weren't aware of the practice. Granted, catch and release wasn't as big a deal back then, but in hindsight it should have been. Thanks to the continued efforts of Muskies Inc. chapters, however, at least the trend they had started in the mid 1960's was growing in popularity.

I also told Dad and my brothers I wouldn't keep any musky that wasn't at least thirty pounds. That was the benchmark I set for myself. Well, I had opened my big mouth and made a commitment I could never disavow. I only hoped the musky gods didn't test my character with a 29 pounder. If they did though, that guy could still put his fish stretcher to good use, if he possessed a high tolerance for pain.

***

Dad liked to fish, he just didn't like to do it all day anymore; actually, he never had. Larry was even less enthused of course, so once again Don and I were on our own the third and last morning of our 1985 trip. Don managed to accomplish two firsts that morning, which is really saying something when you consider how many hours we had logged together on the water.

We like to think we get what we pay for, and true enough, the Zebco combo outfit that came complete in a pre-shrunk package hadn't cost all that much, but it was brand new. Besides, the package said it was designed for "heavy duty action" or something like that. It was a thick pole all right, made of graphite even, and the large, open-faced spinning reel was impressive looking and probably worked really well. We never found out, though.

I told Don he could give it a try, so I rigged it up and told him to have at it. It had an impressive 12 to 14-inch cork handle, which was rendered useless, since that's all that was left after Don had cast. He had let fly with a heavy, homemade bucktail concoction of his own invention and *snap! Kerspash!* It did look cool, the way the pole and reel arch through the sky end over end before hitting the water. Don had managed to get off a really good one, no kidding. It must have traveled at least twenty-five yards, arching away with an optimum vertex of at least thirty feet. Unfortunately, the only part of the entire apparatus that floated was still in Don's hands. We shot over to the spot where it had landed, but it was already assigned to the deep.

Don's next "first" was even more impressive. We hadn't gone another hundred yards, with Don casting in-between partially submerged weed beds when out of nowhere a musky came flying towards his lure as if it were a motorcycle cop making a high-speed bust. It screeched to a halt, checked out Don's lure and took off as fast as it had arrived.

"Did you see that?" Don said as he quickly reeled in. I'd seen it all right. I gave Don honors and he let fly towards the same area, nailing the spot dead on.

"There he is again!" Don exclaimed.

The second time around the musky slammed right into the lure, and with his cat-like reflexes Don immediately set the hooks. That was the good news. The bad news, or what certainly could have been considerably better news, was that the musky in question weighed in at a little under two pounds; all eighteen inches of it. Ever the optimist, Don was nonetheless thrilled with his conquest. Before releasing the tough little guy, Don even gave his first musky a kiss - and fortunately, I was at the ready with my camera. If either of us had needed a visual example to verify Grampa's words - *You can't reel faster than a musky can swim, no one can* - it certainly presented itself that day.

***

Dad got a real kick out of Don's experience after hearing about it. Dad liked to fish all right, but not enough to usually do it if he wasn't with his sons. He looked forward to the trips as much as any of us. Although Don and I appreciated the trips for reasons besides fishing, for Dad those were the most important reasons. Fishing was the excuse, not the rationale for Dad to get together with his sons.

Dad had turned 72 just a week or so before our trip that year, and even though the white hair he'd had since his thirties always made him appear older than his years, one look at the rest of him would tell any observant person he wasn't even close to frail. The term "elderly" simply didn't fit him. His forearms still had their size and strength, as did the rest of him. His voice never took on an old man's quiver, not even in his final years. Whenever he laughed it was genuine; I never knew him to fake it for effect or especially not to placate anyone, so when Don told Dad he had kissed that slippery little critter right on the gill plate, Dad's response made me wish I had kissed my musky too.

Dad was glad both of our muskies were still swimming around out there, but not because of the growing trend to embrace catch and release in order to eventually increase the numbers of large fish. Dad felt good about it just because they were still alive. He wasn't against catching and eating fish or any other food source for that matter. Not the little ones though, regardless of how good they were supposed to taste, he didn't like that. Either that was a recent sentiment on his part, since he had kept a 29-inch musky decades before, or I had failed to notice. Something told me he didn't want to see any life cut short in the springtime of its existence, since he was in the fall of his own.

***

Fall of his existence or not, Dad surprised me over lunch that day when he came up with an idea to circumvent Wisconsin's anti-trolling laws without breaking them. Like most, if not all of Wisconsin's inland lakes, motorized trolling was illegal on Tomahawk. Dad, therefore, offered to row me up and down the shoreline and the adjacent weed beds east of Daniels's Point that afternoon. At first I protested. What kind of a guy has his 72-year-old father row him around a lake on a sunny afternoon with temperatures hovering in the 80's?

Dad wasn't like most 72 year olds though. In the summer months, he still supplemented his income by painting a few houses for old clients from time to time, even two and a half story Victorians. His extension ladders, even the huge one that could reach the highest peaks, were made of wood. Do you know how heavy those things are? I was thirty-seven, lifted weights, and still had to be careful maneuvering that thing. I couldn't do it at all until I was fourteen, and you didn't want to be standing anywhere near the ladder when I did, at least with your back turned.

Dad didn't bother with the small Johnson to get us across the lake. After removing his t-shirt he just started to row. We told Don we'd be out for about an hour, but Dad took me up and down that shoreline for well over two hours. I asked him several times if he wanted to trade places for a while.

"Nope." Was all he said; no reasons why, no "maybe later", no *nothing* except "nope". Classic Pete McCabe – classic Dad.

I wanted to hook into something more than ever that afternoon; I wanted to show off in front of my father in a way that would make him proud of me. I wanted to hook into a lunker musky and experience the fight of a lifetime and land the brute and have Dad take my picture. If big enough, it would go on the wall; if not, I wanted to see the look on Dad's face when it swam away. It didn't happen; not even a follow. Still, it was one of the best times I ever had on a lake, if not *the* best.

When I was a teenager in mindset as well as age, fishing and football were about the only things Dad and I still had in common; two things we could still talk about. It occurred to me, as the steady creaking of his oars was repeated over and over, how some things, the most important things, didn't possess value simply because of what they could bring to me alone, especially that hot afternoon. The value that day was found in what had been created and shared between a father and his son.

Still, it would have been awesome to have caught a trophy musky that afternoon, but the afternoon was awesome anyway.

I knew I'd look back on it someday and wish I could have just one more pass along that shoreline with Dad at the oars. I would like that, but I'm not sorry I can't have it. I had my turn, and was very lucky to have had it at all.

***

The 1985 musky hunt had come to a close, and a few things of major significance closed along with it, or were at least put off for quite a few years. For one thing, Larry wouldn't be coming on future trips for a long time. Also, with one brief exception the following year, we said goodbye to Wisconsin for quite a while as well. It would always remain a very special place to us, and not abandoned forever, but it was time to explore other options. From what I had gathered, the place worth exploring was Lake of the Woods, Canada. I booked an August trip.

Another change would be my attitude towards hiring a guide. It was an expense we could never justify in the past, but as the years had gone by and we were learning just what to do, we were really discovering how little we actually *did* know. I still liked to go over Joe Bucher's book and a few others before a trip, but there was no question it wasn't anywhere near the same as being in Joe Bucher's boat. By then we had heard rumors of what he charged, and besides, he didn't guide in Lake of the Woods as far as I knew.

1986 was going to represent a sea change in the way I approached fulfilling the Quest. I would be on what many believed to be some of the best musky waters in the world, *if* you knew what you were doing. I apparently didn't, but was willing to pay an experienced musky guide to lead the way.

I was going to make it a family affair by bringing Peggy, Danny and Megan along. Our oldest, Cari Ann, was involved with her life at the University of Iowa. Even though her mom had been talked into the trip to Canada because I had booked us in a five-star resort, Cari Ann had other priorities and we sure didn't blame her. Her college years were proving to be very special for her, and my "little blonde tornado" was no longer a little girl.

***

It wasn't going to be cheap, but it was going to be quite a learning experience. Don was content to let me do the learning (and spending) and report my findings. Dad, Don and I would rendezvous at another interesting place we had heard about called Boyd's near Fifield, Wisconsin once September arrived, having decided to put off our farewell to Wisconsin one more year.

All in all, things were beginning to emerge from the fog. We were, and probably always would be unable to just pack and go whenever we felt like it, but the few days a year we had been fortunate enough to cast away on a good musky lake had taught us a few things anyway. We had probably learned more of what not to do than *what* to do. *Where*, exactly, to do it still eluded us. I'm not referring to any given lake because even a great musky lake is worthless if you are casting "where they ain't". The key was where we should be concentrating our efforts all right, and at what depths, plus which lures and retrieve angles should be utilized. The fog was clearing all right, and with a qualified guide to pinpoint the spots, I was banking on it to disappear altogether. I was willing to pay a small fortune to accomplish that goal as well, and to finally fulfill the Quest.

Chapter 13

had been excited about previous trips, very much so, but the anticipation I felt prior to our 1986 trip was so overwhelming I had even packed most of the clothes I planned on bringing and all of my fishing gear well in advance; two *months* in advance, actually. On top of that, I placed all of it under the corner serving-table in the dining room. Peggy thought I was nuts, but her tolerance was appreciated. The only thing she made me put back in the basement was my new rod carrier because it was so long and bulky it took up half the room, or so it seemed, since it was almost always in the way.

I had booked us at a five-star resort called the Totem Lodge located in the general vicinity of Sioux Narrows, Ontario, right on Lake of the Woods. I only remembered Lake of the Woods from what I had heard about it back in 1972. I had a vague memory of hearing it had suffered the same fate as a number of Wisconsin lakes that had fallen victim to excessive fishing pressure, both recreational and sometimes commercial, or so I'd heard. I really had no credible reason to believe Lake of the Woods had been fished out, and once I began reading up on it

I realized almost immediately those claims were exaggerations to say the least.

For one thing, it's a huge body of water; nearly 65 miles long and anywhere from 10 to 55 miles wide. There are over 14,500 islands of every shape and size imaginable, and the overwhelming majority of them are government owned, which means they have remained unchanged for thousands of years. The fishing was supposed to be excellent, at least if you hired an experienced guide, or you were with someone who knew his or her way around. I had specifically requested a musky guide, and the folks at the Totem Lodge told me they had just the guy. I couldn't *wait*.

I had experienced a break-out year selling golf equipment in my territory. I had more than doubled my income, which was good, because up until that time expenses usually out paced appreciable returns. I was in a position to not only take my family on a great Northwoods vacation, but we would be doing it in a style none of us had ever experienced before.

***

As usual, I couldn't stay out of the tackle shops, or any place that sold fishing, camping or hunting equipment. If it was associated with the outdoors, I wanted to at least take a look. I had always acted that way to a degree, but with money scorching my pocket it had grown a little out of hand. I even bought the best snorkeling equipment I could find, because I had read that Lake of the Woods was generally clear and rather deep in places. It wasn't that I was planning to jump in and actually scour the depths for muskies, but I was curious about how things looked down there. I even checked out some scuba gear, but decided against it. Maybe someday.

Cabella's and L.L. Bean owed their third quarter profits to me that year, or at least a thank you note come Christmas. I ended up with so much clothing and equipment for my family and me that we could have gone on the Lewis and Clark expedition. I could have *outfitted* the Lewis and Clark expedition anyway, or so it seemed. I had a brand new, full-sized black and silver Dodge custom van, which we would need to get all that stuff up to Canada. God help us, I thought - if the border guards decided to search everything we would be there all day.

It would take a little under twelve hours to make it from Des Moines to Sioux Narrows if my calculations were correct, so we decided to spend the night somewhere in Minnesota. Besides, the last four hours would undoubtedly take us through some especially beautiful Northwoods country, so I figured it would be best to do it after a good night's sleep. If there was something I hadn't considered, anything I had left out, I sure couldn't think of it. We were all set to go, and everything down to the last possible detail had been considered.

We spent our first night in Cloquet, Minnesota, and upon our departure the following morning the scenery steadily improved the farther north we traveled. From Des Moines, it took any number of hours due north before the corn and soybean fields finally gave way to the Northwoods. The granite outcroppings along the highway, with the tubular drill marks where the dynamite had been inserted were one of the first signs we had arrived. You can bet you're getting close when the roads you're traveling were created by blasting massive amounts of rock out of the way. The streams and rivers go from earthy mud hues, or at best translucent flows, to waters so sparkling you could count the rocks on the riverbeds if you had a mind to stop and do so. Some of the Northwoods streams seemed to rush with a special urgency, as if spring took forever to arrive and winter couldn't wait to return.

It was the first time that Danny, age seventeen, and Megan, eleven, had been out of the United States. I wished our oldest, Cari Ann, could have been there. She would have tired of the fishing, but not the beauty of the Canadian wilderness. As we traveled through Nestor Falls something else peaked my interest.

"See those amphibious planes?" I said as I pointed to an eastern bay close to the highway. "We can book one of those if we want to fish a fly-in lake for a day or so." My comment was met with acute interest or concerned reservation, depending whether Peggy or the kids were doing the contemplating. I changed the subject, an easy thing to do considering our surroundings.

***

The Totem Lodge was a five-star resort all right, and everything about the place left no doubt in our minds as to why it had earned that designation. When we first pulled in I was reminded of that exclusive lodge that Don and I had stumbled across in 1982, the one where that older guy with the stylish Northwoods clothing ensemble had thought best to at least ignore us. I remembered that he had seemed particularly perturbed by the presence of Don's belching pickup truck as it squatted on their perfect parking lot, and the recollection brought a smile to my face. I couldn't help remembering the following year in the Norwood Pines Supper Club when Don had cleared out that guy's entire table of guests.

My smile evolved into a quiet laugh. As I looked around Totem Lodge I knew I was going to miss my brother and father.

***

As impressive as the place looked, the real attraction was Lake of the Woods itself. I could tell you about the nice accommodations and everything else you would expect from a five-star resort, but once we were on the water with our guide Carmen, there was no doubt about what really made that part of the world so exceptional, and that was just our first impression. I had not seen anything that captured the essence of the Northwoods to such a degree since our trips to Perrault Falls in 1962 and 1972.

Our first day on the water substantiated all that and more at every turn. I couldn't get over the incredible number of pristine, tree studded islands that were everywhere. It was as if we were constantly going to one lake after another, all connected, with an unending variety of shapes, sizes and every imaginable type of Northwoods wonderment Mother Nature could have possibly conceived, far as I knew anyway.

To envision Lake of the Woods as a huge body of water 65 miles long and from 10 to 55 miles wide doesn't paint an accurate portrait unless the seemingly infinite variety of all its islands is included.It seldom feels as if you are on a body of water any larger than a lake in Wisconsin or Minnesota, depending where you are. Sometimes it appears to be vast, then a turn or two and you are suddenly in a cozy bay or inlet that resembles a small lake or pond more than anything. A pond situated 15 or 20 miles, perhaps farther still, from the nearest actual shoreline. The Lake of the Woods shoreline is over 300 miles long. If you factor in all of the island shorelines as well, that number swells to a staggering *65,000* miles. I don't know who actually added all that up, but that person sure must have had a lot of time on their hands.

As intricate and immense Lake of the Woods happens to be, it's even more mindboggling to contemplate its origin. It was once a small part of a vast freshwater inland sea called Lake Agassiz. That body of water was over 700 miles long and about 200 miles wide. It covered a great deal of what are now Manitoba, North Dakota, northern Minnesota, Ontario and Saskatchewan; a little over 110,000 square miles in all. The largest existing freshwater lake in the world is Lake Superior, which by comparison is "only" about 32,700 square miles in total size. Around 8,000 years ago, the Laurentide Ice Sheet melted enough to allow Lake Agassiz to drain into Hudson Bay. Along with scores of smaller lakes and other aquatic remnants, Lake of the Woods, Lake Winnipeg and Lake Manitoba are the most notable bodies of water that remain of that once massive inland sea.

The skeletal remains of many of the species of fish swimming around today have been found in areas that used to be submerged in that enormous freshwater behemoth, including (you guessed it) the mighty muskellunge. Well, northern pike anyway, but can zoology professors or their ilk tell the difference between a musky and northern from fossil remains? Can they count the number of submandibular pores in the skin on the underside of a fossil's lower jaw? Are the fossils so intact it can be ascertained whether the fins are pointed enough to be a musky? Maybe. Even though northern pike and muskies are so closely related they can produce hybrids, (try doing that with a walleye and a carp) I suppose the experts might be able to distinguish between the two from fossil remains. Even so, I like to think that for thousands of years there were muskies or their immediate predecessor patrolling the depths of Lake Agassiz.

Imagine the size some of them must have attained. If large bodies of water like Lake of the Woods encourage a species of fish like muskies to grow larger, just as smaller lakes can stunt their ultimate size as some folks maintain, what size muskies did Lake Agassiz produce in its 4,000-plus years of prime existence?

I've had guides and other musky hunters tell me how muskies sometimes charge the boat after being hooked. Maybe Lake Agassiz muskies would have done that too, only not to help them spit a lure. A puny little lure? So much for appetizers. They might have wanted the meal sitting in that funny looking contraption floating on the surface...

Our guide, Carmen, had heard of Lake Agassiz, but apparently hadn't given it a second thought since he'd finished high school, and the subject still didn't seem to hold much interest for him. He was a young guy in his mid-twenties that Eric Brown, owner of the Totem Lodge, told me was the best musky guide he had in his employ. I told Carmen I was primarily interested in catching a trophy musky, but also wanted to take home our limit in walleye unless it would take too much time out of our five-day fishing trip.

"Well," Carmen said as we walked towards the dock the first day, "would the first morning be a short enough time span for you?"

"That'd be fine," I said, "but we have four limits to fill."

"Only four limits, eh?" Carmen said as we approached our boat tethered to the dock. "Might just be needin' half the morning then."

I didn't know whether to laugh, let out a skeptical snort or give thanks to all the fishing gods at once. I helped load stuff in the boat instead. It was an awesome boat, too. A brand new twenty foot Lund with a 115 hp Mercury plus all the other amenities you would expect a five-star resort to offer.

***

The miles flew by as we sped west through Long Bay and into Yellow Girl Bay, a good ten or twelve miles into the wilderness. Peggy, Danny and Megan were truly impressed with the Northwoods splendor that was everywhere, enhanced by a beautifully sunny day with just enough white, billowing clouds to offer a perfect contrast to the astonishingly blue Canadian sky.

I hoped Carmen's declaration was even half true, and that he would make a similar proclamation pertaining to muskies. As I looked around, it sure appeared as if we had arrived at a fishing paradise, but skepticism dies hard when so many days have ended with empty live wells and shattered musky hunting dreams.

Although I strive to avoid clichés like the plague, catching walleye that morning was like shooting fish in a barrel. We not only had all of our limits in less than two hours, but the last hour before shore lunch was spent letting the smaller ones go after replacing them with a bigger catch. Carmen would find a spot, mark it, and then we all started jigging with purple-headed jigs and minnows. Megan and Peggy both caught their first walleye ever, with quite a few more to follow. Danny and I did well too. We had so many fish we either had to stuff ourselves at shore lunch or let some go. We did both.

Carmen found a spectacular spot for shore lunch, not that it was a difficult thing to accomplish. We had a panoramic view and it was a great island for the kids to explore, and they soon discovered the wild blueberries were as plentiful as they were delicious. The crackling fire Carmen built enhanced the clear summer air with an enticing, hardwood and pine incense. If the first morning's fishing and the lunch to follow were indications, I had definitely picked the right place - and perhaps the right time.

"So Carmen," I asked as he was filleting walleye for lunch, "I don't suppose the muskies will be as cooperative as the walleyes, or is it possible we'll get our limits there as well?" At first all Carmen did was smile.

"Well, the limit's two legal's a day for each of you, but I'd be less than honest to promise something like that on any given day even for a week's worth of fishing. We'll get some action, though. Plenty of northern, some big ones too. Mind you, we'll see some muskies. Getting 'em on will be the challenge, eh?"

I told him it was a challenge I was looking forward to, then I headed over to a section of shore, which consisted of a huge, flat section of granite nearly the size of a tennis court. I had put on my trusty Mepps Musky Killer with a gold blade and natural hair, then started to cast as Carmen continued to prepare our Northwoods feast. Peggy was lounging in the sun about twenty feet away and I could hear the kids behind me, their feet snapping dry twigs as they approached, coming back from exploring. It was just our first day, and so many things were falling so perfectly into place. I threw a cast, then a second. The bucktail looked good in the water as the sun created strobe-like glints and flashes off the gold blade.

The water was so clear a boulder fifteen feet down appeared to be less than ten feet away, easily visible. I gazed idly around at the panoramic view as I drank in one of nature's finest accomplishments, reeling in the last twenty or so feet of my second cast. *Wham! Splash!* It was as fast as it was furious. I didn't know what kind of fish had slammed into my small bucktail, but whatever the species, it wasn't kidding around. My new Ugly Stick, one of the stiffest Shakespeare made, was suddenly bent considerably more than it had been made to do by any of the walleye I had caught that morning, and I had brought in two that were over four pounds. Before I managed three turns of my reel after tightening down my drag, it came partially out of the water then splashed back down, but thankfully it was hooked - and it wasn't small.

Carmen had seen the whole thing, yet continued to fillet another walleye as if I were helping the kids pick blueberries.

"Think it might be a musky? Hey Carmen, ya *think?*" I hollered. "Might be a northern, but I think maybe it's a -"

"It's a northern." Was all Carmen said as he deftly sliced another fillet from the other side of the walleye he was working on. A quick glance in his direction told me he was considerably more interested in the quality of the cut he was inspecting than the epic battle I was waging not thirty feet away. "This bay's full of the buggers, as a rule." With that Carmen walked over and began frying up the fillets in a huge iron skillet.

Some of the thrill had disappeared, but not most of it. I horsed the northern to shore then slid it up the level granite I was standing upon. It flopped a few times before I grabbed it, removed the bucktail and put it in the live well. It was almost six pounds, but I had thought it was much bigger when it had first exploded from the water. Still, it had put up a decent fight. I remembered the northern I had caught with Dad manning the boat in Perrault Falls in 1962, and what had just occurred reminded me of that special time.

Right about then, as I walked back from the boat, I wished more than ever Dad and Don were there. Peggy and the kids acted as if they were excited about the northern, and they were I guess, but still, I wished Dad and Don had watched it happen. I couldn't wait to tell them about it, and couldn't help assuming from what had just occurred, that it was merely the beginning of an especially memorable fishing trip.

I was standing on the flat granite rock a few feet from shore, gazing out across the large bay when Megan walked in front of me. She was almost always happy, the type of lucky person who rarely needed a reason to feel that way. Given a reason, like a special family vacation, made her even happier. She smiled at me then stepped closer to the shore for a better look at what was just beyond and beneath the waves.

It happened so fast actual thinking wasn't involved - just instinctive reaction. As if in slow motion but moving fast, I called out and bolted towards her just as her foot stepped on the natural slime that coated the granite at the water line. I arrived at the precise moment she began to slide rapidly into the water, closing in fast towards a fifteen-foot drop off. She could swim, but my heart was pounding in my chest anyway as I grabbed her under the armpits just before she careened into the depths. It wasn't as dramatic as the time I went in after my kid sister when she was four, but it reminded me of that day on Tomahawk way back in 1960. Megan, not surprisingly, considered it a great adventure even if it was a little embarrassing.

"Slipperier than ice, that stuff," Carmen said while he continued to prepare lunch, not missing a beat. "Seen a few fellas end up in the hospital after cracking their heads."

***

We spent the rest of the day musky fishing, or at least casting for them. Megan and Peggy weren't very interested in casting, as in not at all, and brightened considerably when it was suggested we could return to the lodge early if they wanted. The sand beach in front of our A frame cabin sounded considerably more enticing to them than another three hours of watching Danny and me cast, that's for sure. There were a number of kids around Megan's age already swimming and playing when we arrived, and Peggy had at least two murder, mayhem and mystery novels she couldn't wait to explore.

After dropping them off Carmen took us all over the place, and although we didn't see any muskies that first day both Danny and I caught several good-sized northern each, as well as a fair number of smaller ones. The lure that continued to work best for me was a Giant Killer Mepps, black tail with a gold blade. I owned almost every color available. Even so, I hated to switch from the black and gold even when Carmen suggested I do so. I knew it was supposed to be counter productive to dismiss your guide's advice, so I would switch to different lures or colors when Carmen suggested it at a given spot, but invariably a look at the end of my line revealed a black and gold Giant Killer Mepps. I don't know if it mattered all that much or not. Danny experimented with a variety of colors and kept up with my fish count, although he insisted it was the other way around. Other lures, like crankbaits, worked too, but I loved that black and gold Mepps; good thing I had about a dozen of them…

***

Late that afternoon we stopped at the lodge and the girls decided to join us again for a little while, and Peggy hooked into a nice four pound northern using an old Musky Cisco Kid I had found entombed in a mass of lily pads I had reeled in while fishing Perrault Falls in 1972. She had made a good cast right to the edge of some lily pads in a small bay when it hit. Peggy was really excited too; it was fun to see. Maybe a little too excited, but I personally felt all the hooks that ended up imbedded in Carmen's hand were at least partially his fault. I figured any guy who took folks fishing all season should've had the presence of mind to anticipate the potential pitfalls of a fledgling angler. He thought he had; I'll give him that.

"Now Peggy," he had said as the fish was next to the boat, "what*ever* you do, do *not* move the pole, eh? No matter what happens, *do not* move the pole! I'm gonna grab the fish now, Peggy…almost got the little bugger…keep the pole still Peggy, keep it still…"

Two things happened at once. The northern, that had been reeled in as if paralyzed, suddenly must have realized it was now or never. It went berserk, splashing about for its life. Peggy had never experienced anything like it, and her instincts took over. "Yee!" She squealed, jerking the pole just as Carmen had grabbed the back of its head.

"Gaaa! Saints almighty! Gaaa! Gaaa!" Peggy had hooked Carmen better than she had the fish. Worse yet, the fish really went insane then, and between its splashing and Carmen's hysterical screams Peggy again followed her instincts, pulling even harder.

"Hit the release!" Carmen wailed, *"Hit the bloody release! Gaaa!! Quit that damned pullin' woman! Don't pull!* **Please** *quit that damned pullin'! Gaaa!!"* Then he really let fly some choice words when the hooks dug deeper. Decorum doesn't permit me to repeat even one of them.

Later on, Peggy told me the only word she thought she'd understood during all the commotion was "pull!" so that's exactly what she had done. She has always had quick reflexes too, just ask Carmen. We all heard the last things Carmen had said, and although that kind of language in front of my wife and eleven-year-old daughter wasn't appreciated, I couldn't blame the poor guy. Turned out no less than four hooks had found their mark, and I had those things as sharp as needles, even if they were a little rusty.

To his credit, Carmen corrected his string of obscenities immediately, switching to guttural, sustained growling, his eyes pretty much bugged out of his head, teeth clenched. He was shaking quite a bit as well. I thought he conducted himself as well as could be expected, considering all the blood. I also thought I may have heard a "*bless* you man" when I reached over and pushed the release button, but it was hard to tell with all the other face contorting grunts, wheezes and groans going on. Again to Carmen's credit, he never did let go of that northern until it was in the boat.

Peggy was truly sorry for all the blood and bandages, but elated over having caught her first northern. As we were casually strolling along towards the main lodge that evening on our way to supper, she again marveled at how fearless Carmen had been for not letting go of her trophy fish. Personally, I couldn't see what choice he had, since the hooks had him downright conjoined to that northern. I kept my mouth shut though; he had attained a dubious hero status, so who was I to tarnish his hard-won reputation?

***

We again had to hand it to the Totem Lodge. The food was great and our view of the lake during supper was spectacular. A brief storm rolled in, leaving behind a magnificent double rainbow that in its own way made the entire trip worthwhile, at least from Peggy's perspective. We even climbed into a small paddle boat built for two and went out into the tranquil bay by our cabin for a better look. I managed to photograph what, from then on, would be referred to as "Peggy's Rainbows".

It was one of those special times everything was so idyllic, the entire world seemed at ease with itself. Our worries and day-to-day struggles were so far out in the blue, so obscure, they ceased to display any significance at all. We had nearly our entire vacation ahead of us, and if the first day had been any indication it was going to be one of the best ever. It had been so perfect (except for Carmen's hand) I almost allowed it to lull me into a false sense of invincibility, as if nothing the Northwoods had to offer wasn't mine for the taking. I even scoffed at the notion I might not attain my ultimate goal. *Bring it on, musky gods,* I said to myself as I drifted off to sleep that first night, *because I have finally got it right...right place, right time...bring it on...*

***

The next morning my first semi-conscious thought as another gorgeous day dawned wasn't *if* we would catch anything, but when, how many, and how big. I hadn't experienced anything like that for a long, long time, and it sure was a welcomed feeling. I again thought of Dad and Don, and again couldn't wait to tell them what I was certain I had discovered; a fishing paradise, perhaps musky Valhalla itself. I had a new 35mm camera and plenty of film as well, so they would have verification of my enthusiasm.

The next two days were a repeat of the first day, except walleye fishing wasn't necessary. We had great northern action, including a thirteen pounder I nailed the third day, along a thick patch of lily pads in a bay south of Black River. I had heard even larger northern often times didn't put up much of a fight, but that fish went off so hard even Carmen thought I had nailed a musky, at least at first. He expressed disappointment halfway into the fight when he realized it was a northern. His disappointment was understandable; we had been hunting muskies for over two days and had only one verified follow. Fishing Valhalla yes - musky Valhalla? I was beginning to wonder, and Carmen knew it.

Right after we landed my thirteen pounder, Carmen mentioned a three-day tournament that was underway where the two largest fish of a given species landed in the same boat won for that particular day. You didn't even have to enter first, if I had understood Carmen correctly, just be fishing on Lake of the Woods. He no sooner mentioned that when Danny had something absolutely explode going after his bucktail, not twenty feet from where I had just caught my fish.

There had been times when I believed a fish on the other end of my line was a real lunker, only to discover it wasn't nearly as big as I had presumed; even the thirteen pounder I had just landed, although it was big, wasn't as large as I thought it would be after the battle was over. With Danny's fish, there was no doubt from the beginning he had most certainly hooked into something special. As usual, I thought it had to be a musky, but when it surfaced while charging the boat it was obvious Danny had a northern on the end of his line - a *big* northern. Even Carmen was genuinely excited, and he was used to it.

It was the first time Danny had ever hooked a truly big fish. Actually, it was only the third time any McCabe had done so since Grampa, counting the one Don hooked in 1971 on Pelican Lake, the one we never saw that had pulled our boat. Don swears that actually occurred on Carrol Lake in 1960, but I can't shake the memory of it occurring on Pelican, just west of Town Bar. There was also the one that had hit my lure by the boat that night on Lake Tomahawk. Regardless of how Danny's battle ended, at least we were able to get a good look at the brute.

He fought it to the side of the boat but it managed to keep on going, just out of reach of Carmen's net. At that precise moment, just as Carmen made a futile lunge, the northern that looked to be at least twenty pounds made a couple of jerking motions about a foot or two from the end of the net, right in front of Danny who was standing in the center of the boat. Whatever the brute had done, a small amount of slack had probably been created in Danny's line. Before he had time to react the huge fish gave a head shake, spit the lure, and was gone. We all froze, basically in shock, especially Danny. At first all he did was stand there and stare at his bucktail, unable or unwilling to accept what had just happened. Then he slowly sat down, visibly crushed.

Losing fish is part of the sport, and eventually it happens to everyone. Still, the look on my son's face tore my heart out. Losing a fish may be part of the sport, but since it was clearly the biggest fish we had thus far seen and had been so close to being landed, it was hard to take. When you are seventeen and it's your first memorable loss, it is especially devastating. I didn't even try to console Danny. I knew him well enough to realize any attempt to soothe him with encouraging words, at least until he was ready to talk, would have been as useless as they would have been unwelcome. I knew that, but Carmen didn't.

"You lost a beauty there, eh? Must'a weighed in at close to twenty pounds." He said to Danny. One look at Danny should have told Carmen to zip it, but he either didn't notice or for some reason thought a little ribbing was in order.

"Maybe *over* twenty pounds, now that I think on it. We would'a won today's tournament, I'd bet my last dollar. Probably closer to twenty-*five*, wouldn't you say, Tom?" At least Carmen must have correctly interpreted the look I shot him, one that fell somewhere between "put a freakin' cork in it" and "tipping the guide at the end of the week is optional, *eh?*" because he immediately started up the motor and headed to a different spot without another word.

Later on, Danny told me how much Carmen had annoyed him. It was a bizarre way to treat a client, or the son of a client, especially since Carmen was such a good guy. I told Danny that Carmen saw so many fish in the course of his job that he probably failed to realize just how important that particular fish had been to Danny, and to me for that matter, and he honestly hadn't thought his ribbing was anything other than good natured teasing intended to lighten the situation.

Maybe that was a good sign, I rationalized. Maybe Carmen knew we would be seeing (and more importantly catching) fish even larger than the one that got away. Regardless, we pretty much gave Carmen the benefit of the doubt. Besides, he made a promise to us after we were back at the dock that really got our attention. If I would book a fly-in to a place called Lake Carver the next day, he would *guarantee* us a musky.

Fifteen minutes later I was in Eric Brown's office, booking the flight. Peggy wasn't thrilled with the prospect, but she didn't object. Unfortunately, there wasn't room on the plane for her and Megan, but when they heard where we were going and why, neither of them wanted to go anyway, preferring the sandy beach in front of our cabin instead.

***

Lake Carver was in a remote area over twelve miles from the nearest road, or so we were told. The lake experienced very little fishing pressure for that obvious reason, and because it was, according to Carmen, strictly a musky lake. Most fly-in clients preferred a good walleye or northern lake. Carmen said he couldn't promise a wall hanger, but he maintained we would land at least one decent musky.

The flight itself was an experience. It's one thing to look at a map and marvel at the number of lakes in a particular area, and quite another to actually fly over and see them for yourself, especially when you're flying thousands of feet above Lake of the Woods and the surrounding area. How early explorers ever found their way around was a wonderment to me, and as I looked down at all those square miles of literally untouched wilderness it really brought those explorers' achievements into perspective. I recalled that someone had once asked Daniel Boone if he had ever been lost. His response was no, he hadn't, but one time he didn't know where he was for about six weeks. Looking down, that comment almost made sense; it appeared as if it would take forever to go just a few miles.

I didn't mind commercial airline travel, but tires slamming into the runway upon landing could be somewhat unsettling every now and then. A few rough landings had been downright terrifying, having felt as if the tires might end up in the fuselage or something. One of the coolest parts of our Lake Carver trip happened when the pilot touched down, because I couldn't tell when it had happened, as if there was no difference between air and water.

Once, while landing at O'Hare, the plane slammed down so hard quite a number of people shrieked, then grew deathly silent when the airliner started to yaw noticeably to the right. I hadn't screamed (well, maybe yelped a little) but I had sure squeezed my armrests. I was reminded of that when we touched down on Carver because our landing had been its antithesis. It wouldn't have even mattered if we had yawed a little bit, except maybe it would have been fun. Maybe.

Even though we were on a lake that could be accessed only by air or a twelve-mile hike through dense brush and forest, the significance of the actual distance didn't register. I just couldn't feature the concept; not twelve miles of it anyway. Even the small lake that had taken us over a mile to reach with Cecil back in 1972 seemed more remote. I knew the airplane ride had made me lose my perception of distance, but that didn't help bring it back. I figured the only thing that would put it in perspective would be to hike out; or in.

I vowed that one day I would like to hike to a lake in the interior somewhere, backpacking all necessary camping and fishing gear. I also envisaged it being closer to fifty miles from the nearest road so it would take, at the very least, several days to reach. After we were dropped off and the plane was airborne, arching away from us against the blue Canadian sky and white, billowing clouds, I thought better of it. A twelve-mile hike would probably be enough to restore my sense of being wilderness bound; at least it would make a good start. Maybe someday…

***

Carmen brought an outboard motor along and a boat was already there. We spent the entire morning casting into the narrow, deep waters of Lake Carver. It felt much the way it had on Pelican Lake when I was eleven, the year Grampa came with us. Here it was 27 years later and we were on a lake known for its muskies, a lake that was rarely fished and when it was, by just one or two boats at a time. It was a lake where our guide had guaranteed at least one decent musky, therefore I was entitled to feel as confident as when I was eleven – but not as naïve. We spent the entire morning casting all right, and ended up with nothing. Not even a lousy follow.

I was losing faith in Carmen, at least as far as muskies were concerned. Although the northern action had been great and walleye were there for the taking anytime, that wasn't why I was plunking down over $3,000 for a fishing vacation, and that was three thousand 1986 dollars.

Thus far, we had confirmed only three musky follows the whole trip, and nothing close to a strike. A fourth musky, initially estimated to be possibly over forty pounds as it slid a few feet under the surface in a quiet bay on day three, had turned out to be a beaver once it made shore and waddled away. To me, that changed things from "oh well, no one can predict when or if a musky will show up" to "what the hell's going on here, anyway?"

Still, we had an entire afternoon for Carmen to make good on his guarantee. He claimed he had *never* been skunked while musky fishing on Lake Carver, and judging from the look of determination on his face as we continued to cast away, I believed him. He had the look of an accomplished athlete who knew time was running out, a focused athlete who refused to be denied.

***

There was a young Norway spruce in the middle of where we set up for shore lunch. In itself that's not saying much when you're in the middle of unspoiled Canadian wilderness, but that tree had a unique feature - there were about five or six musky heads nailed to it. They were weathered, but no less ferocious looking.

I was standing there gawking at them as I removed that old, Musky Cisco Kid from my leader when Danny asked me to move so he could snap a picture. I told him to take the picture anyway, with me looking at the musky heads. He hated that sort of thing, people posing for pictures and everything. He fancied himself a good photographer, and there was no denying his talent along those lines. I used to believe there was no such thing; if you snap off enough rolls of film you're bound to end up with some keepers. Perhaps, except when I tried to create a great photograph, like a postcard perfect lake / forest / sunset shot and Danny did too, his always looked better. His even looked like postcards. Mine looked like I had to tell you they were postcards, like a kid's drawing when you have to ask "what is it?" Regardless, I didn't break my pose.

Carmen had brought along some walleye fillets for shore lunch. His normally cavalier demeanor, punctuated by mild mood swings that seldom veered towards the negative, were missing as he prepared the food. He was in a funk, plain and simple. I didn't blame him either. He had spent three days on supposedly some of the best musky waters in the world trying to live up to what his boss, Eric Brown, had told me to likely expect. Eric hadn't promised a musky on Lake of the Woods itself, and I had allowed wishful thinking to convince me we should have had more musky action by then, but I felt like I was getting short changed anyway, pouting really, especially when I recalled what had happened the preceding evening.

Several guys who had been at a table near ours during supper were going over their accomplishments on the water that day. Numerous musky follows, with three of them estimated to be over thirty pounds, and two strikes, one of which resulted in the boating of a 26 pound musky. The one that got away was at least 35 pounds, if not in the 40 pound class. And that had happened the day of their arrival. I went from eavesdropping to staring at them like a goof in about half a second once I heard the part about the 26 pounder and especially the possibly 40 pounder that had escaped.

It was, of course, possible they were playing around with the truth, but they didn't display the demeanor I would've normally associated with that sort of thing. They were discussing the day's events analytically, without a hint of bravado. Remember my old pal who dressed like he belonged in a Northwoods clothing catalog? Well, the guys at that table were dressed that way too, only their clothes looked well used - not worn out or sloppy, but well used, like they paid for the best stuff because they needed it to last. The quote by humorist Don Marquis, *fishing is a delusion entirely surrounded by liars in old clothes*, notwithstanding, they had an air of authenticity about them, but then you can't be sure unless you get a chance to really know folks I guess. As it turned out, those guys were the real thing.

Our waitress filled me in. They worked for Field & Stream magazine. She thought they were field editors, or maybe freelancers who just wrote for the magazine, she wasn't sure. Whatever the deal, they were going to be at Totem for only two days; apparently, that was all the time they needed to accomplish their goals. From what I'd overheard, maybe they needed only one day. I stopped staring at them after that, not that I had been in a trance to begin with. They were probably sick of strangers coming up to them once their identity was revealed, asking them a bunch of questions, or someone drunk as a wheelbarrow, going off on some boring fishing or hunting story. Anyway, that's why I stopped paying attention to them - until they went to the bar.

I figured one quick question wouldn't be too bad, unless they were insufferable snobs. If they were just regular snobs, I probably had a shot at an answer, maybe even an honest one. It was worth a try anyway.

"Excuse me guys," I said, after approaching them as they stood with after dinner drinks in hand, "mind if I ask a quick question?"

"You can ask," one of them replied, "don't know if we'll answer."

"Don't know if we *can* answer," one of the others said, eliciting chuckles all around. They seemed like okay guys.

"If you had to choose one general area on Lake of the Woods to catch a trophy musky, where would it be?" I braced myself for the all-too-often "in the water" reply, but thankfully my suspicion about snobs and smart asses was either unfounded, or I hadn't pushed those buttons yet. That, or maybe because of what they did for a living had them thinking that answering such questions by saying something like "in the water" was considered at best verbal plagiarism and at worse (much worse) an indication they lacked creative spontaneity.

Without hesitation, two of them said "Whitefish Bay" and the third guy concurred. I thanked them, put a ten spot on the bar and asked the bartender to set them up again. As I walked away, I hoped for an invitation to join them that never came. Oh well. Maybe, just maybe, I had been given something considerably more valuable than their company.

I hadn't stopped thinking about the previous evening as I helped myself to the shore lunch Carmen had prepared. I took a seat on a rock and complimented Carmen on his cooking, then asked him what he thought about Whitefish Bay for muskies.

"Good a spot as any I suppose," he replied. "Bit of a ways from Totem though, at least the southern half of Whitefish."

"Think we could give it a try tomorrow?" I asked between bites. I had to hand it to him, he was a good cook.

"Well, don't see why not I suppose. Gonna lose some fishing time with the traveling though, and tomorrow's your last day, eh?"

I told him that was okay by me, although I sensed reluctance on his part to make the journey. Still, he had agreed to go, so it was set.

***

As we resumed fishing I was proud of the way Danny never gave up. He kept casting as if the next throw had a musky waiting. Even after the wrenching experience of having lost that huge northern, he had only sat shell shocked for maybe five minutes before he had stood and fired away, one cast after another. I knew Grampa would have been proud of him as well.

The fish don't care who we are of course, or what we think we deserve, or whether our boat, truck and gear are the finest money can buy or the worst products available. All we can do is throw our casts, and see what happens. To a certain extent, fishing has the ability to place us on equal footing.

Some folks who fish for a living concur that often times it's the rookie doing what rookies are known to do that seems to land more muskies than logic would allow; but land them they do, and on more than a few occasions with an experienced musky hunter casting away right next to them. Granted, they often have an experienced guide to cover the basics, the most important being where, exactly, to fish, but it seems as if the rookie can have a disproportionately impressive catch ratio, all else being equal. I was no experienced musky hunter if having caught a few trophies was a prerequisite, but I was standing next to Danny that afternoon on Lake Carver when my theory was somewhat substantiated; when Daniel Corbin McCabe threw the fateful cast.

***

We had been casting for close to two hours after lunch, and we had nothing to show for it. Carmen had warned us Lake Carver didn't have any northern in it, so there would be no action along those lines to break up the tedium. It was muskies or nothing, and since we were expecting the plane in less than three hours, "nothing" seemed to be carrying the day. Then Danny weighed in.

We had just approached the north side of a peninsula that jutted out from the west shoreline when Danny let one fly towards shore. He hadn't made three cranks when he felt either a strike or a snag.

"I think maybe I'm snagged," he said, keeping his line taut just in case. Carmen looked over immediately.

"Then maybe you can explain why your line is headin' away from us, going against the wind? That isn't a snag, so hold tight Danny, you have a musky on!" Carmen exclaimed, causing a rush of adrenalin to shoot through us as if it were riding lightning.

Carmen's words had barely left his mouth before Danny realized he certainly wasn't snagged. The musky had been moving to our right when either the tension Danny had on it, or perhaps a jerking motion had caused it to shoot away with considerably more speed.

"Tighten down your drag, Danny!" Carmen said. Danny responded instantly, causing his rod to bow but at least it slowed down the fleeing musky.

"Keep your rod tip down, Danny, and don't permit any slack to develop, not so much as an inch if you can help it!" Carmen was as intense as I had seen him all week, his eyes staring intently at the end of Danny's line, net already in hand. The musky, however, was still a good forty feet away and fighting furiously. It wanted to head to our right, but Danny kept turning its head, making sure he kept his line tight the whole time by reeling, even when the musky was pulling against the drag and managing to peel off more line as it did so. Danny instinctively tightened the drag further still.

The extra pressure weakened the tiring musky to the extent it stopped fighting as much as it had done at the beginning of its struggle. Danny was able to reel it in the last fifteen feet or so with relative ease, and Carmen managed to get it in the net on his first attempt.

It wasn't a big fish, but had put up an impressive fight. It measured out at 30 inches and weighed a little over five pounds. It was a musky though, and although Danny told Carmen to let it go because it wasn't trophy size, it was still the biggest one landed since Grampa caught his musky out of Pelican Lake back in 1925, if just barely. Sixty-two long years had slipped by since then. I got a snapshot of Danny holding it before Carmen promptly placed it in the water. It didn't need to be resuscitated; it was gone like a shot.

I was happy for Danny, and although it appeared he felt good about his accomplishment something was missing. I suspected it had to do with the day before, and Danny confirmed my suspicions as Carmen was washing out his net before departing to a new spot.

"It wasn't a musky that got away yesterday, but it was huge, and that means a lot." Danny said, as he checked his line for frays. Even so, there was a smile on his face; catching even a small musky will do that, especially your first one.

***

We were listening as well as watching for the plane as we kept casting into a small bay along the west shoreline. I was disappointed Danny's musky had been the only action all day. It wasn't just the expense, although I thought about that too. We were on a fly-in lake with hardly any fishing pressure, and with the exception of Danny's catch we might as well have been casting into a bathtub. Not even a follow, at least any we saw. I was grumbling, feeling sorry for myself more like it, as I threw out another cast. Just as I started to reel in my grumbling ceased, and for good reason.

The huge musky closed in rapidly, coming right towards my bucktail. Due to the clear, relatively shallow water in the bay and the angle of the sun, we could see the fish perfectly. My heart began to pound as I kept reeling, mindful of all I had heard about not slowing up the retrieve, no matter what. It was one thing to acknowledge that bit of advice and quite another to follow it when a musky that appeared to be at least 50 inches long was bearing down on my bucktail.

I kept reeling and the musky kept coming, but for whatever reason it wouldn't make a final commitment. My bucktail was closing in, too, just fifteen feet or so from the boat and moving fast. The musky was right behind it, coming on strong, but the cantankerous brute wasn't quite finished being an exasperating pain in the butt. I couldn't reel anymore and had begun doing figure eights, but rather than slamming into my bucktail the huge fish shot right on by. Carmen and Danny saw it continue for about another twenty feet, turn, and come charging back.

"Keep up the figure eights, Tom!" Carmen yelled. "It's comin' on fast, keep them up!"

I kept them up all right, and the monster musky kept right on going, transforming itself from a pain in the butt to a royal pain in the ass in a matter of seconds. I quickly brought my lure out of the water and let fly in the general direction the musky had taken, but we could no longer see it. That prompted, and justifiably so, Danny and Carmen to throw their lures as well.

I had on a black Mepps Giant Killer with a gold blade and Danny had the same thing with a silver blade; I wasn't sure what Carmen called the lure he was throwing. After three or four turns on my reel the brute showed up again, and just like before showed a great deal of interest in my bucktail, but not quite enough to take a bite. Still, as exasperating as it was, it was a lot more exciting than casting into a bathtub - a fly-in bathtub that cost a substantial amount of money to fish upon to begin with.

I did more figure eights when I could no longer reel, and again it merely swam by, under the boat and out of sight again. Less than two minutes later it zeroed in on Danny's bucktail but broke off the chase half way to the boat. We spotted it again when it decided to check out Carmen's lure, but that particular lure didn't hold its interest like the bucktails had, even if said interest hadn't been enough to trigger a strike.

We were all beside ourselves with exasperation, excitement and anticipation, mainly because we had managed to get a really good look at the fish, and because of that there was no doubt expressed by any of us as to its size; it was over thirty pounds and about fifty inches long - fifty *beautiful* inches long.

I wanted that musky so bad lightning could have been streaking from every direction and I would have kept on casting. Lightning wouldn't have stopped me without scoring a direct hit, but the sound of an approaching plane did, or at least rang a death knell as far as continuing our hunt much longer was concerned.

Unbelievable, I grumbled to myself. We were on that lake all day, yet other than Danny's musky, the only other one we had come in contact with, a thirty-plus pounder that was still hanging around even when the plane touched down a few hundred yards away, would have to be abandoned. I kept casting anyway, and told Carmen I'd slip the pilot a few extra bucks for making him wait, but Carmen said that wouldn't work because there were clients on other lakes who needed to be picked up due to time restraints. Apparently, he couldn't leave and pick the other people up first because of our respective locations, and because he had probably filed a flight plan.

"A *flight* plan?" I responded. "Who needs a flight plan way the hell up here? I've seen maybe three planes in the last four days and one of them was his!"

"Well, not all of them file or even have to I believe, but lake hopping in a wilderness area comes with some risk, so that's usually the way of it, eh? Sorry Tom." Carmen said as he again glanced at his watch.

I kept casting, but unless that musky decided to quit screwing around real soon I knew "now or never" would be the latter, and the only thing at the end of our lines would be the dripping lures. I threw one right down the center of the bay, not three feet from shore and began my last retrieve. I would have continued casting, but the pilot had put one foot on the left wing, leaned out of his plane and then let out a shrill whistle that was meant to be as impatient as it sounded.

My bucktail wasn't ten feet from where it had landed when I spotted that infuriating behemoth for the last time. Instead of attacking my lure, however, it cruised along the shoreline of the bay, right past where my cast had just landed, looking more like a U-boat, a stinking *Unterseeboot* on patrol than a hungry musky, judging by its demeanor. It moved through the water, maybe two feet beneath the surface, then disappeared...or had it?

My musky mania had reached critical mass, because I suspected that fish had *wanted* us to see it, which meant, of course, I was losing my mind. Just as highly intelligent people do virtually everything for effect, perhaps certain muskies do as well, especially a particular Lake Carver musky that was by any rational appraisal a sadist.

It's impossible for a fish to understand the concept of a fly-in, right? Even a much smarter than average fish can't do that any easier than a titmouse can comprehend advanced calculus, not that I could either. No way a musky would notice a boat, keep an eye on it, then tease the crap out of the boat's occupants for about half an hour just before, coincidentally, a plane showed up to retrieve some clients. No way, no way...only a mouth-breathing lunatic would give such nonsense serious consideration, I concluded, just before closing my mouth.

***

Morning arrived and it was our last day - and Carmen was late. He had bolted down to Nester Falls the night before to visit his girlfriend, and didn't make it back until well over an hour past our usual departure time. His boss was pretty upset and offered us a different guide, but I wanted to stick with Carmen. Besides, I had been young and single once, and as far as I was concerned he had a pretty good excuse, since he hadn't been *two* hours late.

As I did every morning, I asked Peggy and Megan if they wanted to head out with us. The thought of all day in a boat far from the resort was all it took to elicit the usual "thanks but no thanks" from Peggy, and Megan had become fast friends with a girl around her age, Liz Johnson. She was from Glenview, Illinois, and for years to come those two remained pen pals. They had the run of the place, so between the beach and the video games in the main lodge, it was no contest when compared to (yawn) fishing all day.

I had spent part of the prior evening going over Lake of the Woods brochures. One in particular, a full color fold out job listed the names, phone numbers and addresses of major and not so major resorts in Ontario's "Sunset Country", and it also contained a basic map of Lake of the Woods from Sabaskong Bay to the south, to well past Yellowgirl Bay to the north and west. The Big Traverse, which made up the extreme southern section of Lake of the Woods was missing, but everything else was there. Different colored circles were used to designate areas where certain fish species were supposedly abundant, with red denoting muskies. There were only two red circles, and both were located in Whitefish Bay, and in the middle of one of them was a smaller black circle with the number 31 on it. That circle represented the only fishing resort located smack in the middle of, according to that map anyway,

Lake of the Woods' primo musky waters - Whitefish Bay - the same thing those Field & Stream guys had told me.

Number 31 caught my eye all right. It was called the Sanctuary Resort, located on an island about five miles west of the mainland. By itself that got my attention, but its location on the map really peaked my interest. Like I said the map was basic, so for the most part only the major islands were on it, including the one where the Sanctuary was located. Carmen was pretty sure he knew where it was or could find it easy enough, even though it was obvious he didn't spend much time on Whitefish Bay.

Most of his clients were after walleye in big numbers, therefore he had few opportunities or at least little reason to head into Whitefish Bay. That section of Lake of the Woods was noted for large walleye as opposed to taking one's limit day after day. Both could be accomplished, but Long Bay and Yellowgirl Bay were the more logical bets for sheer numbers of walleye, or so I was told. Besides, both of those areas were closer to Totem.

I had been told I was hiring a musky guide and I didn't doubt Carmen was one per se, but in 1986 muskies were not the Totem Lodge's specialty, not even close. In their defense, not very many clients insisted muskies were their top priority. Carmen was a good guide, and even if he preferred going after muskies he was rarely given the chance to do so. That meant we had a good guide who seldom had the opportunity to hunt muskies, as opposed to someone who did it for a living.

Except for Lake Carver, we had spent the whole vacation in Yellowgirl Bay, Long Bay and Lobstick Bay hunting muskies. We should have been concentrating our efforts in Whitefish Bay like the map and those Field & Stream guys suggested, because it couldn't have been less productive to at least try. Carmen didn't think so however, or at least had his reasons for avoiding Whitefish Bay, not the least of which was its distance from Totem, near as I could tell. Regardless, I asked him to head over to the island that had the black circle on it along with the number 31. The Sanctuary Resort island; that's what I wanted to check out.

***

We made our way past Reed Narrows, Lobstick Bay and into Regina Bay, surrounded at all times by the magnificent beauty of an unspoiled Northwoods paradise. I inhaled the wilderness air as we sped along, a natural incense of virgin forest and crackling clear water. I never tired of the heady aroma created from air so pure my only regret was I couldn't bottle and drink it.

After heading west for a while we went under the Sioux Narrows Bridge, which we were told was the longest single span wooden bridge in the world. We cruised along, past Hilowjack Island to the north as we entered Whitefish Bay. Although Danny and I had no idea what adventures awaited us and our family members upon that particular body of water in the ensuing years, our senses were overloaded by the sheer Northwoods splendor that was everywhere. I had yet to see any section of Lake of the Woods that was a disappointment, but the farther we ranged into Whitefish Bay the more impressive it became, as if it had been patiently waiting our arrival for years – decades really.

I wasn't a Native Son, far from it. Nor was I inclined to accept mystic musings as they applied to reincarnation or anything else that conveniently eluded my senses, but still…there was a feeling beyond my senses, a sensation that told me somehow, some way, I had found my way home and I was, once again as always, welcome.

Right about then the cops showed up. At least Carmen said they were cops, and it was the nicest thing he had to say about them for the rest of the day. They seemed like friendly enough guys behind their Reflecto sunglasses, but Carmen would have none of that naiveté in his boat. Even though their questions seemed innocent and non-confrontational, Carmen literally growled out his clipped answers when he felt compelled to do more than merely sneer at them. They took it in stride which kind of surprised me, even when Carmen let loose with some colorful language when they asked where Danny and I were from and how long we planned on staying in Ontario. I had to admit their questions struck me as odd, especially when they didn't even ask to see our fishing licenses. I wished they had; it would've made what I had paid for them seem more worthwhile.

Things grew a little tense when they asked if we had any alcoholic beverages onboard. Eric Brown, owner of the Totem Lodge, had warned us it wasn't a good idea to bring booze along, not even a beer or two for shore lunch, which was fine by me. I liked to tip a few after the day was over, but all beer did during the day was make me feel lethargic. Casting for muskies all day was a big enough drain, at least when nothing showed up, without adding beer to the mix.

Even so, "the local Gestapo" as Carmen had begun to call them, kept craning their necks for telltale signs, like a few dozen empty beer cans scattered about or something. It looked like one of them was going to board us for a more thorough search, which increased the tenseness I was telling you about. Carmen looked as if there was a better than 50/50 chance real trouble would ensue if Old Smokey placed so much as a foot in Carmen's boat, even if it was actually the property of the Totem Lodge. They may or may not have been cautious of Carmen, or at least of what they perceived he was capable of trying, but whatever the deal they backed off, waving and wishing us good day and good luck, with smiles on their faces; for Danny and me anyway.

The whole episode struck me as odd all right, if not downright bizarre. Carmen didn't lose the sneer for close to an hour it seemed, which perplexed me further still. Just what *had* occurred between Carmen and the local law enforcement officials over the years? I sure didn't know, but decided not to ask about things that were at least none of my business. Besides, I wanted to concentrate on Whitefish Bay, and more specifically, the muskies the map said were around, hopefully in abundance.

***

"I think the Sanctuary is on the next island south of here, over there to our left." Carmen said as he headed south, past an exposed rock reef to our right with a large navigational marker on it. It held my attention because such markers were rare; at least in hindsight that's what I assumed was the reason I specifically remembered that one in particular amidst all the countless reefs and small islands we passed.

He made a left turn into a short channel between the island he had pointed to and a similar looking island just to the north of it, then proceeded slowly south along the east shore of the nearly half mile long, somewhat narrow island. He slowed further still as we approached a small bay with a large, sturdy log dock protruding out a good sixty feet. There was another, shorter dock of similar construction about twenty feet south of the longer dock with a tired looking boathouse attached to its side, a structure that appeared to be about fifty years old, perhaps older. The roof of the boathouse facing us had THE SANCTUARY RESORT in large green letters printed on it, and it looked as though they had been painted decades ago.

It was the only structure I could see except a small cabin partially hidden in the trees and brush atop a short hill up from the docks. There were no boats around except for an old, Haas wooden rowboat, and no people. It looked like a private residence more than anything, and one that had been there a long, long time. From the look of it I wasn't sure anyone lived there at all.

Assuming I had seen enough, Carmen gunned the motor and we sped away. Too much time had already been wasted, what with Carmen being late, the long ride and the delay caused by Carmen's aquatic police force friends. If nothing else we needed some fish for lunch, and since our last day was ebbing away, it would also be nice if maybe a musky or two found our lures as well.

Danny and I landed several northern between two islands west of the Sanctuary Island. We were about to move on when about halfway into the retrieve of my last cast a musky that appeared to be in the twenty-pound class homed in on my black Mepps Giant Killer with a gold blade. Much like the one in Lake Carver, it followed closely but didn't stick around once I started my figure eight. I had reread the part in Joe Bucher's book about doing figure eights, so I knew I was doing them correctly. At least I thought I was. The muskies were the final judges and they obviously weren't in agreement, or at least not fooled. Even so, my heart wouldn't stop pounding as Danny and I kept casting away. We never saw that fish again though, but it sure was nice to get a bona fide musky follow in Whitefish Bay at our very first fishing spot.

We hit a number of other spots after shore lunch and had two more musky follows, but it was apparent Carmen didn't feel as comfortable fishing Whitefish Bay, or at least navigating it, as he did the others. He reminded me that although we hadn't had any musky success in the northern bays where we had spent almost all of our time, they consistently produced muskies as well as anywhere on Lake of the Woods. Maybe he felt that way because those were the bays he almost always fished, but we had more follows in a little over half a day in Whitefish Bay than we'd had all week, if Lake Carver was factored out of the equation.

I knew muskies were a cagey, fickle, cantankerous lot, and more cautious than any species of fish I had ever chased. Therefore, I had to believe we had stumbled onto something with Lake of the Woods, especially Whitefish Bay. I wasn't inclined to accept mystic musings all right, but still...

***

It was a little past five when Carmen made it back to Totem, which was the time we always ended the day's fishing. It would have been all right with me if we had remained in Whitefish Bay another hour or so, especially since Carmen had been nearly two hours late that morning, but I didn't mention it. It was time to say goodbye to Carmen, which also meant the time had arrived to give him his tip as well.

That's when it occurred to me I didn't know how much to give him. I had failed to ask Eric Brown what the going rate was in that regard, although I did recall him mentioning something about tips being optional or at least entirely up to the client. Whether it was me being put out over our late start or the fact we had seen so few muskies until Whitefish Bay, which had been my idea to begin with, I concluded forty bucks was about right.

After shaking hands with Carmen and thanking him for everything, I handed him two twenties. He didn't stare at the money but he stole a quick glance, enough for him to realize neither bill was at least a fifty as he put them in his pocket. He thanked me, but it was obvious he was disappointed.

About ten minutes or so later I spotted the employee in charge of the dock area, boats and guides. I asked him how much was considered a decent tip for five days of guiding. He repeated what Eric Brown had said, but I pressed him.

"Oh, if you were happy with your guide I suppose twenty a day would be considered about right."

I felt like an idiot, and a cheap one at that. Carmen had already left, or so I thought. I went into the main lodge and checked the bar just in case, but he wasn't there. He would usually be shooting pool and having a beer after a day on the water. I had a beer myself and thought about what a great time we'd had, but the more I thought about it the more guilt I felt about giving Carmen the shaft, even if it hadn't been intentional. I headed back outside since I wasn't in the mood for another brew anyway, and I was glad I did; there was Carmen, heading towards his car. I called out and caught up with him.

"What's your hurry?" I said, a smile on my face.

"Time to call it a day I guess," he replied.

"Yeah? I thought you'd be shooting eight ball and having a cold one." He offered a half-hearted smile and shrugged his shoulders. I put my hand on my forehead then spoke. "Oh, damn, wait a second. I almost forgot. Just one thing before you go, Carmen." I handed him three more twenties.

"You son of a bitch," he said shaking his head, wearing a smile that was anything but half-hearted. "You got me a good one that time, eh? And thanks Tom, I really appreciate it. Well, the money I mean." Again, the smile.

"Your welcome," I responded with a smile to match his. We shook hands again, and that time I could tell he meant it. It cost me only sixty more bucks to feel like a million of them.

***

We had really enjoyed our stay at Totem Lodge all right, and each of us had our stories to tell as we gathered for our last supper the final evening. We had taken plenty of photographs, and I couldn't wait to show Dad and Don all the northern and walleye we had landed. I knew what Don was going to ask about, however. Danny's musky would get his attention, but the follows in Whitefish Bay, and especially the size of them as well as the deranged brute (I still had my suspicions about that s.o.b.) in Lake Carver would really peak his interest.

Canada was a long haul from Illinois, but after hearing about and seeing the results of what we had experienced, I was certain Don and especially Dad would want to make the trip. Dad loved to travel, and even very long distances usually appealed to him. I asked him about that once, not expecting much of an answer. What I mean is, Dad rarely talked about things he truly cared about, as in almost never. He preferred to demonstrate how he felt about family and other things of a personal nature, but not that time. He said one of the things that helped him endure his years in Italy during World War Two (another subject he almost always avoided) was the hope he would make it home alive and relatively unscathed and be able to travel throughout the United States (and apparently Canada) with his family. He said thinking about that had helped him persevere through the more harrowing times, like when he was huddled in a foxhole with enemy artillery shells exploding all around, or firing his 105 Howitzer, returning the favor. Needless to say, he didn't need any prompting as far as heading up to Canada was concerned, but I couldn't wait to ask him anyway – talk about an easy sell.

My chance to really talk up Lake of the Woods came in one short month. We were going to try one more place in Wisconsin after all, that small fishing resort near Fifield, Wisconsin called Boyd's Mason Lake Resort I told you about earlier. Although the lakes around it were small, I had heard muskies were caught in them on a regular basis. It was "On Wisconsin" one more time.

Chapter 14

Kelly Manning, a guy I had known since junior high, told me about Boyd's Mason Lake Resort. Kelly went there often and had landed a musky on his last trip. He made it sound as if it would be unusual if one or more of us *didn't* catch a musky. He said the muskies were rarely, if ever, trophy size, but at least we would probably see some action. I had reported Kelly's experiences to Don and Dad before I had gone to Canada, and it had been all they had needed to hear so I had already booked us there. Believing a fellow Irishman aside, especially one who hunted muskies, we were nonetheless excited about our prospects. There wouldn't be any world-class muskies, but at least our prospects for getting some actual musky catching experience looked promising.

***

"You just missed Route 51," Dad informed me as I sped past our exit near Portage. After a quick check of the map Don told us not to worry, because he was fairly certain we could make good time cutting over to Route 13 and heading north to Fifield from there.

"That's a lot of miles on a two-lane road, boys," was all Dad said. After all the years Don and I had spent with the man, you would have thought we should have acquired at least a modicum of understanding as it related to how Dad's mind worked. The impatience borne from our relative youth insisted we arrive at our destination as soon as possible, and turning back to connect with Route 51 seemed counter to that goal. Dad didn't care when we would get there. After I had ignored his words and continued towards Route 13, he simply adjusted his cap a little lower on his forehead and took a nap. He knew where our impatience was taking us.

Between a few very lengthy bouts with road construction, drivers who considered anything over fifty mph the behavior of the recklessly insane, and more eighteen wheelers than we swore we had ever seen, Fifield finally came into view. Two hours that felt like four had been added to our trip, but at least we had made it, even if it was after dark. Boyd's wasn't hard to find, but when we first arrived a red flag went up when we encountered a guard-house. A *guard*house? Visions of our 1982 Upper Gresham trip came to mind. We only hoped the guardhouse didn't represent a repeat of the first day of that trip four years ago.

Any misgivings were immediately dispelled when the guard, jarred from a sound sleep, sprang to his feet when we pulled up to the small structure. If he didn't have the look and manner of a pirate with his thick black mustache, it was only because he was missing the eye patch and parrot; it wasn't because he didn't sound like one. Not so much in the classic sense, but there was an air about him that was undeniable, something that bordered between a partially subdued Yosemite Sam and a younger version of Wallace Beery.

"Didn't mean to wake you," I said after I had rolled down my window.

"Nah, no big deal. I got all stinkin' winter to sleep! Name's Frank. Who the hell are you?" His eyes grew wide as he spoke. Not crazy wide, but wide enough so you wouldn't feel all that comfortable with him standing directly behind you for any length of time until you got to know him.

"We're the McCabe's," I answered. "We booked reservations for a cabin and -"

"Yep! You're on the list all right. Gonna need a guide?"

"Well, maybe." I said. "What do they charge?"

"Ain't no stinkin' *they,* just me, and I'll cost ya thirty-five bucks a day. I know every damned inch of all the stinkin' lakes around here. You're lookin' for muskies, right? Hope so, 'cause that's the only stinkin' damned fish worth chasin', far as I'm concerned!" Frank's eyes grew incandescently wider with his last comment.

"You're hired." Dad said without further discussion. The man never ceased to amaze me.

***

Dad had turned 73 the week before, and although many would have maintained he looked it, that would have been a casual observation. Dad's hair had begun to turn gray in earnest while still in his thirties, during World War Two, and by the time he was in his forties it was virtually white. I had never known him with dark hair except in photographs, and for that reason a lot people made their misjudgment about his age and let it go at that. Actually, he rarely displayed the demeanor of a man in his seventies, at least up until that year, the fall of 1986. Even then, only the unobservant considered it pervasive. For those of us close to him, the signs of aging were relatively minimal. Still, some things were evident.

His casts were somewhat shorter, and although his natural athletic ability still produced accuracy with most throws, he was in no hurry to make them. As much as he enjoyed being on the water with his sons he tired more easily or so it seemed, although he was reluctant to admit it and was never the first to suggest we head in. Time is as Time was however, and Dad's accumulating days were no exception, although the boy in me refused to accept that completely.

***

"There, right there! Did you see that stinkin' snarly bastard?" Frank hollered as he jumped to his feet and pointed off the port bow.

"Damned near forty inches, that one! Cast over there again, Pete!" Dad's usually slow delivery while casting sped up considerably as he arched one directly where Frank was pointing. I had caught a glimpse of the musky too, and was pretty sure Frank was right about its length. It had a thick body, and had been moving aggressively before it had quickly disappeared. Dad wasn't getting any younger all right, but the gleam in his eyes told me his competitive spirit hadn't waned. He wanted that fish, no doubt about, and Don and I wanted him to catch it, too. We held up our casts so Dad's lure would be the only one out there, and crossed our fingers.

I guess deep down every musky hunter wants to be the one who hooks into a trophy fish, at least that's how I felt. If, however, there were others I wanted to see land a big musky just as much as myself, it was my son and of course Dad. I would have been happy for Don as well, but sibling rivalry with my big brother made me want to get there first. Don probably felt the same way, but being the oldest brother it wasn't as intense - maybe. One thing was for sure, Dad landing a good-sized musky would have meant as much to Don as it would have to Dad, probably more. As Dad threw another cast where Frank had made a second sighting, I hoped more than anything that musky would smack Dad's lure.

Dad had reeled his latest cast to within ten feet of the boat when the musky reappeared, charging Dad's bucktail like a runaway rocket. I had seen fish move rapidly before, but that one charged Dad's lure as fast as any I could recall with the exception of Don's first musky.

"Keep it comin', keep it comin!" Frank yelled, but Dad had run out of liquid real estate so there was nothing left for him to do but a figure eight. Dad began to do just that when his lure was at the side of the boat, but the musky didn't fall for it. It took a hard left and disappeared, just like that.

Frank said Dad hadn't executed his figure eight wide or fast enough, and we should never slow a lure down no matter what. I reminded Dad that the one musky I had landed had grabbed my bucktail while I had been doing just the opposite of Frank's advice, for the most part anyway. One thing was for sure; experts and novices agreed muskies were at least fickle, so who really knew? In the end, it's up to the musky, but Frank's words stayed with us. Good musky guides have the experience and numbers of fish from which to draw their conclusions. Going with the odds made the most sense, but at the time all I cared about was Dad's feelings. That didn't last long. One look at the slight smile on our father's face told Don and me he had just finished experiencing a genuinely exciting event.

"There'll be others," Dad said as he threw out another cast.

"Better man than me," I muttered to Don as both of us hoisted our rods and followed Dad's lead.

***

It was approaching midnight when Don and I stepped outside our lakefront cabin, poles and tackle boxes in hand. It was a magnificent night, with just an occasional small cloud whose presence was exaggerated by a full moon, accompanied by a brilliant display of more stars than we had seen since our nights camping as children in the Colorado Rockies in the early 1950's. Although it was barely fifty degrees, the absence of any breeze whatsoever made for a comfortable night.

Dad had gone to bed after our poker game had ended an hour or so before. I was the big loser as usual, having dropped the better part of five dollars after two hours of fierce nickel and dime gambling. I was hoping my luck would change once we were on the water. If there had ever been the perfect night for having a musky slam into a surface bait, we were convinced we were in the heart of it; all we had to do was convince the muskies. As we made our way down to the dock, even talking in just whispers seemed intrusively loud.

We rowed quietly to the middle of the north end of Mason Lake and began to toss five inch Jitterbugs towards the center.

There was no need to drop an anchor; we weren't going anywhere unless we began rowing again. The only thing that made the boat move a little was our casting and retrieves.

If whispering had almost seemed too loud, the bubbling and gurgling of our surface lures was almost ear shattering. We actually had to get used to the noise; it seemed annoyingly out of place. If someone had been led blindfolded to the opposite end of the lake they would've heard it immediately. If a musky smacked one of them, it would be a watery explosion of monumental proportions, no doubt about it. Still, I wished I had a surface lure that was more subdued as opposed to the PT boats we were using.

Fumbling through my tackle box, I thought maybe I had found one. It was still a Jitterbug, but about half the size of the five-inch jobs we were throwing. Don, employing his own stroke of genius, decided to switch to a shallow running Pikie Minnow, and retrieve it five feet or so behind my pint-sized Jitterbug. Strategies, decoys and plots within plots; with all that going for us we chose to believe that the muskies in Mason Lake didn't stand a chance.

It took us a few casts to get our rhythm down, although it was still a little shaky. Even so, our ploy looked impressive as my small Jitterbug gurgled along, while Don's white and red Pikie Minnow gave chase just beneath the mirror-like surface. We could see the tiny wake from my lure continue to spread until it disappeared as it made its way to shore. It was as if the moon had become a soft, subdued spotlight, making the slightest undulation so visible we wouldn't have been able to see any better if it were high noon. In a sense, daylight would have diminished the effect.

After a few hours or so, we decided to give up. "Best laid plans" and all that crap. We just sat there for a while, staring at the heavens, mesmerized. We were in the middle of a northern Wisconsin lake and experiencing the single most beautiful fall night in memory, but we had begun to fidget. Sitting on a musky lake and not casting will do that to you every time, I swear it will. I don't care if the northern lights are exploding in a once-a-century event with a herd of moose swimming by, musky addicts can't sit still without throwing a cast if it's even rumored there are muskies around somewhere.

You know it's highly unlikely you'll even see a musky when you do cast, let alone catch one. The thing is, that's guaranteed if you just sit there staring wide-eyed at the observable universe, pondering the possibility that long lost galactic civilizations once existed or something. What I mean is, would you rather see a spectacular meteor shower or the surface of a calm lake explode with a trophy musky on the other end of your line? To each their own I guess. Compared to even an average musky explosion, hundred-year events are a dime a dozen anyway to the truly obsessed. Besides, every time you reel in without a musky strike brings you that much closer to the time it will happen, maybe on your very next attempt - try holding your casts with that on your mind.

I let fly with my small Jitterbug, and Don threw a perfect cast that landed about ten feet directly behind my lure. Remember how the slightest undulation was easily detected? Envision a lump in the water the size of a softball, only it's moving with determination as it heads right where your lure had just been.

The first watery explosion occurred about where Don's Pikie Minnow would have been, but Don didn't feel a thing at the end

A Fish Like Grampa's

of his line. Before two seconds had gone by, the surface really exploded right where my little Jitterbug was chugging along. I held on for dear life, waiting for the massive tug that would be my cue to set the hook. Only it didn't happen, and although I denied having done so, Don insisted I had attempted my hookset the instant the frenzied splashing had begun.

I would have continued my denials, adding to them even, but I had no way of explaining just why my Jitterbug, that had been over thirty feet away when the explosion had first occurred, was now floating right next to us tangled up in about thirty feet of line. Once I corrected the mess we both started casting again, first at the spot where the attack had occurred and then outwards from there and back again. It wasn't until we noticed it was after 3:00 a.m. before we decided to call it quits.

***

Don didn't bring up my premature hook set again until the next morning at breakfast, but I hadn't stopped kicking myself since it had happened. Between all I had read about surface lures as well as books written by musky guides, I had known it was a common mistake to react too quickly under those very circumstances. Maybe some folks could absorb what they had read and utilize the information accordingly, but it looked like I was doomed to be the type that learned only through unforgiving experience. I swore the next time I saw splashing I would just squeeze my eyes shut until I felt something solid. That's what I swore all right, but doing it would be another matter.

We all agreed Boyd's was a nice enough place, for what it had to offer. For one thing, we had sighted what started out as an aggressive musky and had tangled with a second one, which was more than we could say about our success rate in most Wisconsin lakes we had fished. It was a well-run place, with clean cabins and grounds, good food and a friendly bunch of folks running it. The three lakes that were part of the place were all small, but that was apparently okay with the people who showed up on a regular basis. Maybe none of the fish were large, not if someone was after a thirty-plus pounder, but given enough time, at least there would probably be something on the end of your line.

***

I couldn't get Lake of the Woods off my mind, however, and wouldn't stop talking about it for long, either. Even when I knew Dad and Don had heard all they cared to on the subject, I found myself keeping a steady discourse going anyway. Don finally told me I could shut up because I had done a good job selling the place, even if I had resorted to overkill. He maintained I had already covered the subject convincingly, especially my favorite phrase: "When you wake up in the morning your first conscious thought isn't *if* you'll catch anything, but how many, when, and how big". I didn't mean I was guaranteeing muskies per se, but tying into large northern on a regular basis and even some good-sized small and largemouth bass while hunting muskies makes for a fun fishing trip as well, just not as fulfilling.

During our last night at Boyd's while playing poker we not only agreed the three of us would go to Lake of the Woods the following fall, we even set specific dates. We would go during the second weekend of September, and it was my job to book everything. I suggested we give the place that advertised musky fishing in Whitefish Bay a try, the Sanctuary Resort. Dad and Don agreed, but I knew I couldn't wait a whole year to give that place a try.

When I arrived home, I contacted the Sanctuary and not only booked our September trip, but a five day stay in late July as well; Danny and I, plus my brother-in-law Jeff Slaney and his son Will; they would be making the trip all the way from Tennessee.

I would have known what to expect if I had booked the Totem Lodge, but not the Sanctuary. I thought I had at least an inkling, at least as far as Lake of the Woods was concerned, but like so many things in life we dream for, what is envisaged all too often doesn't live up to the eventual reality. As far as the Sanctuary Resort was concerned, and especially as it pertained to the people who owned it and called it home, that assumption would become as inaccurate as any I could have ever imagined; the Quest, as it was about to enter its 27th year, was finally coming into focus. That was our belief anyway, even if we had been saying something like that for over a quarter century. Were we ready for the challenge? We had no way of knowing, not for sure, but we were ready to find out once and for all.

Chapter 15

Jeff Slaney was Peggy's older brother by seven years. He had always been the quintessential older brother to his kid sister "Squirt", and since Peggy and I had been married since our teen years some of that had rubbed off on me. He had no brothers, just two sisters, Peggy of course and her older sister Terry, so in a sense I was sort of it I suppose. Having had two older brothers of my own however, I always felt I held a certain advantage because I had learned a long time ago how to deal with the pitfalls and advantages of that particular situation.

Jeff had married a lovely Tennessee girl and had been living there for decades. He flew airplanes for a living, and although his wife Betsy called him the "FOM" (Flight Operations Manager for the State of Tennessee) and was checked out on a variety of aircraft including helicopters, I occasionally reminded him he wasn't cleared to fly amphibious aircraft. I figured once he got a taste of Lake of the Woods, he just might see the error of his ways. If he became hooked on musky fishing while experiencing the magnificence of such a Northwoods paradise, the possibilities with him being able to land on water were virtually endless, or so I reasoned.

Danny had turned eighteen, and after having had such a great time the summer before in Canada, he was definitely looking forward to our upcoming 1987 trip. Because they lived so far apart, Jeff's and Betsy's son Will and Danny never had much of an opportunity to get to know each other very well. They were only a couple years apart with Will being younger. A Canadian fishing adventure held the promise of being the perfect opportunity for them to become friends as well as being cousins. Even though I had obviously known Jeff since marrying his kid sister twenty years before, we hadn't had much of a chance to hang around together for the same reason Danny and Will hadn't. A five-day fishing trip seemed as if it would be perfect for all of us.

Jeff had questioned me about the Sanctuary Resort, wondering if perhaps we wouldn't be better off going to the place Peggy and I had spoken so highly of, the Totem Lodge. I appreciated and somewhat shared his concern, since I didn't know much about the Sanctuary Resort except that it was on its own private island located in the heart of what were supposedly the best musky waters in Lake of the Woods. That had been enough for me to want to give the Sanctuary a try, but not Jeff so much. I couldn't blame him, since he wasn't maniacally obsessed with catching a world class musky. His priorities were along the lines of a father wanting to spend quality time with his teenage son in a place like the Canadian wilderness; to enjoy the entire experience and not just, for the most part anyway, be focused on catching fish, or at least not just muskies.

Danny and I, on the other hand, had been there and done that already. We certainly wanted to do it again, but most of all we wanted large muskies. Failing that, at least a few huge northern, and failing *that,* anything we could get our hooks into.

Danny hadn't forgotten the twenty-plus pound northern that had spit his lure at the side of Carmen's boat, that's for sure. Whenever the subject came up you could see a change come over him. It wouldn't last long, but the fact he had tasted that particular agony was apparent. He was determined to make up for it and knew Lake of the Woods was as good a place as any, if not the best place, to do just that. Throw a good old-fashioned musky camp in the heart of Whitefish Bay into the mix, and the odds looked even better.

***

It never failed. The last three hours of the drive from Des Moines always made up for the monotony of the previous eight or nine. We made record time by getting to Sioux Narrows in less than eleven hours. Bringing people across the border and into the Northwoods splendor Ontario has to offer was another thing that made the last few hours so worthwhile. I especially got a kick out of watching and listening to Will. He had never been farther north than Chicago, so things were really a new and exciting experience for him.

We drove past Nestor Falls with its pontoon planes sitting on the water, and I didn't waste the opportunity to point them out to Jeff, who seemed to remain basically unimpressed with the entire concept. I had to admit not having his own plane would present somewhat of a financial problem, unless Jeff was willing to drop us off in a rental plane, take it back to save money and hike his way to a fly-in lake for a week or so. He worked out a lot and enjoyed nature, as in hiking through it I assumed, but my suggestion didn't merit so much as a response from my brother-in-law, at least at first.

"Tell you what," he finally said. "You buy a floatplane, I'll learn to land it." Good point; you don't hire pilots to fly airplanes as much as you do to land them.

We continued north, catching glimpses of Lake of the Woods from time to time. Occasionally we would see billboards advertising the four and five star resorts in the area. We drove by a couple of them too, and both Jeff and Will remarked at how inviting they appeared to be.

"So," Jeff remarked, "you've never actually been to the Sanctuary Resort?"

"Well, we pulled up to it in a boat." I answered as I drove along, perhaps ten miles south of Sioux Narrows.

"Hmm. Was it similar in appearance to the ones we just drove by?"

"Hard to say. We only got a look at a boat house and a couple of docks."

"There was that small cabin up the hill, Dad." Danny added.

"Oh yeah, the cabin. Couldn't really see it through the trees and brush very well though. Anyway, we're looking for Fickas Road. After that, look for a sign that says The Sanctuary. It'll lead us to the owners' winter quarters and their mainland dock. One of their sons is supposed to meet us there. I believe his name is Rob."

***

We found Fickas Road, mostly washboard that was overdue for several loads of new gravel. My Dodge van was shaking big time, even though I had recently equipped it with new heavy-duty shocks. Rather than a big, beautiful billboard announcing our arrival at the Sanctuary, we instead spotted, and just in time, a small sign with the place's name that had apparently been painted on quite some time ago. We turned in, and the road seemed even bumpier, probably because in my haste I was going too fast. Trees and brush were everywhere, as were a few old, rusted vehicles that obviously hadn't run in years and several pieces of discarded machinery that also looked as if they had been there before any of us were even born. If there was any paint left on anything, it was only because Mother Nature hadn't completed her job disintegrating it yet.

"Hey Uncle Tom, sure doesn't look much like those other places we saw, does it?" Will said as he gazed out the window. His observation wasn't lost on any of us, and I could feel skeptical eyes on the back of my neck.

"It's not supposed to be a fancy resort or anything," I replied, as much for my benefit as anyone's. "Besides, the Sanctuary itself is on an island at least five miles into Whitefish Bay. A little rustic probably, but just what we're looking for." My words sounded more confident than I felt. As we looked around, it was apparent the owners didn't place a whole lot of stock in first impressions. That may or may not have been a good sign.

We made it a little farther and pulled into the parking area about the same time we noticed a young guy in his mid-twenties or so coming up from a large, wooden dock that went a good fifty feet into a sheltered bay. He waved as he approached. We piled out of the van and headed down to meet him.

"You must be the McCabe party then," he said, offering to shake our hands. His name was Rob Horley, the son of Robert Sr. and Carol Horley, the owners of the Sanctuary Resort.

After introductions were made all around I backed my van onto the wide, solidly built dock and we loaded everything into

Rob's boat. It was a good-sized V hull with a level floor, and it had the electronic equipment many of the top guides were using in 1987. It was nothing overly fancy, but it appeared to be a perfectly equipped fishing boat.

It was apparent from the beginning Rob Horley really knew what he was doing. He placed everything in their proper spots from a weight distribution perspective and took off, maneuvering his boat as effortlessly as a Chicago cabby navigating the Loop during rush hour. I asked him about a rusting tugboat that was among the reeds, propped up in shallow water near the shore of Horley's dock. It looked as if it had been there for years, and for good reason.

"Oh, that old thing." Rob said offhandedly as if he hadn't taken notice of it in years, even though it was large enough to be spotted from a commercial jet. "It was used years ago to transport log booms. Been awhile, though." That came as no surprise. If he had said it had been there for several decades no one would have doubted him.

We covered the fives miles or so in good time, although the rolling waves in the open areas made for a bumpy ride. As soon as Rob turned left between the north end of Highrock Island and the island that was home to the Sanctuary Resort, I knew where we were. The two sturdy, wooden docks came into view along with the weathered boathouse I remembered. Even though it didn't appear to be an overly protected bay, the waves calmed considerably as we approached the two docks. The small, shallow bay we entered was nestled in the leeward side of the island, near its southeast corner.

A young boy who appeared to be around ten years old was waiting on the dock next to the boathouse, perched on a three-wheeler with a cart. He was Rob's kid brother, Peter. They wasted no time getting our belongings unloaded and up the short hill to the small, rustic cabin set in the trees with a great eastern view of the wide channel between their island and Highrock Island. There were a few discarded buckets and other items stuck under the front porch, and looking around I was struck by the rustic appearance of our surroundings.

There was no indoor plumbing, just outhouses, and other than the specific areas where a structure had been built, the island remained virtually untouched. There were no indications that any effort had been made to make it even pretend to look like it was in competition with the four and five star resorts in the general area, but that was okay; probably.

Regardless, my initial overall impression was one of ambivalence. It wasn't as if we were staying there for considerably less money than the other places were charging. Besides, the other places had hot and cold running water, showers, and indoor toilets. They had dining rooms with a variety of menu items prepared by chefs, as well as wine lists and well-stocked bars. They had pool tables and video games for the kids, well-manicured grounds while still maintaining a Northwoods ambiance, for the most part.

Noticing some rusting cans and other debris jammed further back under the porch, and a few other old mechanical devices scattered about amidst the untouched brush, I began to wonder just what I had gotten us into. Jeff was wondering the same thing, and although I didn't blame him, I was beginning to appreciate something - it was as if we had stumbled across a 1930's era Canadian fishing camp, and that was more than okay by me as long as the fishing came close to reflecting that era as well. Still, indoor plumbing would have been nice...

Danny and Will didn't care one way or another. As soon as our gear was in the cabin and Jeff and I were following Rob down a timeworn, winding path to the main lodge across the island, the two of them took off to walk the island's entire shoreline. That was no small feat; I estimated the island to be at least twenty heavily wooded acres, and the shoreline was, for the most part, very rocky and covered with thick brush and trees of all sizes.

The main lodge was a one-room log building, with a little over a thousand square feet of living area, which is exactly what the owners, Bob and Carol Horley, used it for from ice-out to ice-in. Their sleeping quarters were upstairs; the only access being through a hole in the middle of the ceiling with a ladder placed in it. The main floor served as a dining room for guests, and also had several long tables along the east wall for magazines and books.

There were also homemade crafts and lures their youngest boy Peter had made. Some of Peter's creations looked like what you might expect from a boy his age, but a few of his handmade, wooden lures sure didn't; especially one he called Fish Rouser. It resembled a Lazy Ike, but Peter's version was considerably larger, fatter actually, designed to catch muskies and had large treble hooks to keep them hooked. As much as I was impressed with his obvious carving abilities, the paint job was downright artistic. I picked it up and noticed the kid was watching me. He was shy, but not enough to stop watching.

"So you made this?" He smiled and walked over.

"I made all of these." Maybe he wasn't so shy after all. Either that, or he knew he was gifted beyond his years. Whatever it was, I bought the lure and a few others as well. Then I noticed a hand carved wooden container. It had been made by hollowing out a five-inch diameter section of a hardwood limb, near as I could tell. It was about six, maybe seven inches high, but it was the amazing job Peter had done with its lid that impressed me most of all. It had been cut from the section and carved so perfectly it went precisely into the top and not only stayed snugly in place, but the artwork was so well done it was hard to believe a boy his age had done it; there was a knot he had transformed into a sun setting on the horizon with pine trees in the foreground, as was the island the trees were growing upon. The detail was amazing. I asked him how much he wanted for it, but only because I needed to know how much money to give him, which I did. I had to believe his creations would only get more refined, especially his hand carved lures, as the years went by; I was right, too. To this day, Mr. Peter M. Horley makes some of the finest hand carved wooden lures you are likely to find anywhere, and the muskies they have caught prove it.

There were also photo albums on the long tables, some of them with pictures decades old, of clients holding up some very impressive fish, especially muskies. Larger, framed photographs were on the walls, most with men hoisting even more muskies; *big* muskies. All of a sudden I didn't care about indoor plumbing, not even a little. If the photographs were any indication of what we could expect to catch, I would have been happy staying in a tent all week, and at that stage of my life I had grown out of tents, or at least spoiled by cabins.

The real clincher came when I had a chance to have a conversation with both Bob Horley and Rob, who was the one Danny and I would have as our guide. Jeff and Will were going to have another of Bob's boys, also named Will, guide for them.

"Been specializing in muskies for decades." Bob told me in response to a question I had asked him. In his sixties, he was as weathered looking as the Sanctuary itself, which, as it turned out, wasn't his only source of income. He and his boys were also loggers, and accomplished hunting guides as well. He may have looked weathered, but I suspected he could still carry his own with men half his age. He picked right up on my musky obsession, understanding it completely.

"If there's a body of water that contains world record muskies, and more than just a few, it would be Lake of the Woods. I'm not saying they're easy to catch, or that you're likely to even see one that big, much less hook into her, but they're out there. I know, because I've seen a few." Bob spoke with the authority of a man who looked you straight in the eye, a look that removed all doubt he was telling you anything but the truth. I liked and trusted him immediately.

"There's never any guarantees when it comes to muskies," he went on to say. "Northern, walleye, bass and lake trout maybe, but not muskies. Even in the old days when my father first homesteaded this island back in the early 1930's, muskies were the exception, not the rule. Back in those days, we could row once around the island and have so many northern, walleye and bass, the bottom of the boat was barely visible, if at all."

"That's a lot of fish," I said. "What did you do with them all?"

"Boiled most of them in a large iron kettle and fed them to our sleigh dogs. Those huskies would devour them in nothing flat. Sure threw off a smell you weren't likely to forget, but the dogs sure didn't mind."

"But not very many muskies?"

"There was no telling when, or even if you'd see a musky, not unlike today, to a degree. We know where to look though, I can promise you that."

I was beside myself. I felt like I was a child again, squirming in bed while waiting for the first rays of sunshine to appear on Christmas morning.

"It would be fantastic to hook a world's record," I said to Bob and Rob, "but any decent sized musky would be awesome. The biggest one, well, the *only* one I've ever caught was only twenty-nine inches, and as fights go it wasn't all that great."

After I said that I caught a gleam in Bob's eye, one coupled with an expression that bordered between being mischievous and highly enlightened. It wouldn't be the last time I'd see that expression, either.

"Well, just maybe we can help you improve on that," he said, that look still gleaming in his eyes.

***

Rob came back with us to our cabin where I showed him my musky fishing gear. He appeared somewhat reserved, not straying an inch from a client-guide relationship, at least at first. He made a few remarks about the number of lures (baits, as he called them) I had brought along, but I couldn't tell if he was impressed or joking around. I considered that a good sign either way. When he got a load of my fishing rod, however, his true personality started to emerge.

Last year, just before our trip to Totem, I had purchased the stoutest Ugly Stick Shakespeare had the audacity to make, unless they had a deep-sea trolling rod I didn't know existed. Mine was a bumblebee yellow job called the Tiger Pro, and it was basically a pain in the ass to cast. There was no finger rest for your casting hand, but at least the butt was a good eighteen inches of high quality foam-like material so the grip was good, especially when wet. Compared to the weight of a graphite rod, the thing felt like it may have been re-enforced with a section of rebar.

"If you tire of musky fishing you can always use this if a pool table floats by, eh?" Rob said as he hoisted it up for further appraisal. "You actually plan on casting all day with this then?" He had a slight smile going as he spoke, and gave a casual glance to gauge my reaction. I told him a little about the year before, and that I had used it all that week.

"Besides," I added, "if I only get one shot at a genuine trophy or maybe a world record, I'd rather have too much pole than too little."

He gave me a look that seemed to say "you're obsessed all right, but could use some direction when it comes to choosing your musky rods".

Rob asked us if we wanted to go out for a couple of hours before dark. Jeff and Will said they would wait for morning, but Danny and I were up for it.

***

Until that evening, my entire experience as it related to guides had consisted of Cecil, Bobo the Clown, Carmen, and of course Frank from the year before. Carmen and Cecil had been great for walleye and northern. Frank had done a good job, considering the waters he had to work with, and at least Abner had supplied a comedic effect, but what happened with Rob Horley in a little over two short hours was the beginning of a genuine musky hunting education.

He started out by inspecting everything Danny and I had brought with us. Nothing escaped him; leaders were okayed or dismissed as being inferior, our lines were checked for frays, hooks on all of our lures were inspected (Rob indicated my hook sharpening skills definitely needed work) and our reels were thoroughly checked out as well. He not only adjusted both our drags, but had us redo it ourselves so we would be able to experience the right feel.

After everything had been examined, he told us let out our lines with just our leaders tied on (he showed us a couple of superior knots as well) then gunned his motor and took off. When almost all of our line was out, he had us reel in against the pressure as he sped along. After having done that our lines were tighter to the spools than ever before.

Rob said it would also keep our lines level on the spools and cut down on backlashes, as would the adjustment of our line tension as it related to our lure's weight. All those years, and I had never known what that little knob on the side of my reel was for. I probably should have kept that to myself, judging by the look Rob gave me. If he still wondered whether he was dealing with a novice, I had answered that question all right, and more than once.

He took us to a spot out in the middle of the lake somewhere, stopped, then fired up a much smaller motor he used for trolling. He sat right on top of the large motor, steering the smaller one with his foot as all three of us began to cast directly towards the specific areas Rob pointed out. He preferred we all use a different type lure, at least at first.

Danny and I were really into our bucktails however, especially our trusty Mepps Giant Killers with black tail dressings and gold blades. That specific lure had caught the overwhelming majority of our fish the year before, so naturally we both had a great deal of confidence in them. I still couldn't pass them up when I found them in tackle shops. By then I must have had at least two dozen still in their boxes, with another boxed dozen or so with silver blades. I had most of the other colors as well, but for the most part they stayed in my tackle boxes. Even so, only one musky had been caught the year before using Giant Killers, but I didn't think that was the lure's fault. Rob didn't either per se, but he knew the value of variety or at least appreciated it more than we did. If nothing else, he wanted us to use different colors and different types of bucktails depending on success rates.

He said red was a very good color, and strongly recommended the bucktails called Eagle Tails. George Wahl was the name of the guy who owned the company, and he was a good friend of the Horley family. He was also the president of a Muskies Inc. chapter back in Minnesota. He spent a lot of time in Whitefish Bay and usually stayed at the Sanctuary. He had plenty of muskies to his credit, having caught almost all of them with Eagle Tails. Rob handed me one, and I had to admit they were very well built. From the heavy gauge wire and hooks to the amount of tail dressing, they were definitely a top quality musky lure.

I preferred the thick, willow leaf style blade used on Mepps Giant Killers to the more rounded, fluted blades on the Eagle Tails though. I liked the way the Mepps would cast and retrieve, and the polished blades threw off an excellent flash. Still, I wanted to get some Eagle Tails, although I wasn't sold on the large, single hooks George Wahl insisted upon using. They were very sturdy, so having one bend on you was highly unlikely, but I preferred treble hooks. It would be easy to switch, although Rob maintained there was a lot to be said about a single hook, especially as it pertained to *keeping* a fish hooked.

I couldn't see how fewer hooks could be an advantage. Even if a single hook had better holding ability, what good did that do if the fish wasn't hooked to begin with? I sure didn't know. I would rather have a semi-good hook set than no hook set at all. It was the first time I questioned someone who had considerably more musky hunting experience than me, which is almost always a bad idea. Still, I was going to stick with treble hooks until I was convinced otherwise.

Rob said he understood my concern with the single hooks, and although it may have been true not as many fish would actually get hooked, it wasn't a large disparity and besides, once a single hook grabbed hold there weren't two other hooks next to it a musky could use, as they sometimes did, to help it dislodge the original hook. I had a hard time picturing that, but not a hard time believing Rob knew exactly what he was talking about.

Rob's knowledge of Whitefish Bay was even more impressive than his knowledge of other aspects of fishing. To me, it was a vast, confounding body of water with more tree studded islands than I cared to count, let alone memorize. Very few of the submerged rocks were marked, and the ones that were could be found only in the main channels, so the loss of lower units wasn't uncommon for those who didn't know their way around. Even those who did could get fooled, depending on water levels and other factors. Not Rob though. He could cover mile after mile and not even come close to hitting anything. When he had been as young as eight he had often explored many of the islands in the general vicinity in a standard sized fishing boat, often by himself.

I had always prided myself with having a good sense of direction, but once we were on the water and away from the Horley island I would become turned around after having gone just a couple of miles, especially if it was cloudy. I wasn't alone. One time an obviously confused fellow in a sharp looking boat hailed Rob over, asking just where, exactly, he was. When told, the guy gave Rob a blank stare, then turned the map he was holding *upside down* and began studying it again, more confused than ever. Now that's lost.

Rob's father said you could take him anywhere on Lake of the Woods after blindfolding him and he would find his way home, and if he had a boat equal to yours he would get there first. Bob wasn't bragging, because I had asked him how well he knew the lake in general. I was convinced if anyone would have been able to make a contest out of it however, it would have been Rob, at least in Whitefish Bay; Bob Horley knew the *entire lake* that well, and if anyone doubted him and wanted to make a friendly wager, well, they had better be able to afford losing.

We worked three different underwater rock reefs whose existence I never would have been able to ascertain, and that was only my first problem. After Rob pulled up to them, he pointed out specific rock formations where he wanted us to place our casts. Half the time I couldn't even see them, and I had always thought I had good eyesight. Sometimes the angle of light and time of day combined with certain wave patterns made the rock structures virtually invisible, but since Rob knew exactly where they were, it didn't matter. He made a complete 360 around each reef, sometimes twice, and if there wasn't a follow we were usually off to the next one.

On my second cast after we had arrived at the third reef, something smacked into the Bagley Rob had told me to throw. It wasn't a light tap either, and just like that the fight was on! My pool cue of a pole didn't bend very much, but enough to get Rob's attention, and although he preferred to land most fish by hand, including muskies, he immediately went for one of his nets; he had two – one standard sized and another that was huge. I tried to horse in whatever I had hooked, but it shot away from the boat taking a good twenty feet of line with it. I tightened down my drag a touch and reeled back those twenty feet and a good deal more. Before long I had a fair sized northern by the side of the boat.

Rob no sooner had it in his burlap bag when Danny nailed another northern that had hit his bucktail. It was about five pounds or so, and both Danny and I mentioned what a good spot Rob had found for us. Rob, however, didn't share our enthusiasm, even though he knew we wanted our full limits of northern so we could bring the fresh fillets home. He also knew that would in no way be a problem even if we had just one day of fishing instead of the five I had booked.

"With this many northern swimming about, especially on this reef, it's a good bet there's likely no sizable muskies around." With that he gunned his engine and we were off to the next spot.

We had told Rob we were after muskies, and that was what he had every intention of finding for us. As much as we wanted to hook into a musky, Danny and I also enjoyed the northern action. I was so used to getting entirely skunked over the years that anything was better than that, therefore good-sized northern were considerably better than having nothing happen. I had been fully conditioned not to catch muskies, and had very rarely even seen them. That justified appreciating northern even more, especially when I had to believe most spots that held northern held muskies as well. We'd go after northern, and any muskies would be a bonus; a self-defeating mindset to be sure, but one ingrained from years of reeling in nothing but a wet lure and maybe a few weeds, and you know you're on a losing streak when even a weed generates a little excitement.

Rob didn't buy into that philosophy at all. He and his clients had landed plenty of big muskies because that was obviously what Rob concentrated upon when clients told him they wanted musky action. He knew where the odds were best, and experience had shown him that it usually wasn't the same places where scores of northern were hanging around, especially if they were smaller northern; those little guys were there to eat, not be eaten.

Rob continued to take us to open areas with submerged rock reefs until darkness fell. He was visibly disappointed we hadn't raised a single musky. By then Danny and I had landed five northern between us so we felt pretty good, yet regardless of our good moods Rob all but apologized anyway.

"There's any number of good spots we didn't have time to visit this evening," he said as we headed back to the Sanctuary. "I've spotted a few big muskies hanging around some of them recently, and they have to eat sometime. The trick is being there when they do."

I liked Rob's style, especially his determination. When we made shore, Danny and I showed off our catch to Jeff and Will. They were nice looking fish all right, but none of them were muskies.

***

Although we were paying guests, gentle reminders made it clear there was a time-honored system in place we were encouraged to follow. A hearty Northwoods breakfast, a specialty of Carol Horley's, was served at seven. It was no time to worry about calories or cholesterol. That would have been nearly impossible to do anyway, once the enticing aroma that permeated the single room main lodge got a hold of us the instant we stepped inside.

Jeff, who was an avid runner and kept a close watch on his diet, realized even his self-control had its limits. Not that anyone blamed him. On my doctor's advice, I had been forced to give up eggs, butter and basically all of my favorite foods or to at least cut way back on them. Yeah, right, like that was going to happen while I was on vacation, sitting in the dining area not far from Carol Horley's kitchen. Four eggs, six bacon strips, a stack of blueberry pancakes (made with fresh picked Canadian blueberries) with real maple syrup and gobs of butter, cold whole milk and cream for my coffee, toast with even more butter and strawberry preserves with as many sausage links that I cared to devour and I was about ready for our first morning on the water, with or without a cardiologist onboard.

Jeff was considerably more conservative than me. In other words, he hadn't behaved like a gluttonous pig. He let me know it too, in true, condescending big brother-in-law fashion. Getting my attention as I was shoveling in another mouthful of delicious heart attack on a fork, he motioned to Rob who was sitting at their family table. His mother had placed a huge bowl of steaming oatmeal in front of him, which he had begun to eat without so much as a word.

"See?" Jeff said so only our table could hear. "That's why he's in such great shape. Works hard all day and eats sensibly." Jeff glanced with disgust at his half-eaten bacon and eggs then held a finger up for Carol. "You know, I'd rather have a bowl of what Rob's having if it's not too much trouble." He asked.

"No trouble at all," Carol answered with a smile, as she disappeared into her kitchen. When she returned, her hands were full but all the plates she was carrying were for Rob. Eggs, bacon, pancakes - well, you get the picture. Without changing expression, Rob dug right in.

"Your oatmeal's almost ready," Carol said to Jeff, still smiling the smile those who love their overall situation are inclined to display, as she walked away with his half-eaten plate of *real* food.

"Live it up, man," I said to Jeff as I stood up slowly and pulled out a Player's non-filtered cigarette. "Think I'll smoke this outside." I would do that, smoke while on vacation, then not touch them until next year's fishing trip. "And good luck with all that oatmeal." I knew he'd finish it though. One thing about my brother-in-law; he seldom shied away from a challenge, even if it turned out to be a self-inflicted wound. Besides, I was pretty sure he really liked oatmeal.

Breakfast at seven, pull away from the dock at eight. That was the preferred routine. If anything needed doing prior to the eight o'clock departure, it was appreciated by those who were on time that it was done by eight or close to it.

Danny and I would again be going out with Rob, while Will and Jeff were getting ready to set out with Rob's brother Will. He was a friendly guy, and close to Rob's age. Like Rob, he knew exactly what he was doing. The Sanctuary Resort, and all it had to offer was coming into focus, and I had a good feeling about all of it. Good things, really good things, were about to happen. I sure hoped so anyway. It was a somewhat breezy, beautiful summer morning with huge cumulous clouds accenting the clear blue sky. All we needed now was a little action.

**

"Dad - check that out." Danny said as he pointed his rod tip to the water directly in front of him. Rob had already spotted the twenty-plus pound musky that had made a move towards Danny's bucktail before veering away at the side of the boat.

"Do a few figure eights, Danny, then throw one to your left, thirty feet out towards eleven o'clock." Rob said. "Tom, aim one to the right, same distance, between two and three o'clock."

I hadn't seen the fish, so I started to do figure eights off the other side of the boat before following Rob's instructions. He watched me do two of them, surveying the immediate area intently. He told me to cast again, but I did another figure eight instead.

"That's enough Tom, now cast!" Rob said. He knew the value of figure eights, but he also knew when to abandon them for a higher percentage maneuver. Another lesson learned - when Rob said to do something, *do* it, and ask questions later, if at all. That time however, we never saw the fish again, which I suspected may have been my fault.

We pounded away at underwater rock reefs and around small islands with submerged rock extensions for the rest of the morning. We had another musky follow but no northern in our boat. Rather than being disappointed, Rob seemed somewhat encouraged. Muskies were moving about, checking out our baits he said, and that was a good sign. Well, okay, I thought, but wouldn't a few decent sized northern be even better along with the musky follows? At first I assumed Rob sensed my frustration, but that wasn't it.

"Hmm, looks like it's about time for shore lunch and we're lacking the entrée. No matter. Finger Bay's not far off." With that, Rob gunned the motor and we sped away.

"There's a decent reef that runs the length of the section of water in front of here," Rob said as he pulled into a long, narrow bay with a high cliff on one side. "We'll hit it after lunch. Pulled a few nice ones from there." And he definitely wasn't talking about northern.

After stopping he pointed to the center of the bay. There was an abundance of mostly submerged weeds that ranged from two to five feet beneath the surface. Half an hour later we had eight northern in the boat. Danny and I had two apiece and a few strikes we hadn't hooked, and Rob had caught four jigging deep into the weeds with a white Mr. Twister. None of his strikes got away. The only reason he hadn't caught more was because he had stopped fishing after ten or fifteen minutes.

"What's the name of this bay again?" I asked.

"Finger Bay, we call it." Rob answered with a slight smile that disappeared as fast as it arrived. We would come to find that not every location had an official name, but thanks to the Horley family and other locals, names were abundant nonetheless, like a large rock called Guppy's Nose, named after a long dead, native fishing guide.

"Must be hundreds of fish in here," I said, impressed with Finger Bay.

"Northern, mostly." Rob said. "I've taken some really big ones out of here in the spring. Not very many muskies though. If they're around, it's usually out by the reef."

As we sped away to meet up with the other boat, Rob told me the biggest northern he had pulled from there had been in the twenty-five to thirty-pound range. He said it wasn't an uncommon occurrence either, at least in the spring and early summer. Not many muskies though, so Rob didn't spend much time there unless he needed a few fish for shore lunch or his clients weren't after muskies, or they were bored from not catching anything all day. And Finger Bay was just one of numerous such spots.

I didn't say anything to Rob, but after so many years of not catching muskies, at least big ones, it felt as if the possibility of doing so ranked right up there with winning the lottery or something. It happened to a select few, but that was about it. If we were catching northern, at least it was a big improvement on what we had been doing before discovering Lake of the Woods.

Besides, I continued to stubbornly (and foolishly) rationalize, muskies didn't just hang around rock reefs and similar structure, right? They entered bays, and crossed the mouth of bays and other areas where the probability of catching northern existed. I still wanted to catch a large musky more than ever, but it was so much fun catching anything, I continued to doubt (again foolishly) it was less likely large muskies would be caught where northern were in abundance. Muskies were caught in those areas from time to time, no doubt about it; except Rob knew we were going to be there only five days, not five months, so going against the odds made no sense at all. I didn't appreciate that at the time, but Rob sure did.

He also knew where our odds were greatest as far as hooking into a truly huge musky was concerned, and that was where he had every intention of spending the majority of our time. If we had told him we weren't interested in muskies as much as upping our catches of northern, he would have changed tactics. Like before, I was still resigned to catching *something* and any muskies would be a bonus, but I kept that self-defeating attitude to myself. Rob probably suspected I felt that way, but he also knew from experience how we would feel once he had guided us to a genuine trophy musky. For me that remained thirty pounds or bigger, or in other words "not likely". For Rob, that was a big "can do" and he was determined to prove it to us.

He turned out to be as good a cook as he was a guide. The brilliant blue skies with large white clouds probably weren't more beautiful than the skies over Des Moines, but as I gazed upwards it sure seemed like they were. One glance at the rest of my surroundings verified what everyone who has been lucky enough to have a shore lunch on Lake of the Woods already knew; it was one of the most beautiful places on Earth, if not beyond.

I again marveled at the foresight and impressive stewardship that had been displayed by the Canadians for not allowing the overwhelming majority of islands to be sold off or otherwise developed. There were a few that were privately owned and that was fine (I would love to own one myself) but with the overwhelming majority of the islands untouched, the pristine Northwoods experience that was the essence of Lake of the Woods would remain unspoiled for at least decades to come, just as they had remained unspoiled for centuries.

After setting everything up, Rob prepared the fresh northern fillets with the Y bones removed, a variety of side dishes cooked over an open fire, and brought out Carol Horley's homemade desserts to finish things off. It sure made for one belt busting shore lunch experience. The only trouble occurred after lunch. Even after several cups of strong, campfire brewed coffee it was still a chore to remain alert the next few hours. I was so stuffed it was all I could do to keep from nodding off.

With Rob Horley as our guide however, that wasn't an option. We'd hit the reefs, pound the daylights out of them and hit some more. If I had thought musky hunting wasn't actual work, I no longer held that opinion, and neither did Danny. By the time five o'clock rolled around we were tired but not defeated, even though we hadn't seen another musky all day. As it turned out, however, there could be a big difference between mid afternoon musky fishing and going out after supper.

***

Even though it was half passed nine that evening, it was still light out. Back in the States, at least in the Midwest, it was dark or close to it by nine, even during the summer solstice. In Whitefish Bay, that didn't happen until ten p.m. or so, at least that time of year.

Although we had put in eight hours during the day, the three hours after supper didn't seem like as much work somehow. For one thing, the fishing was usually better. It was also relaxing to experience the approach of nightfall out on the water, as evening gave way to darkness. After that happened, however, things changed.

Once the sky was black and filled with countless stars, the concept of infinity emerged in a way the daytime sky could never duplicate. Nighttime sounds, especially splashes, seemed to take on mysterious characteristics. It was as if we were intruding upon a nocturnal wilderness world that may or may not have welcomed our presence, or at least seemed compelled to remind us we had entered a somewhat spiritually symbolic place, Northwoods style. Pleasantly surreal you might say, bordering on the mysterious. It was as though there were two distinct realities, one bathed in familiar sunlight and one shrouded in at least incertitude.

The farther we traveled from the Sanctuary, the more those sensations grew. If Rob felt the same way it wasn't apparent. When it was time to head in, he would fly along every bit as fast as if it were high noon, regardless of our location. For him, it was like heading home upon familiar streets of his hometown. We rarely saw other boats even during the day, and that was especially true at night.

It was approaching darkness that evening when it happened. Rob had taken Danny and me to a sheltered rock reef that had produced a large northern and at least two musky follows; the kind of spot that you always felt confident fishing because of past success while it fueled the anticipation of more to come. Rob had no sooner cut the motor when I let fly with a special bucktail I had more or less invented. Rob got a kick out of strange and especially outrageous baits, and it was a safe bet my invention fell in at least one of those categories. Getting carried away with the notion "the more hooks the better" I had attached the tails of three Mepps Giant Killers to the rear section of a similar lure. Totaled up, the thing was almost two feet long in the water - twenty-three inches to be exact.

"I'd like to see you cast that thing just *once* without it ending up in a ball of hooks," Rob said as it went sailing through the air. He couldn't stop chuckling either, or didn't want to, which of course made sense.

Sure enough, when I had it back to the boat it appeared as if something had reached up from the depths and shaped it into a ball. Undaunted, I untangled the mess and tossed it out again, using a slower, more deliberate casting method, like slowly pitching a softball underhanded. I could tell by the way it felt in the water it hadn't tangled up (probably) so I kept reeling with the hope that any decent sized fish within a mile or so couldn't miss noticing it burrowing through the water.

Wham! Followed immediately by frenzied splashing that shattered the evening tranquility with authority.

"Musky!" Rob hollered as he quickly reeled in his own lure just as the brute emerged from the water. "Big one, too!"

Feeling the familiar tug I attempted an unsuccessful hook set just as the water melted back to a smooth, motionless surface, not unlike a movie when a great ship finally disappears under the waves. I stood there dumbfounded and kept reeling, staring at the tranquil surface. Twenty-four hooks and that clumsy son of a musky couldn't find even *one* of them.

My hands were still trembling as we made our way back to the Sanctuary after blasting the immediate area for the better part of half an hour, one cast after another followed by figure eights. Nothing. We never saw that monument to musky buffoonery again. We were on a body of water so large you could probably see it if you were standing on the moon, and I had happened upon the most inept, bumbling musky that massive lake had to offer. It was a miracle it had survived all its years at all, much less fed itself all that time. I wanted to strangle that cross-eyed imposter – odds were, if it tried to bite me it would miss.

Still, it had elevated the Quest to a higher level. We had witnessed musky follows while fishing Lake of the Woods, including a few large muskies, but to finally have one slam into one of our lures changed us from spectators to participants, even if Round One had gone to the musky. There was always tomorrow, and as it turned out for my brother-in-law Jeff, tomorrow would be a day he would never forget; I knew I wouldn't, anyway.

***

It was Jeff, Rob and I who went out the following evening. Danny and Will were on their own, but since they were stranded on an island we figured they'd be okay. Will had already proved he had a healthy sense of humor, if you defined healthy as first scaring the wits out of his uncle then tricking him into torturing himself. We had been walking down the path that led to the dock when Will's creative, though arguably warped sense of humor, first emerged.

"Look out Uncle Tom! *Tree snake!*" Those words reached me just as I heard the urgent rustling in the thin branches directly above my head, followed immediately by something that landed on the back of my head.

"*Gaaa!!*" Was the only sound I was capable of producing as I repeatedly slapped the back of my scalp like I was putting out fire. I shot down the rocky path, nearly falling on at least two occasions. I didn't regain my composure until I was safely on the dock, and when I did there was Will, laughing and clearly proud of himself, holding the stick he had so deftly tossed into the tree branches just moments before.

"Hey Uncle Tom," he finally managed to get out, "you're not gonna have a heart attack on me now, are ya?" He wasn't through with me, either.

There was something he hadn't known but discovered in no uncertain terms that day - I was deathly afraid of any snake that wasn't a garter snake, and I wasn't exactly enamored with those critters, either. When I was a kid, out in a boat with Don manning the oars on Carrol Lake, we had inadvertently drifted directly under a pine tree growing out at an angle from shore. The branches were so thick they scratched and dragged against us and the sides of the boat just as we ran aground, wedged in-between the rocks with the bow portion (where I was located) closest to shore. I was completely surrounded by branches, but I wasn't alone - oh no no no - not by a stinking long shot. Not *twelve inches* from the tip of my nose was the biggest damn snake I had ever seen outside of a Walt Disney nature show. It knew I was invading its space too, and boy was it pissed. Or something.

"Uh, Don, *Don,* we really need to get outta here..." I was barely capable of breathing the words. The snake moved menacingly closer for a better look, or a meal, forked tongue darting in and out, as I waited for my short sweet life to begin flashing through what was left of my panic-stricken mind. I thought I heard a funny rattling noise, too. "I mean *now* Don!"

Sensing my urgency and almost controlling his laughter, Don managed to free the boat from the rocks and inch us back into the safety of that suddenly wonderful body of water. After getting away from that tree, a sewage pond would have seemed wonderful to me. Anyway, that was the beginning of my snake phobia, and it wasn't diminished when two days later a camper killed a timber rattler (you guessed it) not ten feet from that very tree. Okay, maybe it hadn't been the same snake – maybe.

"Never did see a snake near Tom the other day." Don casually remarked to Dad after the timber rattler had been killed. "Heard a rattle though."

As I was saying however, Will wasn't done with me. Tell you one thing, I must have been whacked especially hard with a stupid stick that day, that's for sure.

"Heck Uncle Tom," Will assured me as we knelt down upon the dock for a closer look at a baby crawfish he had caught, "little ole thing like that can't hurt ya none. Must'a pinched me twice before I put it down. Go on, put your finger right in that tiny little pincer. Won't hurt none, you'll see."

"Daaamn!" Pathetic, painful sounds from an equally pathetic musky hunter filled the air. It felt like two red-hot hat pins had been shoved into my index finger. I shook that evil little sadist (the crawfish) until it went flying through the air and landed directly upon the table where Rob was filleting our day's catch of northern. Without missing a beat, he poked it with the tip of his fillet knife and flicked it into the water. I kept a real close eye on "the Willer" after that. Real close. It was good to get out on the water and away from whatever else he had in store for me. I owed him big time, and payback was a forgone conclusion.

***

Rob took Jeff and me somewhere south of Timber Island, to one of my favorite parts of Whitefish Bay. It was another beautiful evening just before twilight, made even more so by the growing prospect of a spectacular sunset. Awe inspiring sunsets can occur all over the world I suppose, but with the exception of a few truly remarkable ones in Colorado as a child, nothing I had experienced could compare to the summer and fall masterpieces that frequently burst forth over Whitefish Bay like hushed, slow-motion fireworks.

I had loaned Jeff my yellow pool-cue Ugly Stick for the evening. He had never used exceptionally stout musky gear and wanted to give it a try. We entered a sheltered, narrow portion of water surrounded by small islands with an abundance of rock reefs, both submerged and exposed. There was one section in particular Rob wanted us to work.

It happened so fast it felt like it was over before it had begun. Jeff had floated a perfect cast between two submerged boulders that jutted out from the reef then cranked the handle once, twice...*Wham!* Suddenly, what looked like an enraged football with teeth broke the tranquil surface and began to shake its head. Jeff delivered a hook set with everything he had, and for a split second the lure's hooks seemed to have been driven home. My Ugly Stick was bent over more than it had ever been before, except when I had snagged rocks while trolling. Jeff kept the tension on as the beast kept its head out of the water, shaking it as violently as ever. The monster was about twenty-five feet from the side of the boat.

"Well over forty pounds, that one!" Rob exclaimed as he quickly grabbed his largest net. At that precise moment the huge fish, its entire head out of the water, made another exceptionally violent head shake and the bucktail dislodged. Jeff had applied so much pressure to avoid any slack that the bucktail flew back not ten inches above the water the whole way and slammed into the side of the boat with a resounding *wap!* Then all was quiet, as quiet as Death as far as I was concerned, and no more appealing. I began casting immediately, as did Jeff once he had reeled in. We both made a number of fruitless casts before Rob finally spoke, utter disappointment in his voice.

"Well, we best try another spot, eh? This one's done for the night." With that he started up the motor and proceeded to leave, slower than usual. That was when Jeff said something for the first time since losing what was easily the fish of a lifetime, if not several lifetimes.

"What a beautiful sunset." Was all he said.

I could not believe my ears; didn't believe them actually, until I looked at my brother-in-law. Jeff had a serene expression on his face without a hint of pensiveness as he gazed at what was indeed a truly remarkable sight, even by Lake of the Woods standards.

Personally, if that had happened to me I wouldn't have cared if it had been the most spectacular sunset in the history of the known universe. I was certain any sane person would have seen nothing but funeral gray, or would have expected to at any rate. Not Jeff though. There he was, a former Navy pilot no less, and all he did after losing the biggest musky any of us would probably ever see again in our lives, was gaze at the setting sun as if he wanted to ask it for a date. I glanced at Rob right after Jeff spoke, and from the look I received I knew I wasn't alone in thinking my brother-in-law was indeed off his rocker.

It eventually occurred to me that Jeff wasn't crazy, the rest of us were; at least those of us who were obsessed with catching huge muskies. That night however, as I drifted off to sleep, I was grateful it hadn't been me who had lost that monster fish. My only son was in the room right next to mine. How pathetic would it have been for him to hear his father sobbing and blubbering himself to sleep, or beating his head against the wall? I sure didn't know, and I never wanted to find out.

Jeff, on the other hand, was doing just fine. He loved baseball, and had managed to find a game on the DX radio he had brought along for that express purpose. It wasn't his beloved Chicago White Sox, but no matter. He had a good book, a good ball game, and he was on vacation; all was right with the world - his world, anyway.

That point was brought into clearer focus on our last day when he surprised all of us again by actually landing a musky while out with Bob Horley Sr. It wasn't over thirty inches, so of course it was released, but it was still a musky; the only one caught by any of us on that trip.

During shore lunch that day we got to hear all about it, and more than once. Will had been there when it had happened, so when the second telling got underway he headed off to explore the small island. I figured he had just let his guard down a little too far. He knew I was out to get him and had kept a close watch on all my movements, or so he thought.

There were certain clients who just couldn't bring themselves to urinate over the side of the boat no matter how bad they had to go. There was a metal cup in Bob's boat for just that purpose. Those particular clients with their shy kidneys would relieve themselves into the cup then pour it over the side. It was marked with a large X that had been scratched into the bottom so it wouldn't be confused for a drinking cup.

My trap was set when the Willer accepted the cup of coffee I offered him during another great shore lunch. I wish you could have seen the look on his face when, upon my urging, he had glanced at the bottom of the metal cup after finishing his coffee.

Then his look of utter shock turned into a calculated smile that I just *knew* had crossed his face on purpose. I was just being a little paranoid I assured myself. Still…

My suspicions were confirmed when I finished my coffee and went down to the water's edge to rinse out my own metal cup. How he had pulled it off remains a mystery to this day. There it was though. The only thing missing was the background music from the shower scene in the movie *Psycho* as I stared in horror at the large, mysterious X scratched into the bottom of my cup. The Willer had struck again.

Chapter 16

Dad had turned 74 a couple weeks before our 1987 fall trip to the Sanctuary. As excited as he was when he and Don arrived at my new house in Des Moines, I suspected he may have been reverting back to his childhood. You usually had to look close to notice it though, and listen even closer in order to sense his moods, but not that day; he was genuinely looking forward to a Canadian fishing adventure with his sons, and had abandoned his usual restraint.

It had been fifteen years since Dad, Don and I had made our way to Canada, and memories of all the fish we had landed (no muskies, of course) coupled with my glowing accounts of what we could expect to find in Whitefish Bay had all three of us filled with anticipation. Even so, there was that ever present, underlying sense of eventual failure, borne from almost thirty years of us trying but not catching a fish like Grampa's.

I had to believe the expertise of the Horley family in general, coupled with having Rob as our guide, was bound to change that sad state of affairs. Still, it was just as easy to accept the opposite. You just don't throw that many casts for nearly three decades into waters that contain muskies, including *big* muskies, and end up with nothing memorable.

Well, actually you do. At least we did. The very real suspicion it might never happen certainly existed - not unlike yearning for a Chicago Cubs World Series championship - yet we refused to give up until it *did* happen, and not stop there. Welcome to the jungle of musky lunacy.

Our predicament reminded me of a quote from Jack Brickhouse, the legendary Chicago Cubs announcer: *Any team can have a bad century.* If nothing else, his words allowed us a respite from our frustration, but there was always that underlying feeling caused by, among other things, our foolish superstition; after all, Grampa was the last McCabe my generation had known personally who had actually seen his beloved Cubs win a game in a World Series they went on to win as well.

Grampa had been in attendance for the second game in 1908. It was so long ago the Cubs hadn't even been playing their games at Wrigley Field yet, but at West Side Grounds a few blocks south of where the Eisenhower Expressway is today, near West Taylor Street - and Grampa was the only McCabe who had caught a trophy musky. Good God, were we condemned to failure until the Cubs *weren't?* Welcome to the jungle of musky lunacy indeed.

Grampa and his Chicago Cubs; he had loved that team all right, and of course his six sons knew it. Dad and his brothers had also been well aware of the incalculable stress their parents had endured while all six of their sons were in combat overseas during World War Two. It took the Six Micks a number of years before they could raise the money, but in 1953 they were finally able to at least partially pay their parents back for what they had endured; they bought Grampa and Gramma their first TV.

Much to the surprise of her sons and their spouses, Gramma became addicted to the soap opera Guiding Light, but they weren't surprised that Grampa felt the same way about watching the Cubs on TV. Radio broadcasts hadn't even been around in 1908, and suddenly Grampa was listening *and* seeing the Cubs play. Grampa was mesmerized by it all, and even though I had been only five, it struck me that he seemed just as excited as I was on birthdays and Christmas the day the TV had been delivered. Baseball bored me back then because I didn't really understand more than the basics, but sitting there with Grampa changed all that. He not only explained things so I could understand them, but did so by intertwining stories considerably more colorful than anything on the black and white TV.

The technology was amazing to him all right, which shouldn't have surprised me. After all, not long before the TV had arrived I had been with him in Dad's car. Our whole family was packed in there, on a Sunday drive into the countryside south of Naperville. We passed a meadow and I exclaimed "Look! A horse!" Grampa chuckled as he looked my way and spoke:

"Doesn't seem that long ago when folks would've said, 'Look! A car!' and been just as awestruck, Tommy boy."

***

You know how it is when a fishing trip is still quite a ways off but you start going half-crazy with anticipation anyway? You find yourself sharpening hooks that are already honed to a point capable of penetrating boot leather, or wandering around tackle shops or getting "lost" while shopping with your wife in a big discount or department store, only to have her find you inspecting a display of bucktails or gazing at the new reels under a glass counter. I had come up with another pre-trip diversion, one I had actually started the year before.

It was officially called **THE BENJAMIN FRANKLIN McCABE FAMILY MUSKY TROPHY.** I had gone to a local trophy shop in Des Moines and explained what I wanted. It was 12 x 30 inches, made from hard maple stained chestnut brown. Attached diagonally from lower left to upper right was the actual gaff hook used to hoist Grampa's musky out of the choppy waters of Pelican Lake way back in 1925. Grampa had replaced the wooden handle in the 1930's, but it was the original hook. Dad had given it to me years before, but I had never felt comfortable carrying it along on fishing trips for fear of losing it. Now it was as safe as could be expected. I also had a 5x7 inch copy of Grampa's photograph made and placed behind a clear plastic cover that was screwed on near the upper left portion of the trophy. Covering the rest of it were thirteen 1x3 inch metal plaques, either blank in anticipation of a future catch, or with the name of the person, size of the musky, along with when and where it had been landed.

Grampa's, of course, was the first plaque that had been engraved. It wasn't gold colored like the others though; any legal musky taken from the sacred waters of Pelican Lake had a silver colored plaque, in honor of Grampa. He had always spurned anything that even whiffed at being ostentatious, and besides, I wanted his plaque to stand out from the rest. That's why I had the most revered plaque (and hopefully one day "plaques") colored proletariat silver, as opposed to bourgeoisie colored gold. A little over the top on my part I suppose, but in a way "over the top" helped define the entire concept of chasing muskies. If you don't understand that or don't want to, well, keep casting. We're all in this together.

When I had first shown the finished trophy to Dad and Don earlier that year in Aurora, they had liked the whole idea; at least for the most part. Don was a little put out that along with Grampa's plaque, there were also plaques denoting Dad's musky caught from Carrol Lake and the one I landed out of Tomahawk, plus Danny's Carver Lake catch. Not Don's catch out of Tomahawk in 1985 though. Since Dad and I hadn't landed legal sized muskies (both were 29 inches - an inch shy of being legal at the time) and Danny's 30 incher wasn't legal in Ontario, Don thought his first musky should have been given a plaque as well. Since his musky hadn't been much bigger than the little plaque it would have adorned (okay, eighteen inches *is* bigger than three inches) it hadn't occurred to me to include it on what promised to be such a revered trophy. Besides, I had a picture of Don kissing that near fingerling prior to its release. I maintained any musky small enough to kiss, on the side of its face no less, had no business being on **THE BENJAMIN FRANKLIN McCABE FAMILY MUSKY TROPHY**, period.

Don heard me out, but it was obvious he didn't agree. I finally told him if he ever won the trophy, he could use an extra plaque for Moby Guppy if he didn't mind the humiliation of having its size engraved upon it for all to see, including yet-to-be born generations. Later on, the "Board of Elders" which originally consisted of just Dad, Don and me, wrote up a couple pages of by-laws, most of which I won't bore you with. Basically, biggest musky in a given year wins, as long as it's legal. The winner holds onto the trophy until someone else wins it, as long as that someone else is a direct descendant of Keith Allen "Pete"

McCabe, or a spouse thereof. We didn't use "direct descendant" of Grampa because we had too many uncles and cousins, even if most of them never fished for muskies. If any of them really wanted in though, the Board of Elders had authorized itself to review cases on a one by one basis. Godspeed.

Anyway, we now had something tangible to go along with the Quest itself. Danny was the current trophy holder due to his 1986 catch. We (okay, I) grandfathered in non-legal catches already made (with one obvious exception) but hopefully the trophy would change hands once Dad, Don and I made it to the pristine waters of Whitefish Bay. As his father, however, I also hoped Danny would win it right back again.

There were not only big muskies roaming the waters of Lake of the Woods, but as previously stated world record muskies as well. Bob Horley Sr. or his clients had even raised a few over the decades, and musky hunter or not, he was not the type of man who was prone to exaggeration; he didn't have to be, not having lived most of his life up there.

He told of one musky that had followed a client's lure that was easily longer than the boat's oars, and they were over *six feet* long. He said he got a very good look at the behemoth, mainly because it wasn't moving all that fast, as if it had *nothing* to fear in its watery world. Bob said it was easily in the eighty-pound class, perhaps bigger, making it more than ten pounds larger than the current world's record. Here was a man in his sixties who had spent much of his time, from ice out to ice in, since before he was ten years old, fishing for muskies in Whitefish Bay and points beyond. Although the biggest musky he had ever caught was "only" fifty-six pounds, he said he wouldn't be surprised if muskies over *one hundred pounds* were lurking about in the depths of Lake of the Woods. If anything, he said he would be surprised if there *weren't*.

If you're going to cast for muskies, why not throw your casts into waters that can produce the ultimate dream? How great would that plaque look on a trophy? Oh yeah, that was another by-law. Any world's record musky automatically retired the trophy, and if the world record musky was caught in Pelican Lake off Indian Point, all family members from that day forward had to refer to the person who had caught the fish as Grand Master, and were allowed to leave that person's presence only by walking away backwards. There was a time when royalty could have had someone beheaded for turning their back while leaving the presence of his or her Majesty, but we decided to leave that out - subject to further review by the Board of Elders.

***

Even though it took around eleven hours to drive from Des Moines to Sioux Narrows, we never dreaded the prospect, quite the opposite. I still had my big custom van, so once Dad and Don arrived from Illinois and we headed out the next day, there was plenty of room for everyone. Dad especially liked the way the rear seats folded down into a double bed. He had always been a nap-oholic, and having reached his 74th year sure hadn't diminished his appreciation of a good nap.

Even though I had been telling and re-telling stories about my two previous trips to Lake of the Woods, something inside of them still refused to let go of their skepticism. The many photos I had of the fish caught were impressive, but so were the photos in fishing magazines - until Dad and Don were in on the action themselves, on a lake with good-sized northern and more importantly muskies striking their lures, their skepticism wasn't going anywhere.

Even though their justifiable skepticism was never mentioned, it was as much a part of those two as breathing. I could go on about the Sanctuary, the Horleys, Whitefish Bay and its fish-filled waters until those two were left snoring in their seats (that only happened once) but until they wetted their own lines, had cast successfully towards submerged rock formations themselves, it was all but meaningless. That changed within the first thirty minutes we were in Rob's boat.

***

After introductions were made and we had settled into our cabin by the main dock, it was time to hit the water for a few hours. Our first stop didn't produce anything, but along an island shoreline at the next stop a five-pound northern slammed into my black Giant Killer with a gold blade. Dad and Don were beside themselves with excitement as they fumbled about for their cameras. Back in the day, we had gone years without landing such a beautiful fish. There we were, less than half an hour into our first time together in the middle of Whitefish Bay, and I was holding up a five-pound freshwater feast.

Rob got a kick out of the way those two made such a big deal out of a five-pound fish that wasn't even a musky. I saw a slight smile on his face, the one that usually meant his subtle, low-key sense of humor was about to emerge.

"Well then," he remarked after putting the northern in a wet gunnysack and rinsing his hands, "hopefully the two of you brought enough film, eh?"

If they hadn't grasped Rob's meaning right away, they no doubt understood it by the time we headed in that evening. I had caught four more keepers, Don had three and Dad two, plus a follow from a twenty-plus pound musky that had teased Dad's Pikie Minnow before giving us the fin finger and moving on.

***

Before long, nearly all human emotions find a way into musky fishing as one cast, one day and even one trip follows another. The excitement of a first catch of the day by one of us was acknowledged by the lowly fishless ones with congratulations, which really meant "it's nice the fish are biting; too bad it wasn't my lure". If the same person catches another before anyone else, no verbal congratulations will likely be heard, as if it is assumed the others still feel it was a good, or at least a positive sign. If that same person does it again, the others go from thinking *well, okay, at least the fish are hitting,* to *this is beginning to really suck.* Then a decent northern finds their lure and they don't even remember the gut shots of envy and childish self-pity that had consumed them just moments before.

Still, all of that was nothing more than dress rehearsal, regardless of how many northern were caught, including large ones; if it wasn't a musky, it wasn't worth getting overly excited about. Well, for the most part anyway. Rob's father told us something that sure challenged that concept.

Bob Horley Sr. was a man who weaved as good a story as anyone. Only Grampa, as far as my subjective reasoning is concerned, could have bested him. Bob had been fishing Lake of the Woods most of his life all right, as well as many other lakes in Ontario that had a reputation for being worth a try. He didn't have to rely on the stories of others, not with all the amazing experiences of his own to draw from - like the farmer from Minnesota for instance:

The hardworking Swede deserved a vacation although he never would have admitted that was the purpose of his trip, not even to himself. It was the 1940's, and a young Bob Horley was his guide. They were in pursuit of large fish - and Bob not only knew the best spots for trophy muskies, but every other species of fish that attained impressive size as well. The more pounds the better, as far as the farmer was concerned. He had a large family to feed back in Minnesota, and returning home with anything less than a large quantity of fresh fish fillets was not only out of the question, but negated the entire purpose of his time away from the farm, or so the farmer maintained.

As of this writing, the IGFA world record northern pike is the fifty-five pound, one ounce behemoth taken from Greffen Lake in Germany. There were other northerns reportedly larger caught in Europe and North America, but never verified as official records. Back when the farmer caught his northern, the North American record was 46 pounds, 2 ounces caught by Peter Dubuc out of Sacandaga Lake in New York. It's safe to say northern can get pretty huge all right, regardless of the continent.

Bob had already guided the farmer to prodigious amounts of northern, bass and walleye when it happened. The fight lasted over half an hour before the huge fish, at first believed to be a musky, was finally brought close enough for proper identification. It turned out not to be a musky at all, but a fifty-pound northern.

After it had been hauled into the boat, it actually weighed out at a few ounces over fifty pounds. Bob told the Minnesota farmer what he had, but records meant nothing to the man, at least not as much as feeding his family. Besides, back in those days it wasn't like someone would glean a tidy sum through various channels because they had landed a record northern, or any other record fish for that matter. You wouldn't exactly be able to retire on it today, either. Regardless, the farmer didn't care. He gutted it and put it on ice. That year, he announced with pride, his large family would have more than they could eat at one sitting, and all from one fish – a *world record* fish.

***

Rob, of course, knew exactly where that magnificent beast had been prowling the day it had been caught, even if it had happened a few decades before Rob's birth. He didn't, however, tell us until later we were casting at that very spot that particular afternoon; the day after we had first heard his father's story. It was a very small island; the exposed, highest point of yet another rock reef of which Lake of the Woods boasts tens of thousands. Reeds were around part of it, and that's where I had been concentrating my casts whenever the position of the boat allowed.

Dad had been casting in the opposite direction of the island and the reef in general, in an attempt to entice a suspended musky with an old fashioned, non-jointed Pikie Minnow. It was wooden with a classic red head, white body and genuine amber eyes; the very same battle-scarred lure Grampa had used when he had caught his musky. It was cracked, worn and beat up, but it was Dad's favorite lure; rusty hooks and all. Dad had over a dozen old lures and feathered bucktails that had been Grampa's, but none of them inspired as much awe as *the* Pikie Minnow.

Dad wasn't very impressed with fishing lure innovations, although in 1959 he did purchase an original Suick, from a Pelican Lake tackle shop no less – I still have that lure. He acknowledged the latest and greatest Don and I always showed up with, but that was about it. You could usually tell when Dad wasn't very impressed with something; he would barely acknowledge it then fade away on you. He wasn't very impressed with the latest innovations in fishing lures and never had been because, for the most part, he knew what a well-placed Pikie Minnow could accomplish. Thing was though, he never bought into the concept of changing his line, or even checking for frays very often.

Don and I held our breath every time Dad threw the famed Pikie Minnow. It was the only time we truly hoped there were no huge fish in the vicinity, at least if they thought Dad's lure appeared delectable. We could just envision even a relatively small northern smacking our most precious family fishing heirloom and Dad's line snapping like so much sewing thread.

Since Dad had no intention of not throwing Grampa's Pikie Minnow, Don and I took it upon ourselves to not only check Dad's line constantly (he didn't grumble out loud, but it was there) as well as loosen the drag when necessary, but we also made sure one of us brought along new line every year. Even so, on that day neither of us had bothered to check Dad's line or drag until it was almost too late.

None of us, not even Rob, got a very good look at it. Dad probably got the best look at what he described as "a genuine whopper" before it disappeared as suddenly as it had arrived. It had either missed the Pikie Minnow or changed its mind at the last second.

I had just placed my bucktail in front of the reeds that grew from the shore of the small island, but Don had finished reeling in when Dad let out one of his classic "Jysus!" yells upon spotting the fish. It was a variation of "Jesus!" but Dad seldom swore in front of his children, even if he was with his adult sons on a fishing trip in the middle of the Canadian wilderness on a body of water bigger than the state of Rhode Island.

Don placed his bucktail in the general direction that Rob thought the fish had headed. Before he had a chance to complete three turns on his reel, something that Don later maintained felt like he had snagged a creature that resembled a fish only bigger, was on the other end of his line. If it was a rock or a log, it had somehow acquired the uncanny ability to swim, tug and fight. Don's pole bent quickly into a half moon before he had a chance to let up on his drag a little, and the fight was on!

One thing became evident, at least to Don and Rob; it wasn't some average northern that had taken off swiftly for the deep. So far, the largest fish any of us had caught that year was around eight pounds. What Don suspected, and Rob pretty much knew, was the fish that had gone after Dad's Pikie Minnow was tugging and thrashing at the end of Don's line.

Unlike other fights, the fish stayed deep even after Don had managed to horse it close enough so it was under the boat. Even in the clear waters of Whitefish Bay, none of us could see what was directly beneath us, over fifteen feet down. By then we all knew one thing though; it was big, and as far as Don was concerned it was, in all likelihood, a musky. In fact, he became so overwhelmed by subjective jubilance, he was convinced that it *had* to be a musky, and a very big one, too.

Don had always possessed lightning reflexes, so he was certain he had delivered a deeply imbedded hook set. Unable to control his excitement, he actually began to do something that resembled either a dance or a jig, right there in the boat while holding onto his rod, all the while singing some little ditty he had spontaneously made up, the type of simple tune most of us would be too embarrassed to sing even if we were alone in a shower or something. Not Don though, since he was convinced he knew what was tugging at the end of his line. Besides, shy and Don never got along very well. They'd never even *met*.

"~I've caught a musky! I've won the trophy! La la la la, la! I've caught a musky, I've won the trophy! La la la la, la! I've caught a ~ - "

"It's a northern," Rob observed loud enough for all to hear the moment its form was visible, still a good ten feet down. How he could determine that was a wonderment to me; all I could see was a vague outline of a big fish. Don looked as if someone had plopped a straight flush on top of his four aces.

"What? No way! Gotta be a musky. It's *huge*." He had the huge part right, relatively speaking, but no amount of denial or wishful thinking could alter the cold, cruel fact that indeed, Don had hooked into a northern.

He was finally able to horse it up just below the surface, where Rob boated it immediately by hand. It turned out to be the biggest fish any of us had ever caught - a beautifully marked, eighteen pound northern. Several photos were taken, and if the expression on Don's face was any indication, he had overcome his disappointment over his inept species identification prowess;

a deficiency shared by two others in the boat, and I ain't talkin' about Rob Horley.

Rob asked Don if he wanted to keep it, but Don said no. You could tell Rob appreciated Don's decision, especially since the growing trend of catch and release wasn't as common on Lake of the Woods in the 1980's as it is today. Rob had told us large northern didn't taste as good as the three and four pounders, and besides, since Don's beauty was probably a female, the amount of eggs she would produce in the spring would likely be considerable. There had been no gill damage, so it wasn't going to bleed to death. Rob began coaxing it back and forth in the water while holding onto its tail, and after awhile it sprang to life and was off like a shot. It was an awesome sight to see as it sped away, to watery safe havens she knew so well.

Later that night over a few Labatts during our evening poker game, Don suggested we start a northern trophy. It sounded like a good enough idea, and still does, but no one has gotten around to it yet. I would imagine the person who had the biggest northern caught in our family (and since then Don has caught larger ones than that) would be the natural choice to initiate such an endeavor...

***

The last day of our 1987 trip turned out to be beautiful; if magnificent blue skies dotted with billowing clouds and a light breeze counted for anything. I had heard and read where musky hunters reported catching the beasts in what otherwise passes for perfect weather, and tales of rain-swept days, or immediately prior to them, with a good chop on the water being best for musky fishing were just that - tales. There were musky guides who maintained weather didn't matter, but the skeptic in me had to wonder if what they told some of their clients, and what they discussed over a few brews without any clients around, was the same.

Rob displayed above average intelligence to say the least, and above average integrity. He knew our time in Canada would always be extremely limited and therefore hostage to whatever weather developed, and he was well aware of how important it was for his clients to maintain a positive attitude. Musky fishing, at least the full-bore attack mode he insisted upon, was a lot of work. Sometimes, however, he acknowledged that certain weather patterns could be more productive than others. Occasionally that was obvious by what he didn't say.

We had become friends, and Rob's moral compass had a hard time pointing towards anything deceitful under those circumstances or other situations of any significance I could ascertain, unless he was joking around. Besides, he had witnessed some impressive results in weather conditions that were considered less than ideal for landing muskies, so he wasn't being disingenuous when he insisted we stood as good a chance as the next person as long as we kept casting. If nothing else, he was more than capable of jump-starting our morale, and mentioning George Wahl's success during so-called "bad fishing weather" was a prime example.

Year after year, no one who stayed at the Sanctuary caught more muskies than George, and the large chart the Horley's kept on a wall in the main lodge proved it. High, sunny skies with little or no wind after a storm front passed through? Not necessarily a problem, according to George. He even said sometimes he preferred that weather, and there was no arguing with that chart...

***

Although we had again caught our fair share of northern, we didn't see a musky all that day. When we made it out after supper, however, all that changed dramatically, and in a way none of us had anticipated; none of us except Rob. There wasn't much he hadn't witnessed while musky hunting, and what occurred that evening was no exception.

Back then he rarely use leaders, had an open-faced spinning reel and used monofilament line. For the life of me, I didn't get it. He was as obsessed as any of us when it came to hunting muskies, yet I thought he chose most of his fishing gear as if he was going after anything but muskies. That, or he was interested in getting more follows and hits even if the odds of losing them were greater. If nothing else, I suspected he wanted to raise more muskies that in turn might go after his clients' lures. It was possible, if not probable, leaders cut down on follows and hits, especially in the exceptionally clear waters of Whitefish Bay. Lure movement could be at least partially inhibited as well.

Even so, we went with the odds; the odds that leaned towards *landing* any muskies we were fortunate enough to hook. It would have been just our luck to hook into a genuine trophy only to have it bite off our line. Rob said that could happen all right, but it wasn't necessarily a rule set in stone. However, when we factored in the entire McCabe family musky success rate over the years, the fact that it only had to happen once was difficult to ignore.

We knew who it would probably happen to all right, so we used top quality leaders that were at least eighteen inches long and our line was at least 36 pound braided Dacron - usually. We had the right line, leaders, rods (okay, not rods so much) Garcia Ambassedeur baitcasting reels and Giant Killer Mepps, and a large assortment of other musky lures. He approved of our choices, too, not unlike someone who was an expert with a trick yo-yo who knew guys like us should stick with a beginner's model, the kind that come back right away as opposed to the advanced models that stay spinning at the end of the string until the expert wants it to start flying all over the place. You know, like a guy who actually knows what he's doing.

Rob also had the smoothest, most accurate cast any of us had ever seen. We knew all about casting too, believe me. We had tens of thousands of casts between us and considered ourselves accomplished and accurate, even if the muskies hadn't been overly impressed for the better part of thirty years. It was casting prowess that set things in motion that evening as Rob guided us through a somewhat narrow channel, with plenty of submerged and exposed boulders to test our abilities, but any demonstration of casting prowess didn't come from a McCabe that evening.

Halfway into the channel Rob pointed to a partially sub-merged outcropping of boulders, and instructed us to spray our casts all around it. Don and I let fly again and again, while Dad worked a white twister tail over the side, all the time watching our casts – classic Dad – he wanted one of his sons to catch a musky. Rob, sitting atop the large motor at the stern, watched our lures intently, or rather just behind and to the sides of them as we worked our way past the outcropping. Nothing. No follows, no hits; nothing.

We finally passed beyond what Don and I knew was our casting range. Regardless, Rob sent one soaring. It landed exactly where he had been aiming, a good twenty feet farther than either Don or I could have achieved with our baitcasting reels. We weren't paying close attention though, hardly any at all. We had been out all day and evening, and even though it was our last day we had seen so many fruitless casts over the last few days it was easy to let our attention wander. Besides, we had pretty much resigned ourselves to our usual fate - musky skunked for another year.

"I was afraid of that." Was all Rob said as he performed a lightning quick hook set. We figured he had hooked into another northern, but the instant Rob had set the hooks he knew better.

"Here." Just like that, he handed me his rod. "It's at least in the twenty-pound class, maybe bigger." He said, watching the end of the line intently. I couldn't see a thing. I sure felt it though.

I was immediately shocked not once, but twice. Not only was I suddenly fighting the biggest fish of my life, but I was doing it with an open faced spinning reel set up for a right-hander. I was "left" everything, especially left-handed. It was all backwards; if it hadn't been for the tension Rob urged me to maintain, I wouldn't have known if I was reeling in or out, at least at first. It was kind of like suddenly being forced to switch-hit in a baseball game for the first time, then having to fight an urge to race towards third after somehow making contact.

"Keep it coming, Tom, that's it, no slack mind you, keep it coming…"

The huge creature may not have understood what was happening, but seemed to know enough to realize it was fighting for its life. Its thrashing, tugging movements moved me as well, or at least my arms. I had never felt anything quite like it before, although it vaguely resembled trying to control a large dog on a leash after the hound had located a rabbit or something.

After just a few minutes that seemed longer, we finally got our first look at the magnificent creature when it slid across the surface, then attempted to lumber quickly away. It was a musky all right; a big one. Try as it would, it wasn't able to spit Rob's Eagle Tail even when I messed up a little with that spinning reel and accidentally gave it some slack. Rob had drilled that musky with one well-timed hook set - that was for sure – a single hook set, not a treble.

Even though Rob had been using monofilament, it was a heavy test. Besides, his drag was set perfectly so I could horse that musky all I wanted. Sometimes I'd gain ground, and sometimes the musky would simply pull out more line on one of its runs. Before ten minutes were up I had it next to the boat and Rob reached into the water and managed, after several attempts, to grab it by hand and lift it aboard. It all happened so fast I'm not sure Dad, Don and I had really grasped what had just occurred. We had of course, I don't mean that, but for a moment or so it was as if illusion hadn't caught up to reality. Ultimately, it didn't matter.

After weighing it (it came in at 48 inches, 28 pounds even) Rob asked if I wanted to keep it, but that was out of the question. It wasn't my fish; not even close. Nor was its size acceptable, which didn't matter to begin with; well, if it had been a world's record... We took a few photos then Rob carefully placed it back in the water and began moving it back and forth while holding onto its tail. After enough oxygen found her gills, she sped away in a blur. It was, as with other fish, an amazing sight to watch her torpedo into the deep. It reminded me of Fourth of July fireworks - they don't last long and you want to see more, but at least you had been able to see the spectacular sight. Even though it wasn't an official McCabe catch by any definition, it had still been exciting.

Rob kicked himself for (in his opinion) having had the misfortune of hooking into a big musky instead of it happening to one of us. That would have been great all right, but at least the way it turned out had rekindled our hope that catching a trophy was bound to happen to one of us sooner or later. Maybe it wasn't *bound* to happen, but at least we could feel it go from unlikely to maybe, leaning towards probably? Besides, since I (and eventually Don) had agreed we wouldn't keep any musky under thirty pounds, it was a relief neither of us had actually caught a twenty-eight pounder - sort of. Dad said he'd let any size go, but Don and I wanted to have a trophy musky mounted. In 1987 it was still a common practice, so if we ever did catch a fish like Grampa's, it was going on the wall.

Keeping a twenty-eight pounder, especially one as beautifully marked as the one Rob had caught and I had been lucky enough to land, would have been tempting. It also would have been a true test of character to decide whether or not to let it go and watch it swim away; a musky that was perhaps a meal or two away from being a keeper.

Contemplating all those things could be set aside for a while. We would no doubt mull them over, and discuss those and other things during dead-of-winter phone calls, but 1987 was in the books. All that was left was to head home, have all the photos developed and put in photo albums, and make plans for next year.

***

The entire Horley family always came down to the dock to say goodbye for the year. The contrast between the excitement of arriving and the melancholy of leaving stayed with us the entire morning, but had really come into focus as we shook hands with everyone before stepping aboard Rob's boat for the ride back to the mainland. Carol Horley took a few snapshots, and then we were off. It was impossible to avoid that feeling of melancholy, no matter how hard you tried to look forward to getting home.

We had only been there three days, which was part of it I guess. With Jeff, Will and Danny it had been five days. Dad was retired and my schedule was usually flexible, but Don could only get away from his job on the railroad for so long.

If the fates allowed, there was always next year. I would be turning forty come March of 1988. It would mark the twenty-ninth year since Grampa had called me over to that storefront cooler and I had stared wide-eyed at that huge Pelican Lake musky stretched out on the ice. Twenty-nine years is a long time by most standards, but it can be no time at all if vivid memories are used as bridges. Just thinking of that moment-in-time makes all the years vanish. I'm eleven again, the smoke from Grampa's Kentucky Club Mixture is curling in the air and his calm, baritone voice is again holding me and my brothers spellbound:

When it happens though, when you finally hook into one, you'll be a cut above the bobber and worm crowd. They'll never know the thrill of thrills, because they gave up...

One thing was certain, and it was Grampa who had instilled it in us; giving up just wasn't an option. There were others; guides, professional fishermen and such who had the knowledge, time and experience to out-fish us on our best days. Even so, Don and I believed in the essence of Grampa's words, believed that you weren't a loser if you failed, only if you gave up. There was no guarantee that day would come in 1988, but there was every reason to believe it couldn't hide forever - not with Grampa and Dad being the best part of us.

Chapter 17

guess you could say the whole thing was my fault, although my intentions had been good. I had been exercising for years with free weights and a running regimen. Don, on the other hand, distained most, if not all, forms of exercise. As a teenager he had been an excellent athlete until a serious knee injury ended sports for him, for the most part anyway. His exercise options were therefore limited to begin with, and the ones that were options didn't appeal to him. He had put on weight and I was concerned for his overall health. That was my story anyway. If the road to hell is paved with good intentions, you can bet I laid some of the bricks. Just ask Don.

Perhaps you've heard of it; psyllium husk. It's derived from the crushed or whole seeds of the *plantago ovata* plant, and most experts agree it is nature's richest or at least most concentrated form of soluble and non-soluble fiber, bar none. It's native to parts of Asia, Mediterranean regions of Europe as well as North Africa. It's the stuff Metamucil and its generic equivalents are made from, but my favorite brand was "Colon Cleanse".

The only drawback of that brand, for me at least, is the picture of this colon right on the front of the container. It's a real doozy too. It's got your inner lining, outer lining, transverse colon, ascending and descending colons clearly displayed for your viewing pleasure. Worse yet, the bar codes are on the opposite side. When the checkout girl scans it, there's a picture of some goof's upper and lower tract staring back at her, and since I'm the guy buying the stuff you can bet who she figures the real goof happens to be, and a constipated one at that. Then she sneaks a little peak to see what a constipated goof really looks like, and there I stand, pretending to be engrossed with nuances of the ceiling.

Even so, it's worth it. More than one doctor has told me it not only reduces cholesterol, but is helpful in preventing diseases like colon and other upper and lower tract cancers, at least for quite a few people. And talk about keeping you regular; the stuff is amazing along those lines, no kidding.

If you're wondering what any of that has to do with musky fishing, I can help; just like I wanted to help Don, only different. I figured since he obviously had such poor eating habits, he could use something to offset some of the carnage. Not only that, but we could both use something when vacationing at the Sanctuary because we ate so well, or like gluttonous pigs, depending on one's point of view. We only had half an hour or so to respond to nature's call after breakfast, and sometimes nature didn't call at all within that time frame. Ever been in a boat when Mother Nature finally hollered out? You know, when she's gone basically insane? Not good, not good.

At first Don wanted nothing to do with the stuff. Even after I clearly explained the effectiveness and reliability of psyllium husk, he still wouldn't budge. A few times during our previous trip to the Sanctuary I had really laid on the old sales pitch too, and since I was a sales rep it eventually took hold - only not in Canada. Don figured he'd give it a try once he arrived back home, to kind of work his way into the routine. He took the recommended dose the first day then doubled it on the second. Nothing. If anything, the opposite effect had taken place; his kid brother's alleged propensity to over-dramatize something's effectiveness was probably the culprit, so on the third day he tripled the dose then left for work.

Being an engineer for the railroad has its advantages - and its disadvantages. Depending on the run, some of the disadvantages have a way of magnifying, like when the engineer is on a non-stop run in a switch engine with no bathroom facilities. Non-stop means just that; nothing short of a heart attack or attempting to avoid smashing into a school bus or something would be considered acceptable reasons to hit the brakes. A psyllium attack would be considered short of a heart attack by upper management, but not necessarily by the person having one, if that person was trapped in an engine with no toilet.

I'll spare you the gruesome details. It's enough to know Don eventually radioed ahead and told the yardmaster to contact his wife Linda and have her show up at the train station with some clean pants and underwear, since what Don had on was no longer salvageable. Worse yet, the psyllium explosion had occurred with *way* too many miles to go.

When Don told me what had happened as we were heading up to Canada in 1988, I displayed all the maturity of a ten-year-old; especially when it became obvious he was still traumatized over the incident. One recommended daily dose of psyllium husk is usually effective, but it generally takes time to make it through your system. In hindsight, perhaps I hadn't made that clear enough. A double dose is flirting with danger, and a triple dose on top of the other two borders on a soluble fiber holocaust, all but nuclear in its proportion. I wouldn't let it go, either. The image of Don in that train engine, bug-eyed and panic-stricken, would form in my mind and I was back to being ten again.

It was a good thing there was something to laugh about, because the bad news was Dad couldn't make it that year. He was recovering from an eye operation, so a September trip was out. It was just Don and me, all our equipment and gear, and my trusty container of "Colon Cleanse" psyllium husk. What goes around comes around however, and that unwritten law was brought home full force the very first morning of our fateful trip.

***

We had been out the evening of our arrival with Rob, and I had managed to catch the first fish, a four-pound northern. That meant I won a dollar, and was one up for the most fish of the trip as well. We had quite a few bets going all right; a buck each for first fish, most fish and biggest northern both for each day and for the entire trip. There was also five bucks riding on the first musky and another fiver for biggest musky and yet another five for the most muskies. Needless to say, if one of us caught just one musky, that guy would likely clean up. Catching the first fish of the trip was a good start all right, and I was feeling pretty cocky. What goes around comes around…eh?

***

I was a little put out when we left the dock the following morning. My normally reliable dose of Colon Cleanse had let me down, for the second day in a row no less, and that meant there would probably have to be a pit stop at one of the islands before the morning was out. Not that big a deal, but it was, or should have been, an avoidable inconvenience for which I thought I had planned accordingly.

I preferred having everything considered, prepared for and in its proper place when a fishing trip was underway. Musky fishing by its own definition is unpredictable enough, therefore anything that can be controlled should be. That goes for avoiding certain things as well, like unscheduled stops on deserted islands that may or may not have a bear or two wandering around, but I'm getting ahead of myself. Things were okay for the first hour or so, same with the second. For a while I even thought I'd be fine until shore lunch; a classic example of wishful thinking if there ever was one, not unlike a hissing grenade landing in your foxhole that you hope will be a dud – but isn't.

To truly appreciate my dilemma takes a brief biology lesson as it pertains to the effect psyllium husk has on the human body. That stuff doesn't fool around, *period*. When it's time, *it is time,* savvy? There's no negotiating a compromise, forestalling a final resolution or tabling the issue for a later date. When Doctor Insanity Psyllium decides it's time to bolt, especially if he is behind schedule, any chance of stopping him simply does not exist. You might just as well try to stop a river of molten lava by spitting at it, an even more fitting analogy if you overdid it with chips, habanero salsa and beer the evening before.

Think you're a tough guy? Played high school or maybe even college football and can take and deliver a punch? If psylium husk has your number, it will change your name to Alice so fast you'll barely have time to lift your skirt. No amount of pleading or craven blubbering will save you. You will be on your knees, begging for just a little more time, but none will be forthcoming. Either you find a place to go right away, or suffer the consequences of a remorseless Psyllium Tsunami – game over, you lose, end of story.

Rob wasted absolutely no time getting me to the nearest island the instant he heard my blubbering and saw the panic in my eyes. He knew nothing about psyllium husk other than what Don had told him about his train experience, which was more than enough for Rob to want me the hell out of his boat as fast as possible - fine by me - I didn't even wait for him to stop. I was over the side and sloshing frantically towards shore. I finally made it, walking quickly with compressed buttocks only because running would have been disastrous. Still, the humiliation from the snickering and wise-ass remarks coming from the boat was enough for me to at least find a little privacy. I found it too, about forty feet into the heavily wooded island; forty-one feet may well have been too late – way too late.

Okay, maybe it wasn't a growl, although whatever it was sounded deep enough to definitely resemble one. I can tell you one thing - as fast as I had undone my pants before taking care of business was nothing compared to how fast I had them back on. That's when I actually *did* hear a growl, I swore I did, and if I had it figured right, it had come from something huge that was closer to me than I was to the boat. It was as if those forty feet had become forty miles, especially when something Rob had once mentioned shot through me like the unheeded warning it had become: *You can't out run, out climb or out swim a determined bear.* The words didn't go through my panic-stricken mind per se, I don't mean that, but the message sure did.

Wise move or not, I took off like the ground wasn't even there. I had always been a fast runner, but that day I wished my favorite high school football coaches, Coach Nordengren and Coach Adolf, had me on there stopwatches. Ever had one of those dreams where no matter how hard you try, you just can't run fast at all? It was nothing like that. My toes barely touched the ground. I felt airborne. **Grraawww!** That tore it. I *was* airborne.

When my feet did come in contact with the ground the sound of snapping twigs and crackling brush could be heard, but it was nothing compared to the same type of noises that, in my fevered mind, were bearing down behind me. It sounded as if an Indiana Jones boulder had been catapulted in my direction, but there was no way I was going to turn around to verify what was careening towards me - so much for bears being more afraid of humans than we of them.

"Bear! *Bear!*" I screamed as I flew past a small clearing and into the boat, all wide-eyed, my chest heaving. I had even gone into the lake up to my knees for a few lunging steps, but if the water slowed me down I sure hadn't noticed, I can tell you that.

Rob had begun to scan the tree and brush line as soon as he'd heard my caterwauling, but other than that he merely went about his business, relaxed as ever.

"Let's get the hell *outta* here, man! I'm tellin' ya, there's a *bear* coming!" I was panic-stricken all right, red-faced and panting like a lunatic.

"Well," Rob observed as he glanced back at the island, "If it was a bear, and I'm not denying that for a minute mind you, it's the first one I've ever seen with a white tail."

"But I heard it growl, I swear I heard that thing *growl...*" When Rob heard that he lost all semblance of control.

"Makes perfect sense, eh?" He managed to say, still laughing. "This island is famous for its growling white-tailed deer population." Then he lost it again, and took Don along for the ride. What goes around comes around...

***

It was a bright, sunny day with high skies, and although Don and I threw cast after cast until our arms and backs ached, we didn't catch another fish all day except for one small northern each. We had some musky follows but no strikes. That's one of the reasons why a lot folks who fish stay away from musky fishing. It's bad enough when you go all day without even seeing one, but when they follow your lure to the boat then casually swim away, snickering at your pathetic attempts to execute a figure eight, it's downright infuriating.

Another depressing situation occurred after shore lunch. Rob spotted two older guys fishing who had been coming to the Sanctuary for decades, Art and Sy. Bob Horley Sr. was, as always, guiding them. We headed over to their boat to see how their morning had gone. Art had the look and demeanor of a retired college professor, while his old fishing pal Sy bore an uncanny resemblance to the Scarecrow from the 1939 *Wizard of Oz* movie, except a lot older and nowhere near as sane, as if he were way past due to have his medication adjusted.

Art said it had been slow, except for several northern and
the twenty-pound musky he had caught and released. I wasn't
depressed because he had caught the fish. What depressed me was
the lackluster way Art had announced it, as if remembering such
an insignificant accomplishment was something barely worth
the effort, all in a day's work kind of thing. I was pretty sure
both of them acted that way for effect, like they were pretending
not to be smug and doing a lousy job of it on purpose, but the
possibility that they really hadn't cared one way or the other was
difficult to dismiss. It was as if they not only were members of
a very select club (those who had landed trophy muskies) but
had been members for so long that nothing short of a world's
record, or at the very least a fifty-pound class musky, would ever
truly excite them again.

For his part, Sy had most certainly earned his reputation
for being colorful and more than a little crazy, especially in
his younger days. When the opportunity would present itself
back in the day, he enjoyed sneaking up hills and rolling huge
boulders (the bigger the better) past people savoring a peaceful
shore lunch. Feeling the ground move as a mass of granite that's
half the size of a Volkswagen careens by must be a real knee
slapper all right.

Sy had definitely caught his fair share of muskies though,
despite himself. What I mean is, he liked to shake his pole and
let the line go slack; anything to get the fish to fight more, or at
least longer, all the while hollering insults at the musky while
flirting with disaster. Naturally he lost his fair share as well, but
that was something he apparently felt he could easily afford.

Not the two McCabe brothers. Sure, we had caught a couple
small muskies in Wisconsin, but so what? The one Rob hooked

the year before and I reeled in didn't count. We were in the heart of the Canadian wilderness on one of the most beautiful bodies of water in the world; water so pure you could dip in a cup right from the boat and drink it without concern, at least in most of Whitefish Bay. We were surrounded by countless islands, untouched as if we were gazing at them in 88 A.D. instead of 1988 A.D. In the midst of that unspoiled splendor it was easy to imagine two free souls without a care between them, leisurely casting away, at one with the Universe…

Well, not exactly. Try two guys making cast after cast with nothing much to show for it except sore backs, arms and wrists; might as well throw in Don's tennis elbow for good measure, even if he didn't play tennis anymore. Not only that, but we had been at that wild goose chase, off and on, for nearly thirty years. We were used to not catching muskies.

At least northern displayed the decency to strike your lure from time to time, which is why we would occasionally hint to Rob that a nice northern bay out of the wind would be okay with us for a little while; anything to mute the frustration, to allow us a false sense of accomplishment. Regardless, there was the impending let down we both just knew would likely be our fate; no trophy musky for you two dopes.

Rob would have none of that in his boat because he knew going after northern would likely reduce our odds further still. We had told him repeatedly we wanted to land trophy muskies and that was what he was determined to deliver. He knew how seductive, if not addictive it could be to hook into something that at least resembled a musky, but what he also realized, which we apparently did not, was the excitement generated by hooking into and landing a truly large musky; he also knew the price that had to be paid in order to do so. He kept us out on the submerged rock reefs in open water because more often than not that was where the big ones came to feed. He had us throwing different colored bucktails even though we both preferred black, and sometimes different types of lures like jerkbaits and surface lures, but that's what we were paying him for, his expertise. We could be stubborn about using our favorite lures, but we would grudgingly comply because he knew what he was talking about and besides, we didn't want to upset him. Upset guides have been known to take their clients to some pretty unusual places, like back to the parking lot.

We hit one reef that had become infamous the month before when I had again gone up with Danny, Jeff and Will. A musky Rob had estimated to be in the thirty-pound class had slammed into my bucktail and held on for ten or fifteen seconds before spitting the lure. Talk about depression taking on a whole new meaning. Things like that can really do a job on your self-confidence, let me tell you. You begin to think it will never happen, at least not on this day, or this reef, or especially this cast. When that sets in, especially as your trip is drawing to a close, it's just like going into the championship game with high hopes and tons of confidence and determination, only to find your team trailing by thirty late in the fourth quarter.

After that, most of us just go through the motions, ensuring a slow and inevitable demise, void of any hope for success. *Just don't give up, don't **ever** give up...* Grampa's words from long ago would come to me, and I was casting again; and again, and again and again.

Musky...

***

Another awesome cholesterol bomb for breakfast coupled with a few of Sy's colorful one minute stories that took five to tell and we were ready to give chase once more. The weather was sunny and in the low seventies. Not our favorite fishing weather, but at least the wind had picked up. As usual, we wanted overcast skies with drizzling rain or have it in our immediate future. High, cloudless skies may be great for sightseeing, but it wasn't what we were looking for and not what Grampa would have looked for either, which was enough for us despite what others had to say.

It was a good thing we had decided to forego shore lunch. By noon we seemed to be lacking the key ingredient for that particular Northwoods tradition, since Rob had us chasing nothing but muskies. We could have found a northern spot easy enough, but some quick sandwiches were just fine. Besides, skipping the catching, cooking and cleaning everything up gave us more time on the water.

Things picked up a little after lunch, though. Rob must have sensed our increasing frustration (or was sick of our pouting) and decided to pull into a good northern bay. We hadn't made five casts when I got a strike from a good-sized northern about sixty feet from the boat. It was putting up a good fight as I horsed it to within ten feet of us. Rob had grabbed his smaller net and was making his way towards the bow where I was standing, but before he got there the fish turned, shook its head and was gone. Things were getting ridiculous. I had never experienced a day of fishing on Lake of the Woods where I had failed to catch at least one fish (Rob was sick of hearing about that, too, hence the net) and what I had estimated as a six pounder was almost in the boat then gone, just like that.

"Six? Hell, that fish was at least eight pounds, maybe ten." Don felt compelled to add.

"Six tops," I muttered back. The thought of losing one bigger was more than I wanted to deal with at that moment.

"Naw, eight easy, probably ten!" Don exclaimed with so much authority it was as if he had managed to mysteriously weigh the thing.

"Six, *damn it*. Maybe just five." I was beginning to lose it. The fact there were just a few hours left in the day had also begun to play on my nerves. Mid-afternoon was no time to screw around losing a fish that should have been caught, especially when you have nothing or no one to blame but yourself. I had failed to check my drag (or my hooks) for who knew how long, and it had been tightened down so much one of the rear treble hooks, which was probably bent to begin with, on my Mepps Giant Killer had been bent enough for the fish to spit the lure. Dumb, dumb, dumb - it also meant Don had been right – if anything, his estimate had probably been conservative.

Rob took us to another northern spot, and within half an hour I had three decent fish in the boat, as if they had been hitting all day. I lost a fourth one on a short strike. I wasn't upset to have lost the fish, but there was a cloud of gloom in the boat hovering directly above my big brother's head. He had been glad to see me catch the first one, tolerated the second, but fell silent with the third, since he hadn't been catching anything either. Landing that fourth one would have been a little embarrassing. I could have handled the embarrassment all right, but I was almost relieved the fish had escaped. Then Don nailed two in a row, just like that. Does wonders for one's mood.

Satisfied he had extinguished our lust for something, *any*thing that swam, Rob highballed it back to the open water reefs, with the attendant wind and waves. We only had a few more hours left, and the following day was our last one on the water until next year. We pounded away, cast after cast, and although we had a couple of decent follows, the wary muskies had other plans.

The wind had increased and brought along plenty of clouds and a noticeable chill, with just enough bite to remind us we were indeed in Canada, and fall had definitely arrived. It was time to grit our teeth and cast away with added determination and put every mean faced, snarly toothed son of a musky on notice; even though it sure felt like it was the other way around.

***

I'm about as relaxed as I can be when standing on the Sanctuary's solid wooden dock with an ice-cold Labatts in my hand, watching Rob or Bob Horley Sr. fillet the day's catch. The Horley's had indeed become more than just our hosts and guides, they had become friends, and going over the day's adventures and misadventures with them was always enjoyable.

As much as I had wanted to own a small place on the water in northern Wisconsin, the appeal of Lake of the Woods made me reconsider that nearly lifelong dream as I gazed out across the wide channel. Ever since my first trip to Pelican Lake back in 1959, I had wanted a small cabin on the water either there or somewhere in northern Wisconsin. I still loved northern Wisconsin, but as I stood there and gazed about at the untouched

Northwoods paradise, I knew Lake of the Woods had indeed seduced me.

Gazing east, past the small, protected Sanctuary bay and the channel beyond, was Highrock Island several hundred yards away, maybe farther. It was true to its name, at least for the general vicinity; only Painted Rock Island was higher, as far as I knew anyway. Maybe I felt that way because earlier that day I had hiked to the summit of Painted Rock.

***

Rob had pointed out the ancient images about two thirds of the way up the sheer granite face of Painted Rock Island while we were fishing just to the east of it. Ojibways were the likely artists, who centuries ago had used a mixture of fish oil and iron oxide to create the images of fish, deer and other local wildlife. There was a narrow granite ledge they had stood on, but I couldn't see how they had possibly been able to get there.

"Oh, it isn't that difficult to reach," Rob said. "I've been up there a few times. You start on the left side and work your way up is all."

"Holding onto what?" I said. "All I see is a sheer wall of rock."

"There's small crag's here and there to grab until you're even with the ledge. It's a fair distance away though, so you need to leap about five or six feet. Pretty narrow, that ledge, so a decent sense of balance is helpful."

"I guess so," I said. "Looks like about a sixty-foot drop if you screw up."

"A hundred more like it," Rob said, a smile on his face. "The dicey part comes when you have to jump back. You need to get your hand hold and footing just so when you land, but at least you've got those jagged rocks at the bottom to break your fall."

I wanted to see the images close up, but there was no way in hell I was going anywhere near that granite wall. Still, the view from the top of the summit would be awesome, so I decided to hike my way up, starting from the southeast shore of the large island. It would take time away from fishing, but as far as that small adventure was concerned, "maybe someday" had finally arrived. I couldn't talk Don or Rob into it though, so I headed up alone.

It took me half an hour, fighting through thick brush and over huge boulders and fallen trees, at least most of the way. I finally located what I assumed was an overgrown deer path only more narrow, except it kept disappearing. I never was able to see through the brush and trees more than ten, maybe fifteen feet in any direction, and usually a lot less than that; if claustrophobia freaks you out, don't even *try* going through that Northwoods jungle.

I made it to the top, though. There was a fairly large clearing on the summit, and the view was every bit as spectacular as I had hoped it would be. I must have been at least a hundred and fifty feet straight up, probably higher. Mile after mile of islands and water to the east, south and north, all the way to the horizon. To the west, just the large island itself, angling down, thick with growth. It took me almost as long to get back.

"That was really something," I said once I was back in the boat, breathing heavily. "Good thing I located that narrow deer path for part of the way." Rob glanced at me and chuckled.

"A path, eh? Didn't know there was one. If there is, I doubt it's a deer path though, since there aren't any deer on that island."

"You sure about that, Rob? It's a fairly big island."

"Pretty sure I guess. If there are any deer, they don't stick around long enough to make a path."

"How come?"

"Too many damned bears."

***

I thought about my adventure as I stood there on the dock that late afternoon gazing at Highrock Island. I smiled and shook my head as I recalled Rob's comment. He never did admit he'd been joking, assuming he had been. If nothing else, he had accomplished keeping me in the boat and concentrating on musky hunting, and that brought a smile to my face as well.

I continued gazing across the water. Just like I had been doing ever since I was fourteen, I imagined Ojibways or members of a different tribe, hundreds and even thousands of years ago, gliding by in their canoes, seeing the very things that had me so mesmerized; can you imagine the amazing stories those guys must have had about some truly massive muskies? Sure you can. I hope so anyway.

A fish jumped out in the bay, breaking my reverie. A small one, then two larger ones did the same in rapid succession.

"Things are stirring," was all Bob Horley Sr. said without looking up from the northern he was filleting.

***

The small, antique wood-burner kept our cabin as warm as we cared to make it. Don and I went over what we believed was a logical game plan for our last day on the water for the year. It was getting chilly, flirting with downright cold, so we needed to keep the fire cranking out the BTU's. A damp north wind had picked up, and brought enough clouds along with it to blot out the stars.

We were completely worn out, enjoying the warmth of the fire and the taste of Labatts and Players, even if by then those things were losing their allure, especially the cigarettes. We had some music playing, but not the usual New Christy Minstrels or big band tapes. It was Dan Gibson's original *Solitudes* tape, *Exploring Nature With Music*. After ten hours of casting, riding high on the waves most of the time and still feeling the undulating motion while sitting in our cabin, we weren't capable of doing much more than sit there like a couple of zombie musky morons and let the music sooth our battle worn minds and bodies. The beer didn't hurt either, although we both knew it was going to be a short night.

When the tape ended we just sat there on our respective butts like a couple of slugs, basically numb to the world, our motionless chairs still being rocked by non-existent waves. That's when we first heard it, first heard the rain as it tap-danced against the rolled asphalt and wooden roof. We decided another beer would be a waste of good Canadian brew, and called it a night.

Our definition of an ideal day for musky fishing hadn't changed; it would be in the low sixties to upper fifties, heavily overcast with sporadic rain or drizzle. We would want it to be somewhat windy; enough to put a chop on the water anyway. As luck would have it, that was almost exactly the conditions we found ourselves in when we awoke around 6:30 a.m. on September 16, 1988.

***

The first thing I did after breakfast was put on my camouflage rain suit. I already had on a thick, wool shirt and a down vest which was good, because last night's chill hadn't diminished with the dawn. Since the Sanctuary bay is located on the leeward side of the island you aren't sure how intense conditions on the water are from the vicinity of our cabin so much, until you see the tops of the huge pine trees. If they are oscillating haphazardly in time with the gusts, you can bet the conditions out on the water will be rough.

If there had been any doubts about that, they were dispelled after looking out the paneled picture window in the main lodge during breakfast. The large window had a western exposure and a panoramic view of the sweeping expanse of water in that direction. The islands on the horizon, well over a thousand yards away, were shrouded in fog and drizzle, barely visible; what a beautiful sight. We couldn't wait to get out there.

Bob Horley Sr. entered the lodge while we were eating, brushing water off his raingear, having just made it back from the mainland. He looked at us and nodded good morning, but there was something else in his eyes, something unmistakable, and it prompted me to ask a question.

"So Bob, are things still stirring out there?" He didn't answer. He didn't have to. All he did was offer his signature cagey smile.

***

Rob drove through the rain and wind to a spot across the channel east of the dock area, off the southwest corner of Highrock Island. I hadn't made six casts when a good-sized northern shot up to my bucktail, hit short then sped off. It was definitely gratifying to see some action so early on, even if it did get away. *Things are stirring out there...*

As the morning wore on we saw several muskies follow our lures to the boat, then move on. Occasionally one would hang around for a while, following someone's lure one time and some-one else's the next. God that was frustrating; I mean there they were, approaching the side of the boat, and all we could do was watch them ignore our figure eights as they went by.

Although the weather may have been ideal for musky fishing, it was tough on the fishermen. The temperature was a wet and chilly fifty degrees or so and dropping, accompanied by an increasingly stiff north by northwest wind that made it a lot colder. The wind never let up much either, just shifted from time to time. Sometimes the rain would slow down to a drizzle, even stop for ten minutes or so, but before long it was back stronger than ever.

It didn't take long to realize I hadn't dressed warm enough. My old down vest felt as if it had lost half its feathers, the sort of thing you don't notice until it's too late. The old running shoes I was wearing were okay for traction, but once your feet are wet in that kind of weather, well, you know what I mean. We weren't complaining without joking about it though. It was exactly the type of weather we had hoped for. Next time though, I was going to have the best double-down vest Cabala's had to offer, and a pair of Gor-tex boots like Rob's.

The bone-chilling weather, coupled with three ten hour days of steady casting were beginning to take their toll. The old musky adage "the fish of 10,000 casts" seemed too conservative; it felt like I had made a million. The cold, stinging rain started coming in sideways on sustained gusts...

We were heading for another spot when Rob abruptly pulled into a small bay where he had raised a good-sized musky not too long ago. On about my third or fourth cast I felt a strike more powerful than any since the musky that had slammed into my bucktail the month before, when I had been there with Danny, Jeff and Will. This time however, I managed to set the hooks better, or so I thought. It pulled my drag twice as it bent my new graphite musky rod a good forty degrees. With the aid of an adrenalin rush I could feel pulsating in my temples, all my concentration was focused on keeping my line tight, the tip of my pole close to the water and my eyes riveted on the end of my line. It was really happening, I just knew it, and it felt as if my heart would pound right out of my chest.

All of a sudden there was muted *"pop"* not unlike the hollow report of a small caliber handgun coming from a distant field. The sickening realization that my twenty-pound braided Dacron had just snapped washed over me. I *knew* I should have been using 36-pound test. The 20-pound test was allegedly camouflaged, but there hadn't been a stronger test available of that type when I had purchased the line. Besides, I figured by setting my drag properly the 20-pound test would be enough; maybe for Rob Horley, but apparently not for me. My last black Giant Killer was gone as well – I had messed up and left the rest in my other tackle box, and had left *that* in the boathouse which was about ten miles away.

I thought I had been checking my line often enough to avoid such a disaster. Rechecking it again, I noticed some really bad frays farther back on the line. I had only been checking farther back about four or five feet, but the frays I found after losing that fish, most likely *that musky,* were back a good ten to twelve feet.

I pulled that much out and more, cut and retied. Rob checked the eyelet on the end of my new pole, and told me to replace it with a high grade aluminium oxide eyelet at my first opportunity, and in the meantime check for frays on a more regular basis.

As the adrenalin rush abated it became, or at least felt colder than ever, as if the unrelenting wind and rain were chanting *never, never*. Rob tried to help by saying it had probably been a northern, but I knew better, or thought I did. I'd had some decent northern strikes over the years, but none of them were like what had just occurred, unless they actually had been, but I needed an excuse to justify feeling sorry for myself. *Don't give up, don't **ever** give up…* Grampa's words came to me like they had so many times before, and before along I was casting away, one after the other.

Rob was a study in determination if there ever was one. Any attempt by either Don or me to coax an hour or so of fishing on the leeward side of some island in a less windy northern bay was dismissed diplomatically, but dismissed nonetheless. We wanted to get out of the biting wind as much as anything, but Rob knew time was running out even if we didn't.

"Ya know Rob," Don called out through the wind and biting rain, only half joking, "Tom and I could be in a little trouble on the home front if we show up without our limits of northerns!" We were still several fish short. Rob, however, was hunting muskies, and was making sure we were too, come hell *and* high water. In other words, his gloves were off. Off with a vengeance.

"No need to worry, Don, we have plenty of fresh fillets in the freezer back at the lodge you're welcome to," Rob called back as he pointed across the water. "Now aim one towards that crevice next to the outcropping…"

*Ah, the lodge...the lodge...*my fevered brain envisaged, while my teeth chattered. The potbellied stove was no doubt keeping things glowingly warm...warmer than warm really...there's Carol coming from her kitchen with a pot of strong, fresh brewed coffee...think I'll just settle into that overstuffed recliner next to the stove with the latest Cabela's catalog...there's got to be a few things in there I can't live without...more hot coffee, Tom? Why sure, thank you Carol...

"Tom! Put one right where Don just did, I'll work us around the reef, put your baits closer to the rocks, don't get snagged mind you, that cast's too close, raise your rod tip, reel faster!"

Keep casting, keep casting, keep casting...

***

Don and I felt some relief when Rob took us to the leeward side of a pine-studded island for shore lunch. We made our way up a hill to a small campsite nestled in the pines that offered some relief from the frigid, biting wind and pounding rain. I had always been proud of my ability to start and maintain fires, but on that windswept day with everything completely soaked, I was having trouble. I failed to get even a flicker of flame after three attempts, so Rob took over.

The three of us were huddled around a roaring fire in less than five minutes drinking apple juice, wishing it was hot coffee. Rob always brewed strong coffee for shore lunch, but we didn't have any. We had planned on heading back to the lodge for a quick lunch so there had been no need to bring coffee or food. We ended up so focused on musky hunting it was decided not to waste the added time heading in. We had known we were in for a chilly, wet and windy day, but the sudden intensity had been unexpected, an intensity that appeared to foretell what we could expect for the rest of the day - our last day for an entire year.

We had only one bone chilling afternoon left until next year all right, so we wasted no time getting back out there. Not surprisingly, the wind and rain picked up after our stop, and the temperature had dropped at least another ten degrees. No telling how cold it was from a wind chill perspective. Rob asked if we had brought along any gloves. We hadn't.

For a couple of guys who fancied themselves musky fishermen, we were sure a sorry pair of unprepared, freezing dopes. My teeth had gone from chattering to chattering uncontrollably, and the only sensation my hands could muster was dull pain. Regardless, Rob kept us in the jaws of that inclement weather because that's where the best rock reefs were located and that's where the muskies came to feed - as soon as we left. That's how it felt anyway.

We headed to the reef where the year before, when Dad had been with us, Rob had hooked that 28-pound musky and handed me his pole. Memories of that adventure were enhanced because Dad had been with us. I wondered how he would have held up under the extreme conditions we were enduring, but I knew the answer. He wouldn't have said anything, but he wouldn't have argued if the rest of us decided to head in - maybe. *Damn,* it was getting cold...

My thoughts were interrupted by a strike Don received from a northern off that very reef. He had it on for a little while before it spat the lure. It seemed as if they had been hitting short all day. Don reeled in then asked me if that was an orange Giant Killer he had spotted in my tackle box. I said it sure was orange as I removed the red bucktail I had put on to let Rob know I was paying attention to his advice; besides, I was out of black. Don then proposed the following fateful deal - he'd give me his last remaining black bucktail if I would let him have my orange one. As I quickly handed Don that orange beauty, Rob looked at it and declared "That just might be the ticket." Don thought so anyway, and he was well known to display an uncanny intuition about such things, let me tell you.

I threw a few casts with the black one for a while, but I didn't think it threw off enough flash. I had put that very lure together for Don just a few days before. That was probably why he reminded me, and in no uncertain terms the way older brothers are prone to do, that I had thought it had thrown off enough flash while *he* was using it. No sense taking his accusation personally I rationalized, especially since he was right, but I set about changing the blade anyway.

***

The afternoon wore on with no relief in the weather, not even close. We were cold, wet, and tired. I glanced at my watch. It was just past 1:30 - I fantasized that I would catch the musky of my dreams around, oh, 3:30 or so. I thought about things like that all the time, usually to sidestep the boredom and especially the frustration on a slow day. That afternoon I did it to keep my mind off of what was happening to my half-frozen body. Could it *get* any damn colder? At least if you kept casting fast and furious it took away some of the chill, or pretended to more like it...

We went to a reef where I thought for sure something big had hit my bucktail, but all I did was set the hooks into a clump of weeds instead. Wonderful. Now I was becoming delusional, perhaps flirting with full-blown dementia. I was approaching a point where just maybe I would have been willing to trade a few years of my life for a warm fire.

I had always thought I could handle the cold as good as the next guy, but when it doesn't let up and you're standing or sitting in it for hours on end…I was reminded of an interview given by a Chicago Bear prior to a game where brutal cold with wind chills below zero had been forecasted. He was bare armed, and maintained all you had to do was snarl at it with contempt, along the lines of "Is this all ya got? *Bring it.*" It worked, too, for damn near three minutes.

Rob decided it was time to try another spot so off we went, plowing through waves that continued to grow in size as the storm system intensified. Open water was of course the worst, and the wind that howled across the larger expanses did so with such velocity it actually snatched the frothy tips of the whitecaps and send them flying ahead of the waves they had been attached to. I had never seen that before, the frothy tips accelerating at the speed of the wind, which was of course substantial.

If there was comfort to be found anywhere, it was that Rob was manning the boat. Also, if there had been any question regarding why he insisted upon using only deep V hulled boats, they would have been answered for anyone aboard his craft that afternoon. If we had been in Don's flat bottom, we would have likely needed scuba gear.

Some people swear by the luck of the Irish, but I've known some pretty unlucky Irishmen, in my own family even. Not Don though. His luck transcends any nationality including his own, I swear it does. He has never been lucky because he hoped or prayed for it, or even because he wanted it. He was lucky because he expected it to come calling, and he accepted no substitutes. You could usually see it in his eyes, and when you did you'd better do some praying of your own that you're not competing with Don McCabe whether it's a game of horse while shooting baskets, playing poker or fishing. Good fortune seems to gravitate towards him with ease once he acquires "the look".

It was that very look I noticed as he pounded away with my orange bucktail towards the latest reef Rob had chosen. Orange. I couldn't believe it. I also had a hot pink Mepps Musky Killer I had received as a gag gift. He might as well have been throwing that beauty. Regardless, he nailed two northern and had a follow from a large musky that paid absolutely no attention to my black bucktail or Rob's red one. Just the orange bucktail, and that brute of a fish checked it out several times before disappearing into the deep; you know, where it was *warmer*.

Don't get me wrong; I really wanted Don to catch a trophy musky. Someday. I doubt there's a musky hunter alive who wouldn't prefer the fish of a lifetime hit his or her lure first. I know I did. Only Dad felt otherwise, but it wouldn't exactly break his heart if he landed the first big one. Needless to say, Don's blood was up as he stood there casting away. He set a good example so I stood up as well, but before long I was sitting again, convinced it felt warmer to do so while not feeling any warmer at all.

When the musky Don had raised refused to reappear, Rob gunned the engine and headed north, right into the teeth of that howling wind and stinging rain. If we had been wearing our sunglasses, we wouldn't have been able to see much past our noses except indistinct, dripping gray images.

We headed to an exposed reef about a mile southeast of Three Sisters Islands with a big triangular marker on it. It was just before 3:00 when we began casting on its northwest side, working our way down the west side of the reef. When we approached the southwest corner, Rob said it was at that very spot where he had hooked into a thirty-pound class musky just a few weeks before. I didn't doubt him, but I had to believe he had mentioned that for my benefit. Both Don and Rob were still standing, but not me. I was huddled in the middle of the boat sitting in a swivel chair, too cold, wet and exhausted to do much more than go through the motions of throwing one cast after another, not paying much attention to where they landed as long as it was near the boulders.

We were all cold, but I was the one least prepared for such conditions. That's what I told myself anyway, even if it was just an excuse to justify my recent decision to spend, along with the new vest and boots, several hundred bucks on some insulated Gor-tex raingear like Rob's. Only the promise of a roaring fire, hot coffee with a shot of cognac and a burning Players non-filter kept me going, and just barely at that. Still...I kept casting.

We made our way around the southeast corner and played a little rock tag to ease the frustration and everything else that was gnawing at us; in our own way we were having fun, even if we had to pretend we weren't lying to ourselves to find it. The idea was to get as close to an exposed rock as possible without actually hitting it. Rob usually won, but Don was very accurate as well. We kept on casting, working our way up the east side of the reef. Rob remarked he had rarely seen a musky on the northeast end. That type of comment usually meant he was getting ready to take us to another spot. At that point I didn't really care, even though I did. I'd had it. Wait till next year, all that defeatist garbage.

As we approached the northeast corner I found myself leaning wearily back in my swivel chair, done in by the unrelenting weather and my own negative attitude. Sitting in that position I noticed Don's cast heading out from the bow on the port side, straight towards the northeast end of the reef. He was still standing, braced against the pounding wind and rain, not giving up.

Don't give up, don't *ever* give up…

"Okay Grampa, whatever you say." I muttered as I clenched my chattering teeth. I was done with all that pathetic whining. Wind? What wind? What rain? I have an Iowa winter waiting for me in a couple of months, I'll freeze to death then, I said to myself. Sitting up, I let one soar to within five feet of the exposed rocks. I gave the handle of my Ambassadeur 5000C reel three quick turns and was in the process of making a fourth…*WHAM!*

I bolted to my feet immediately, delivering a solid hook set as I did so. My heart pounded in my chest as I felt a tremendous surge of raw power tugging relentlessly at the end of my line. It resembled the machine-gun-like tugging of certain northerns and especially a large smallmouth only slower, with considerably more strength. Each tug seemed to shoot through my entire upper body.

About ten seconds elapsed before we finally got a glimpse of just what was pulling so desperately at the end of my line. I could not believe my eyes. A huge musky slid sideways across the choppy surface then headed straight for the deep, a good sixty feet away from the boat. I kept the tension on as I reeled in methodically, or at least tried to. Every few feet of progress would be followed by a short burst of power that pulled my tightly set drag out with ease. I only hoped it wasn't set too tight, or too loose; things were happening so fast I didn't know what to think. Things were happening quickly all right, but it was like they were speeding along in slow motion. That makes no sense at all, which was exactly how I felt at the time; nothing made sense, everything made sense…

I had never, nor have I since, concentrated so intently upon anything in my life. The howling wind and slashing rain battered away, but of course I didn't feel a thing. There was a musky on the end of my line, a *big* musky, a Lake of the *Woods* musky, and that's all I knew, or cared to know.

Keep your line taut Tommy boy, no slack, no slack!

"I hear you Grampa, I hear you…" I did, too, in a way. I didn't actually hear a voice, I don't mean that, but it sure seemed like he was with me somehow.

I didn't want to get carried away and lose it by trying to horse it in, because the only way that could have been done was tightening down the drag. Even if I was tempted to do so, and I was, I couldn't feature myself moving my fingers long enough to attempt such a maneuver. Besides, how much strain could my twenty-pound test line handle? I had already lost what was most likely a musky earlier that day from a line break, and that fish didn't compare to what I had just tangled into the second time around. The huge fish would allow itself to be reeled in ten feet or so, then make powerful surges in whatever direction it felt like going.

I didn't really notice what else was going on in the boat as it tossed about on the waves. At one point, I heard Don ask about the camera's location, but I felt like I couldn't break off my concentration long enough to point and say "Under the trap door." or even nod my head in that direction. I started to, but instantly returned to the musky I had never really left without so much as a word.

By then I had worked the musky to within twenty feet from the boat. Rob's practiced eye caught something that caused him to grab the large net, the one he used when trying to improve the odds. Not a good sign, I thought, since Rob and his father landed most muskies by hand, regardless of size. They implemented that practice to cause as little damage to a musky as possible. Sometimes, however, Rob had been known to go for the big net if he felt something was amiss, like if a large fish had a good chance of getting away. I didn't know if that was the reason Rob had grabbed the big net, or because I had told him I wanted to keep any musky that was at least thirty pounds. I hoped the latter was the reason Rob had gone for the net, but I sure wasn't convinced of it.

Standing in the middle of the boat, I had the musky to within ten feet from the stern off the port side. It immediately rumbled straight away from the stern and port, staying a good fifteen feet out; then it turned and made its way towards the bow. Rob had a large net all right, but not large enough to cover that distance. All we could do was watch it glide by while I held on for dear life, keeping the line taut and the tip of my rod close to the water. I reeled like a madman as well, but when that brute was on the move my drag system, as it was supposed to in order to avoid a variety of problems, made it impossible for me to gain so much as an inch. I continued to keep a tight line though. Still, it was nerve racking in an exciting kind of way, especially since Rob continued to stand there as deep in concentration as I was, perhaps more. He resembled a cougar ready to pounce.

If I could just get that magnificent beast a little closer, my fervid mind envisioned, I could loosen the drag so Rob would have more flexibility to work with; another idea that tried to make sense but fell flat on its face - if Rob got the net on it, all I had to do was hit the release button. Before those thoughts had a chance to dissipate, I felt an awesome surge that pulled my line out so fast it was as if the drag hadn't been tightened at all.

"Feels like it's loosening the drag itself!" I exclaimed, getting a mouthful of sideways rain for my trouble. The howling wind and pounding waves continued to buck us around as well.

Right at that precise moment my heart stopped. I couldn't feel the pressure anymore. Panic shot through me as I frantically reeled in the line, refusing to admit the musky of my dreams had managed to escape. The more the line kept coming in without any resistance however, the deeper my panic grew. More line was retrieved, and with each turn of the reel handle my panic increased then melted into a dismal pool of profound depression. *Whizzz!* My line all but screamed as the powerful musky made its most spectacular run of the afternoon. The heartfelt relief that washed over me was so intense I became lightheaded, and I'm not kidding.

My rod arched as I kept the tip inches from the waves, leaning back and to my right with everything I had as I reeled like a man possessed, which was exactly what I had become. If I was going to lose that fish, that magnificent trophy, it would occur due to line breakage while the both of us were putting up the battle of a lifetime. Spitting the bucktail because slack had developed was not an option. Never again would I allow that to happen, never again - maybe. I had been extremely lucky, although at the time I didn't know how much. Rob sure knew...

It was during that last, mighty run that the musky seemed to have realized it was indeed fighting for its life. That's how it felt anyway. Before, although it had been putting up an impressive struggle, I had sensed it hadn't considered the hooks much more than an annoying inconvenience. Not anymore. It thrashed and pulled like a creature fully aware of its plight then made an abrupt left turn and shot towards the stern; and directly for the large, sharp blades of Rob's 175 hp Yamaha, its prop positioned just under the churning surface. I was determined to keep it away from those blades, just as much as the musky was to wrap around them. Fifteen years ago I had lost a huge walleye that way fishing Diamond Lake in Michigan. That had been disappointing - what the musky had in mind would be a tragedy of the first order. I went for broke.

The only drag system Grampa had was his thumb. If that was good enough for him it would work for me; I had to believe that was true. I had, of course, never been in a boat with him while fighting a monster fish. He had taught me how to cast though: *Cast smooth, not hard...keep your thumb lightly on the spool as you cast, lightly now, as if you are stroking the head of a canary...*no, I had never been with him during a street brawl of a musky fight, but I had to believe he would say the antithesis of his casting advice was the only way to go at that particular moment.

Just as the massive head approached those blades, its muscular body plowing through the water with everything it had, I jammed my thumb down on the spool and pulled back with everything *I* had. It was now or never. Either the huge fish would make it to those blades or its head would be turned, unless my line snapped or the lure came out. The tip of my graphite pole was bent so much I wasn't so sure there wasn't a potential problem with that as well.

Thankfully the head turned, and the musky slid to the surface off the port stern and headed in my direction - and right past Rob Horley. As he lowered the net into the choppy water the musky made a final lunge, and almost avoided the big net. Rob was, however, a veteran of many such battles and immediately shoved the front of the net in exactly the optimum position to encircle the huge head without knocking the bucktail out of its mouth. As he put his back into hauling the massive fish into the boat it almost careened right out of the net, teetering on the brink of the frame; once again my heart leapt into my throat. One last heave however, and at long last my dream had come true. It had actually come true. After twenty-nine long years, the Quest had finally been fulfilled, and I could scarcely believe it was happening.

I was visibly shaking as I watched Rob wrestle that beast, trying to keep it on the floor of the boat; it was anything but tired out. I was so awestruck I hadn't even pushed the release button to free the spool. When I finally did, the musky opened its large, white mouth and the bucktail simply fell out, just like that. The only reason that musky was in the boat was because it hadn't done an open mouth headshake when it had stolen all that slack just moments before. Only one hook on the rear treble had been sticking just inside its lower lip the whole time, and it was bent. One bent hook! I could see the small hole where the hook had been. The northern from the day before had bent one just like it and had gotten away.

Rob said he had spotted the dubious hook-set when the fish had been a good twenty feet from the boat, and that was why he had grabbed the big net. He said he couldn't believe the line hadn't snapped as he leaned over and picked it up and pointed out a large fray about six or seven feet up from the leader. At first, we just stared at each other.

"How you turned that fish without this giving way I'll never know," he finally said. "I can only imagine the diminished test of your line with a fray like this. Probably less than ten pounds, eh? Tom, you surely had help from above."

I looked at Don; my big brother knew *exactly* what I was thinking, without a word spoken. Yes, it was hard to believe such a powerful creature hadn't managed to get away. Maybe someone was watching over me, someone I had known a long, long time ago and still revered, still loved. Maybe Grampa figured it was time.

Rob had his hands full trying to subdue that fish while Don was snapping as many pictures as he could. I think he was as excited as me. History was being made and the two biggest gluttons for punishment throughout the entire Pete and Benjamin Franklin McCabe Family Musky Quest were there, live and in person.

There was plenty of fight left in that musky, and it had no intention of cooperating with Rob. He asked, no *told* me to grab another gunnysack from the hatch up front. He was trying to keep it from flopping all over the place and still had quite a battle on his hands. At one point it even moved Rob's upper body about, not unlike a high school wrestler. He managed to get it under control long enough to weigh it. The boat was rocking so much it was difficult for him to get a precise reading, but he said it was around thirty to thirty-one pounds and close to fifty inches in length. I asked him if he was sure it was at least thirty pounds. He said yes. That made it official - it was going on the wall!

When the fish was finally wrapped up in two wet gunnysacks and secured with rope, Rob asked if we wanted to continue fishing or call it quits. I half-heartedly mentioned something about it not mattering to me one way or the other, realizing as I spoke it was Don's call, not mine. He opted for the Sanctuary. It had been a long day for him, too.

***

As we plowed through the waves, I looked around at all the scenery and familiar landmarks. The storm was still blowing, but with less intensity or so it seemed. The gulls were gliding about, riding the air currents as they soared through the gray-white skies. The diverse, natural order of things on Lake of the Woods continued, with the strong and able doing what they had been doing for millenniums; surviving. Looking at my musky that appeared even larger wrapped up in the gunnysacks, I felt a kinship with the pristine yet unforgiving Northwoods surroundings. It was as if I had finally succeeded in forcing its hand and had made it give up something very special, something few people are allowed to have because they aren't willing to pay the price. Grampa had, of course, been right all along: *When it happens though, when you finally hook into one, you'll be a cut above the bobber and worm crowd. They'll never know the thrill of thrills, because they gave up...*

I was actually living a decades old dream. I had reached the summit, and it was every bit as rewarding as I had imagined it would be. It was hard to feature that less than an hour before

I had been ready to call it quits for another year as I prepared myself for the inevitable let down. Instead, thanks in large part to Grampa, I was in a boat plowing through whitecaps, my trophy musky at my feet, as happy as I had ever wanted to be.

***

We returned to an almost empty camp. Don and I headed up the small hill to our cabin as Rob placed the musky upon the dock and began to unwrap it for more photographs and more accurate measurements. Once inside, I stoked up the fire to finally relieve the chill, and although I hadn't stopped shaking, I honestly hadn't noticed the cold since hooking into my musky. I poured two snifters of Courvoisier VSOP and Don and I shared a toast that was long overdue. Our only regret was Dad's absence, so we toasted him as well. We would toast Grampa during supper, because he had never touched spirits of any kind, but had loved his coffee.

After supper, I went back to our cabin for a while to collect my thoughts. I was leaning against the front porch contemplating all that had happened. I don't recall vivid thoughts as much as just letting the waves of elation wash over me. I had arrived, I had actually *arrived*.

I stayed there for a while, just soaking it all in. I decided to walk down to the dock and look out across the water like I had done countless times before, only on those occasions I would, as often as not, wonder if that incredible body of water would ever give up the musky I had always wanted so badly. The light rain felt good against my face as I glanced at Highrock Island across the channel, shrouded in mist, where the day's adventure had begun. Like the rest of my surroundings it didn't look different, yet felt like it was, all at the same time.

I remembered a small northern I had caught before lunch. He was maybe two pounds, and at the time was the only assurance I wouldn't get skunked that day. In all the excitement Rob had overlooked filleting it. We were still short of our northern limit, but I didn't care, not anymore. I got in the boat and lifted the lid of the live well. He was as lively as ever. I reached in, and after several futile attempts I finally got a hold of that slippery little guy. I admonished him to be more careful of what he decided to bite in the future then placed him in the lake. He took off like a shot and was gone. One mighty fish died that day, one little fish survived. That summed up Lake of the Woods.

As much as I had wanted that trophy hanging on my wall, and as much as I thought I understood the inevitable cycle of birth, life and death within, upon and surrounding that magnificent body of water, I knew I had killed my last musky. I was proud of my catch, very proud, but it was time to move on.

Fifteen years later:

The heel strikes of my boots sounded louder than usual against the wooden basement stairs. That made perfect sense, since I was carrying my three-year-old grandson in my arms. It wasn't the first time we had made the journey down to "Grampa's fishing room" and most certainly wouldn't be the last. There was something down there amidst the lures, rods, reels and fishing mementos; something hanging on the wall that never failed to open my grandson's eyes all the wider once he pulled the string that filled the room with light. It had become a ritual:

"Grampa, can I see the musky?" He would ask. Then our trip downstairs would begin. There was an old, battle-scared Mepps spinner blade tied to the end of the string, and it was my grandson's job to pull it. Once the room was filled with light, I knew where his eyes would be.

"Can I touch its teeth?" He always asked.

"Be careful, they're sharp." He would reach up then, and tentatively place a fingertip on one of the needle-sharp teeth, then pull his hand away in mock fear. It was my job to pretend he had poked his finger, and to over-act in the process.

"How did you catch it, Grampa?" Then the story would begin.

He would listen intently, as intently as a three-year-old can anyway. His eyes would always go back to the musky though…as my calm, baritone voice explained something about the fish. He would be listening all right, but his eyes told me all I had to know about what was on his mind - what he really wanted.

A fish like Grampa's…

The Quest had been joined.

TO GRANDFATHER
BENJAMIN FRANKLIN McCABE

On the shores of Upper Gresham
In late fall of '82
We renewed again a Quest
That had ended once with you.

Thru bodies chilled and numb to the bone
We made to you this pledge
Across generations etched in stone
A fish like yours we'd catch

So they sent us out in snow and rain
To fish a place that had no fish.
We numbly laughed at cold and pain,
"Hey! It just don't get no better than this!"

Six years of adventures t'would fill a book
As we slowly learned just what to do.
And many's the musky that missed the hook,
Cause they wuz laughin' at us too.

A Fish Like Grampa's

But on September 16th, 1988,
All that was delegated…to the past.
Because at 3:22 p.m. that day,
Tom delivered the fateful cast.

Thirty pounds of power hit the lure
And, took off swiftly for the deep.
But Tom was on him fast and sure,
He played that musky beautifully.

When it was landed at 3:29,
The guide looked around…took off his glove,
And noticing the hook and line
Said, "Tom you surely - had help from Above."

"One hook from the treble was under his lip,
So all he had to do was open his mouth there, eh?
And give that frayed old line a flip,
Then your musky, Tom, 'd been headin' south ,eh?"

Well, Tom's my brother, and I was there,
And I'll tell you all just what I saw.
A better fisherman than Wisconsin's Joe Bucher,
Put that trophy on the wall!

Thomas McCabe

This then Gramps, is how the story ran,
We know you're thrilled for K.A.'s T.K.,
I can see you smiling, as Tom says to Dan,
"C'mon son…now cast away."

"Nothing's forever - nothing's sure
Nothing stands the test of Time.
A bigger musky found my lure;
Another, could be right behind."

So Gramps, o'er sixty years you've been the one,
The only McCabe to feel this thrill of thrills,
And I know how proud you must be of Tom;
Who, in your honor, the Quest fulfilled.

- Donald Corbin McCabe
October, 1988

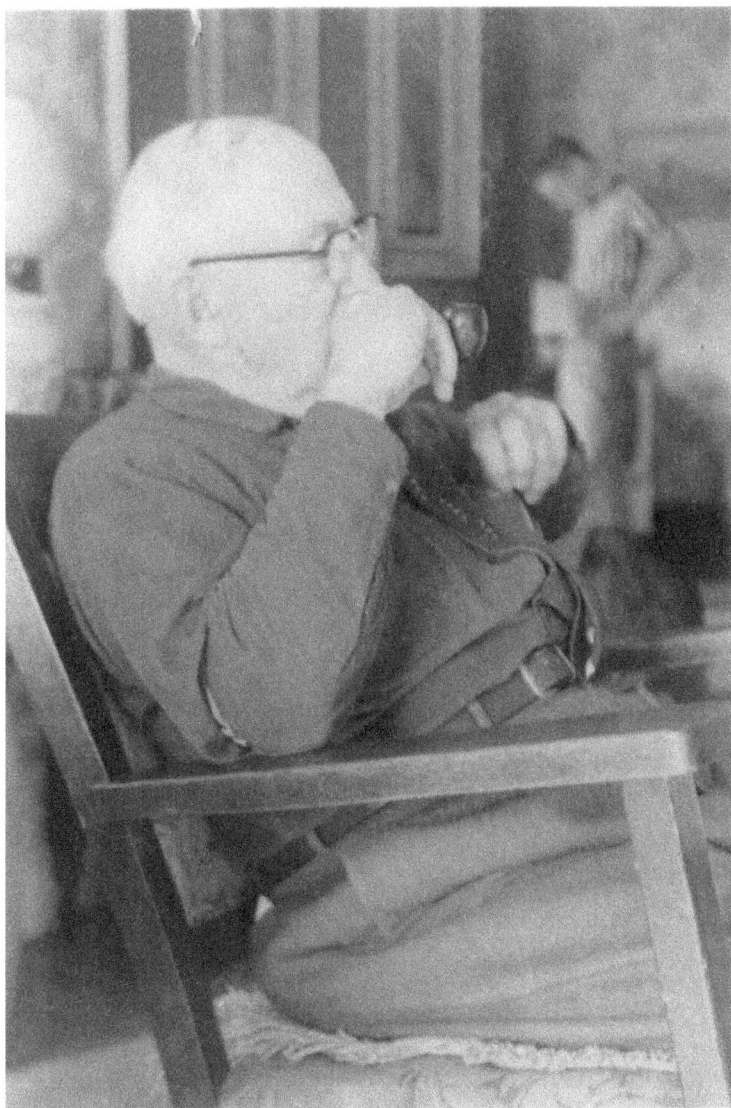

Benjamin F. McCabe

www.ingramcontent.com/pod-product-compliance
Lightning Source LLC
Chambersburg PA
CBHW032032080426
42733CB00006B/66